Advance Praise for *America, The Owner's Manual*

"If you want to be a part of the political action instead of sitting in the grandstands, then Bob Graham's *America, the Owner's Manual* is for you. Not only has he been one of America's most effective political leaders, along the way he became a first-rate teacher of his art."

—Sen. Lamar Alexander, Former U.S. Secretary of Education and Former Governor of Tennessee

"Bob Graham is a true statesman who has spent a lifetime developing future leaders and encouraging the youth of our country to participate in public service—we are a nation incredibly grateful for all of his gifts. This is an extremely important book and a crucial undertaking that will teach generations of Americans about our government and the very special impact of their contributions."

—Sen. John D. (Jay) Rockefeller IV

"At a time when the United States needs an engaged citizenry more than ever, *America, the Owner's Manual* provides a road map on what it takes to be involved and how individuals can actually influence the political system. Calling on a long and distinguished career in public service, Sen. Bob Graham illustrates each of his chapters with real-world examples of success, failure, and the stops in between. It's a must-read for anyone who cares about what is going on around them and the future of our country."

—Christine Todd Whitman, Former EPA Administrator and Governor of New Jersey

America, The
Owner's Manual

Engaged citizens
are fundamental
& the quality
environment.

Bob Graham

March 1, 2016

America, The Owner's Manual

Making Government Work for You

Sen. Bob Graham

with

Chris Hand

CQ PRESS

A Division of SAGE
Washington, D.C.

CQ Press
2300 N Street, NW, Suite 800
Washington, DC 20037

Phone: 202-729-1900; toll-free, 1-866-4CQ-PRESS (1-866-427-7737)

Web: www.cqpress.com

Cover design: Matthew Simmons

⊗ The paper used in this publication exceeds the requirements of the
American National Standard for Information Sciences—Permanence of
Paper for Printed Library Materials, ANSI Z39.48-1992.

Printed and bound in the United States of America

17   16   15   14   6   7   8   9

Library of Congress Cataloging-in-Publication Data

Graham, Bob,
America, the owner's manual : making government work for you /
Bob Graham, with Chris Hand.
     p. cm.
   Includes bibliographical references and index.
   ISBN 978-1-60426-476-0 (alk. paper)
   1. Political participation—United States. 2. Politics,
Practical—United States. I. Hand, Chris, II. Title.

JK1764.G71 2009
322.40973—dc22

                                        2009007769

For the late Donnell Morris and his Miami Carol City Senior High School students, who fueled my passion for participatory citizenship

For the Harvard University undergraduates who attended my Fall 2005 citizenship seminar and inspired this owner's manual

About the Authors

Bob Graham was elected governor of Florida in 1978 and served two successful terms. He was nationally recognized for reforms in education, environmental protection, and economic diversification. Graham was elected to the U.S. Senate in 1986, serving three consecutive terms. As a member of the Senate Finance Committee, he was a leader on health, trade, and tax issues. One of his most important contributions came during his last term, when he was named chairman of the Senate Select Committee on Intelligence. He cosponsored the bill to create the Director of National Intelligence position and cochaired the "Joint Inquiry into Intelligence Community Activities before and after the Terrorist Attacks on September 11, 2001." Graham later authored the 2004 book *Intelligence Matters,* revealing serious faults in the U.S. national security system.

After retiring from public office in early 2005, Graham spent the 2005–2006 academic year at Harvard University's Kennedy School of Government as a senior fellow. He is focusing his efforts on training the next generation of public leaders by mobilizing the academic resources of the University of Florida to solve public policy challenges facing Florida, the nation, and the Americas.

Chris Hand is an attorney in Jacksonville, Florida, with a long history of public service. He previously served as press secretary, speechwriter, and campaign press secretary for Senator Graham and as campaign manager for Florida's statewide elected chief financial officer, Alex Sink. A graduate of Princeton University's Woodrow Wilson School of Public and International Affairs, Hand is active in a variety of local and state civic issues.

Contents

Preface

In recent years, doctors, scientists, and fitness experts have decried our nation's increasingly sedentary lifestyle and made clear its negative effects on our health. Research shows that people who regularly exercise and engage in other physical activity are much less likely to suffer from heart disease, diabetes, premature aging, and other serious medical conditions than are those who are inactive. The fact that many Americans do not lead active lives accounts for alarmingly high rates of dangerous conditions such as obesity—and the biggest concern is for children.

This book addresses another health crisis in which activity produces beneficial effects and inactivity poses unacceptable risks, particularly for our youngest generation. Although the excitement surrounding the 2008 elections temporarily obscured concerns about our civic health, American democracy suffers from a pervasive lack of active participation among our citizens. For a variety of reasons, many of our fellow Americans view civics as a kind of spectator sport—something to be viewed from afar through the filters of media outlets and personalities.

Since my retirement from the U.S. Senate in 2005, I have become increasingly involved in the effort to transform civics from a spectator sport into a participatory sport—one in which citizens directly engage in democracy and shape local, state, and federal policies to the betterment of their families and communities. Through my involvement in this effort, I have become convinced that many Americans would embrace active citizenship if they just knew how. Thus the title of this book: *America, the Owner's Manual: Making Government Work for You.* In order for citizens to realize the benefits of direct civic engagement, it is not enough to understand the structure or the history of American democracy. My goal is to help citizens, particularly those who are currently pursuing the study of civics, interact directly with their government and make it respond to their concerns and hopes.

In the planning stages of this owner's manual, I drew on the expert advice of many civic advocates as well as on my own thirty-eight years in public service—twelve in the Florida Legislature, eight as governor of Florida, and eighteen in the U.S. Senate—to identify the skills most critical to effective citizenship. Each of the ten chapters in this book provides instruction on a different skill: defining the problem to which you want government to respond; gathering the facts you need to generate solutions and influence public officials; identifying which level of government and which agencies and officials are authorized to act on your concerns; determining public opinion; persuading decision makers; using deadlines, trends, and cycles to your advantage; building coalitions; engaging the media; raising funds; and capitalizing on victory and rebounding from defeat. Many of the chapters include valuable practice tips—"Tips from the Pros"—from professionals who have worked in government or politics.

One of the biggest roadblocks to participation in democracy is the perception that it isn't possible—that privileged citizens and special interests command the levers of power, that bureaucracy makes change impossible, and that everyday Americans can't fight City Hall. In writing this book, I didn't expect readers to simply take my word that they can make a difference. In this owner's manual I provide case studies that show what a single person or a group of people can accomplish. The prologue tells how campus leaders at Georgetown University in Washington,

D.C., when faced with local government decisions that threatened their off-campus parking and housing options, were able to mobilize and elect students to the commission making those decisions. Each chapter begins with a story about citizens who used the skill outlined in that chapter to make democracy respond to a problem they had identified and wanted to solve. If reading these stories of citizen participation inspires you to share your own story or others of which you are aware, please e-mail me at americaownersmanual@cqpress.com.

Although the case studies provide meaningful examples of citizens who have made a difference, they still represent learning by reading. The exercises at the end of each chapter are my attempt to help you learn by doing. I hope that actively using your citizenship skills through these exercises will generate lively discussions and make you eager to compete in the democratic arena time and time again throughout your life.

Keep two caveats in mind as you explore the pages of this book. First, I have provided multiple Web links to help you access resources and real-life examples that may assist you in your own civic engagement. If you find that one of these links has changed since this book was published, use a Web search engine to track down the source. Second, please remember that the law is subject to change and often does. You would be wise to check the status of any of the local, state, or federal laws or regulations referenced in this owner's manual.

This book would not have been possible without the help of many people who share my passion for civic engagement. I want to acknowledge them here.

The inspiration to teach participatory democracy came early in my political career when I taught a semester of twelfth-grade civics at Miami Carol City Senior High School. My colleague, the late Donnell Morris, was one of the most effective and passionate educators I have ever known. Together with our students we learned what committed and trained citizens of any age can do to make their community a better place.

The idea for this book took root during the fall of 2005 when I was a senior fellow at the Kennedy School of Government at Harvard. During that fall semester, I led a group of undergraduates in a weekly seminar about effective citizenship. Hayley Fink, Matt Greenfield, Rachel Johnson, Steven Johnston, Richard Krumholz, Nicholas Melvoin, John Oxtoby, Baruch Shemtov, Zak Tanjeloff, and Jarrett Zafran were highly motivated students who helped me understand the skills required to take a citizen from a seat in the audience to the arena floor.

Several members of the Kennedy School faculty—including Professors Archon Fung, David King, and Robert D. Putnam—greatly facilitated the task of putting concepts onto paper. I was fortunate to have the support of remarkable people at the Institute of Politics, including Eric R. Andersen, Sarah Bieging, and Amy Howell. Professor Graham Allison, director of the Belfer Center for Science and International Affairs and Douglas Dillon Professor of Government at the Kennedy School, has been for many years a mentor. He is responsible for the title of this book.

No officeholder could survive without an effective staff. I've been blessed to work with dedicated staff members for my entire career, including the two who worked with me during the writing of this book. Chip Burpee and Thomas White played critical roles in the completion of this project. They kept me on schedule, provided research assistance, and performed the many other tasks that have enabled me to stay actively engaged in local, state, and national issues following my retirement from public office.

Since 2007 I have chaired the board of oversight of the Bob Graham Center for Public Service at the University of Florida. I have received generous support from its interim director, Walter A. Rosenbaum; associate directors, Michael Bowen and David Hedge; program assistant, Kimberly Martin; and administrator, Sherry C. Feagle.

I am very grateful to the citizen leaders who helped in crafting the eleven case studies in this book that powerfully illustrate democracy in action. James Fogarty, Chad Griffin, Dan Leistikow, and Rebecca Sinderbrand were instrumental in telling the story of Campaign Georgetown in the prologue. For chapter 1, Roger Turner and Bob and Susan Leveille, members of the Jackson County Smart Roads Alliance, and Walter Kulash, the Smart Roads Alliance's invaluable consultant, generously gave of their time and materials in narrating this ongoing saga. The chapter 2 case study would not have been possible without Cindy DeRocher, a leader of the successful initiatives for fair insurance rates in Monroe County, and Heather Carruthers, a Monroe County commissioner.

South Florida's leading historian, Arva Parks McCabe, and one of its most distinguished civic leaders, Ruth Shack, lived through and were invaluable sources on the revitalization of South Beach, described in chapter 3. Dr. Cyndy Simms, Bob Maddox, and Dr. David Hill, three of the principal figures in the educational reform initiative in Steamboat Springs discussed in chapter 4, shared several hours with me explaining how confrontation evolved into highly successful consensus. Thanks also to Hill Research Consultants for allowing me to display part of the Steamboat Springs poll at the end of chapter 4. In chapter 5 the case study benefitted greatly from the insights of Karolyn Nunnallee, former president of Mothers Against Drink Driving (MADD). The unnamed (but known to me) university professor in chapter 6 refreshed my memory and added details to his lesson in clock management. I also owe thanks to Professor Burdett Loomis of the University of Kansas for his counsel on the importance of deadlines, trends, and cycles in the political process. My telephone conversations with him, as well as the wisdom in his book *Time, Politics, and Policies: A Legislative Year*, greatly assisted in the development of chapter 6.

For more than three decades I have maintained a friendship with Tom Fiedler, former *Miami Herald* reporter and editor and now dean of the College of Communications at Boston University, because we always have understood the boundaries and standards of a relationship between a journalist and a politician. His willingness to contribute the Max Rameau story, as well as substantial advice on engaging the media, for chapter 8 is but the latest expression of that friendship. Rick Reilly of ESPN and Elizabeth Gore of the United Nations Foundation were as generous with their contributions to chapter 9 as supporters of Nothing But Nets have been in reducing deaths caused by malaria. I also greatly appreciate the assistance of George Deukmejian, former governor of California, and his former chief of staff, Steve Merksamer, with the East L.A. case study in chapter 10.

For two of the chapters, I owe enormous thanks to the President and Fellows of Harvard College and the John F. Kennedy School of Government's Case Program. Harvey Simon originally told the unabridged story of Fairlawn in "The Orange Hats of Fairlawn: A Washington, DC Neighborhood Battles Drugs" (C16-91-1034.0). I am grateful for permission to condense that case study and use it in chapter 7. Two Harvard Kennedy School case studies written by Pamela Varley: "No Prison in East L.A.! Birth of a Grassroots Movement" (C14-00-1541.0) and "No Prison in East L.A.! Birth of a Grassroots Movement Sequel" (C14-00-1541.1) were important sources for the case study in chapter 10.

Several professionals generously shared their insights into the workings of government and politics in the "Tips from the Pros" segments in this owner's manual. I am grateful to Alyce Robertson, executive director of the Miami Downtown Development Authority; Tom Eldon of Schroth Eldon and Associates; Geoff Garin of Peter D. Hart Research Associates; Mark Block, director of external relations for *Newsweek;* and Josh Koster of Chong Designs for providing readers with practical advice on how citizens can maximize their effectiveness.

I am very fortunate that CQ Press took such a strong interest in this book and wanted to publish it. You are reading these pages thanks to the tireless work of CQ Press editors Charisse Kiino,

Dwain Smith, Ann Davies, Lorna Notsch, and Steve Pazdan; marketing manager Chris O'Brien and associate marketing manager Erin Snow; and other CQ Press employees.

Five women who have long influenced my life and work played critical roles in this project. My four daughters—Gwen Graham, Cissy McCullough, Suzanne Gibson, and Kendall Elias—have not only provided love, support, and eleven wonderful grandchildren but also helped me by suggesting ideas and reviewing chapters.

Throughout this process, as she has been for more than fifty years, my wife, Adele, was an invaluable source of inspiration, encouragement, and—drawing on her decades of experience as a teacher and civic activist—advice on the skills of participatory citizenship. Without her, this project would long ago have lost momentum.

Chris Hand greatly appreciates the many people mentioned above for their contributions of time, insights, and suggestions to this owner's manual, particularly those who were on the receiving end of his frequent telephone calls and e-mails. He is also deeply grateful to the friends, colleagues, and family members whose support made his participation possible—Heather Sarra; Jack and Grace Hand; Mike, Sarah, and Liam Hand; Marcellite Baker; Wayne Hogan; J. J. Balaban; and Stephen Schmier.

Prologue

Student Government[1]

For most Americans the major news event on November 5, 1996, was Bill Clinton's reelection as president of the United States. Clinton's victory was historic. For the first time since Franklin Delano Roosevelt won his fourth presidential contest in 1944, voters had chosen the same Democratic president for a second consecutive election. Clinton's triumph was especially significant in the nation's capital. It meant that residents of Washington, D.C., could avoid the upheaval that often accompanies a change in the presidency. White House aides and other executive branch officials could start working on Clinton's second-term agenda. Members of Congress and various Washington-based interest groups could set their own legislative priorities with knowledge of who would have the power to sign or veto bills. National print and television media outlets could begin reporting on the new faces and new policies that might appear in a second Clinton term.

But in one corner of the nation's capital, the big story of the November 1996 election was not the presidential contest but

---

[1] In addition to contemporaneous news accounts from such sources as the Associated Press, *Washington Post, Washington Times, New York Times, The Hoya, Georgetown Voice,* and *Washington City Paper,* the preparation of this case study would not have been possible without the generous assistance of former Campaign Georgetown leaders James Fogarty, Chad Griffin, Dan Leistikow, and Rebecca Sinderbrand.

one with historic meaning of its own. Voters in one of the city's Advisory Neighborhood Commission districts—ANC-2E (www .anc2e.com)—elected two new members who were barely old enough to cast ballots for themselves: James Fogarty and Rebecca Sinderbrand, both nineteen years old and students at Georgetown University. That these new commissioners were precocious was newsworthy in itself. But the events that led to and followed their election were even more significant. For good or ill, Georgetown University student leaders had determined that the ANC did not represent their interests and decided to influence the commission by electing new members. Whether one agreed or disagreed with the movement to elect Fogarty and Sinderbrand, the effort was an indisputably powerful example of effective citizen participation in the democratic process.

THE DISTRICT OF COLUMBIA AND NEIGHBORHOOD DEMOCRACY

The District of Columbia, which comprises the city of Washington, is by design more than a typical city but less than a sovereign state. Its governance has long reflected that unique status. From the District's official organization in 1801 until the last quarter of the twentieth century, the federal government held strict jurisdiction over D.C. government. During that time, citizens who lived in Washington did not have the power to vote in presidential elections, elect representatives to the U.S. Senate or House of Representatives, or choose local governing officials. For most of this time the District was governed by a board of commissioners appointed by the president and overseen by Congress.

The wall of federal control over the District began to crack in the 1960s and 1970s in favor of more self-government. In March 1961 the constitutionally required number of states to amend the U.S. Constitution voted to ratify the Twenty-Third Amendment, which permits D.C. citizens to cast ballots in presidential elections.

Twelve years later, in 1973, Congress passed home-rule legislation for the District, which allowed for the direct election of a mayor and a thirteen-member council—eight elected from individual, geographic-based districts, or wards, and five elected at-large from the District as a whole.

The layers of citizen involvement in the administration of Washington did not stop there. The fledgling D.C. government established a network of thirty-seven Advisory Neighborhood Commissions to give citizens a greater voice on issues related to their specific communities. Each ANC is responsible for a certain boundaried section of Washington. For example, ANC-2E covers the neighborhoods of Georgetown, Burleith, and Hillandale. Additionally, each commissioner represents a specific part of the ANC territory called a Single Member District (SMD). Each commissioner serves a two-year term and is accountable to approximately 2,000 constituents in his or her SMD. Commissioners are not paid, but they control a small annual budget for supplies and neighborhood grants. The D.C. government describes the role of ANCs as follows:

> The Advisory Neighborhood Commissions consider a wide range of policies and programs affecting their neighborhoods, including traffic, parking, recreation, street improvements, liquor licenses, zoning, economic development, police protection, sanitation and trash collection, and the District's annual budget.
>
> In each of these areas, the intent of the ANC legislation is to ensure input from an advisory board that is made up of the residents of the neighborhoods that are directly affected by government action. The ANCs are the body of government with the closest official ties to the people in a neighborhood.
>
> The ANCs present their positions and recommendations on issues to various District government agencies, the Executive Branch, and the Council. They

also present testimony to independent agencies, boards, and commissions, usually under the rules of procedure specific to those entities. By law, the ANCs may also present their positions to Federal agencies.[2]

District of Columbia law requires that the D.C. Council and various appointed bodies, such as the Zoning Commission, give "great weight" to ANC resolutions and decisions. In 1997 Councilman Jack Evans said that he and his colleagues on the council "really take them [the ANCs] seriously. We look to them to get their advice. Ninety-five percent of the time, we follow the lead of the ANC."[3] Although others questioned the influence of ANCs, Evans's opinion had real significance for Georgetown University students: Since 1991 he has represented the district that includes Georgetown, Burleith, and Hillandale—all neighborhoods where students live and park, and all within ANC-2E.[4]

TOWN VS. GOWN

Conflicts between town and gown date back to the Middle Ages. Back then, differences of opinion between local community members and university residents were not to be taken lightly. In 1355 an argument in a tavern near Oxford University exploded into a two-day battle between townspeople and Oxford scholars that left scores on both sides dead.[5] Although bloody disputes are uncommon today, universities and their surrounding neighborhoods still have heated clashes. The tension between residents in Washington's

---

[2] Advisory Neighborhood Commissions, http://anc.dc.gov/anc/site/default.asp.

[3] Todd Beamon, "Even After 2 Decades, ANCs Fall Short of a D.C. Dream," *Washington Post*, March 30, 1997, B1.

[4] Jack Evans, Ward 2, www.dccouncil.washington.dc.us/EVANS/about.html.

[5] Oxford City Council, "Top Ten Astonishing Facts," www.oxford.gov.uk/community/interesting-facts.cfm.

storied Georgetown neighborhood and the highly regarded Jesuit academic institution of the same name is a classic example.

Georgetown University (www.georgetown.edu), founded in 1789, sits on high ground north of M Street N.W. and west of Wisconsin Avenue. The university's elevated topography, which offers breathtaking views of the Potomac River, the nearby Virginia suburbs, and parts of the D.C. skyline, matches its towering heights in the academic world. But unlike most university communities, where the college is the undisputed center of attention, the surrounding neighborhood has a rich history all its own. Georgetown, which was established as a municipality in 1751, when the area still belonged to the British colony of Maryland, was an early hub of commerce and shipping. It was incorporated into the District of Columbia in 1871. Today, Georgetown's cobblestone streets and brick townhouses, convenience to downtown Washington, noted restaurants, and high-end shopping have attracted many of Washington's most prominent and affluent citizens as residents.[6]

For much of their recent history, the two Georgetowns—university and neighborhood—have experienced a rocky coexistence. Neighbors have long griped about the university's expanding footprint in the community. In August 1990 residents appeared before a Washington zoning board meeting and asked the members not to approve a university development plan until the university agreed to cap enrollment and require that students live on campus. As one citizen leader complained, "[s]lumlords are willing to stuff six or eight students in a house. Late at night they will come pouring out of the houses, drinking beer and screaming at each other."[7] In the early 1990s forty residents formed a group called Residents for a Safe Georgetown to pressure some of the neighborhood's most popular bars—largely frequented by

---

[6] Georgetown Historic District, www.nps.gov/history/nR/travel/wash/dc15.htm.

[7] "Campus Life: Georgetown, Neighbors Fight Student Housing Off Campus," *New York Times,* August 5, 1992.

students—into meeting several demands, including more aggressively cracking down on underage drinking and refusing service to intoxicated customers. In 1994 a flood of complaints about student renters making loud noise, littering, leaving lawns uncut, increasing traffic, and taking up parking spaces throughout Northwest Washington led three D.C. Council members to introduce legislation that would have limited the formation of group houses. Neighborhood activists also fought the university over its desire to build a campus power plant.

But it was not until the eight-member ANC took direct action against students that they decided to flex their civic muscles. In the summer of 1996 the ANC endorsed a proposal to limit student parking privileges in the neighborhoods around campus. The limitations were to take effect on October 1, 1996. The ANC also supported a rezoning plan that would limit each home to no more than three unrelated residents—a move that would make it very difficult for Georgetown students to rent nearby houses and apartments. Since more than 1,200 students lived off campus in surrounding neighborhoods, the ANC plan would have affected a large section of the student body. Faced with the threat of the ANC taking action to deprive them of parking and housing options, Georgetown student leaders decided to fight back at the ballot box. They figured their best opportunity was November 5, 1996, the next time that all eight ANC seats would be up for reelection.

CAMPAIGN GEORGETOWN

The entity through which students fought back was not originally intended to mobilize voters for particular candidates. In early 1996 approximately two dozen Georgetown students formed a nonpartisan organization called Campaign Georgetown. Their primary goals were to register Georgetown students for the fall presidential election and to foster conversation about local issues. But when the ANC voted for the parking restrictions and supported a crackdown on group homes, Campaign Georgetown leaders made a last-minute decision to compete in the ANC election.

It would have been overly ambitious for Georgetown students to try to win all eight seats on the ANC. The map made it impossible. In 1991, when the District redrew ANC political boundaries as part of the reapportionment required every ten years, the Georgetown ANC had grown from six seats to eight. The new lines spread student housing across all eight districts—an effort to dilute the potential impact of student voting.[8] But Hoya students didn't need all eight seats on the ANC. Some of the commissioners were open to student participation in neighborhood affairs.[9] If students could organize and elect one or two commissioners, they might have a chance to recruit allies and prevent anti-university policies from seeing the light of day.

Although it was pressed for time—like most jurisdictions the District of Columbia required candidates to put their names on the ballot several months before an election, and the deadline was fast approaching—Campaign Georgetown paid close attention to details when selecting its candidates. The group decided that each candidate should be someone who had lived at the same address for a significant period of time; who had been registered to vote at that address for a similar period of time; and who would be

[8] Shaun Sutner, "New Boundaries to Redefine ANC Politics," *Washington Post,* September 12, 1991, J1; Tracy Zupancis, "ANC Districts Redrawn," *The Hoya,* August 31, 2001.

[9] In October 1996 two ANC-2E commissioners—Judith Dollenmayer and Jonda McFarlane—wrote a letter to the *Washington Post* in which they distanced themselves from anti-university forces on the ANC. Dollenmayer and McFarlane, "Education with Representation," *Washington Post,* October 5, 1996, A21. McFarlane repeatedly encouraged student participation on the ANC. See Linda Wheeler, "Student's Election Riles Some in Georgetown," *Washington Post,* November 14, 1996, J1; and Julie Goodman, "Some Say College Aggravates Area's Decline," *Washington Post,* January 9, 1997.

able to serve the full, two-year ANC term if elected. With those restrictions, Campaign Georgetown selected two candidates from its leadership: James Fogarty, a junior from San Francisco, and Rebecca Sinderbrand, a junior from Brooklyn. Because Fogarty and Sinderbrand could not qualify for the ballot unless each secured the signatures of at least twenty-five registered voters in their respective ANC districts, the two candidates canvassed the Georgetown campus and the neighborhoods until they found enough signatories. Sinderbrand's effort was hampered by Mother Nature but saved by divine intervention. With only a couple of days to gather signatures before the filing deadline, and a tropical storm bearing down on Washington, it appeared that she might fall short. But, at the last minute, Sinderbrand's campaign team visited a convent in Burleith and found enough nuns to put her over the top.

With two candidates on the ballot—Fogarty in district ANC-2E05 and Sinderbrand in ANC-2E03—Campaign Georgetown next resumed its effort to register as many Georgetown students as possible. This was no easy task. At nearly every campus in America, students are often reluctant to give up their home registration. Most employ the same reasoning: College is just the place where I am staying for the next four years; home will always be there. Campaign Georgetown faced another challenge. In a presidential election year, on-campus political organizations, such as the College Democrats and College Republicans, wanted students to cast their ballots where they would do the most good for their preferred candidates. Since the District of Columbia's vote is historically conceded to the Democratic candidate even before the campaign begins, a student from a swing state, such as Florida, Ohio, Michigan, or Pennsylvania, would help President Clinton or his chief opponent, Sen. Bob Dole, more by voting at home.

Fortunately for Campaign Georgetown, the loss of parking and the threat of losing prime housing proved much more powerful than the presidential election. But Campaign Georgetown was fighting more than home-state loyalty and strategic voting. It also had to contend with an aggressive effort from some ANC incumbents and their allies to discourage students from voting. In September 2006 an anonymous flier appeared in dorms and student houses. As one newspaper reported, "[t]he flier told students that registering to vote in the District could cause them to lose grant money from their home states." The fliers also stated that students must pay D.C. income taxes and obtain D.C. driver's licenses.[10]

The flier turned out to be a stroke of good fortune for Campaign Georgetown. When the document was traced back to an ANC commissioner who opposed the student candidacies, students reacted with anger at what they saw as voter intimidation and misleading advertising. Dan Leistikow, the chair of Campaign Georgetown, filed a complaint with the D.C. Board of Elections and Ethics, and student voter registration gained new momentum in the critical days before the deadline. By the time voter registration closed in October 1996, Campaign Georgetown had registered more than 1,000 students living on campus and in the nearby neighborhoods—including one-fourth of all undergraduates.

As Campaign Georgetown focused on the task of registering voters, Fogarty and Sinderbrand each embarked upon their campaigns. Both candidates ran on a platform of change. Fogarty expressed concern about the parking and housing restrictions and the failure of the ANC to include students in the decision process. "We didn't get to say anything about that," he told the *Washington Post.* "We should be included in these decisions because we, too, are residents."[11] After both candidates attended their first ANC meeting in the fall of 1996 and were met with

---

[10] Julie Goodman, "Residents Decry Georgetown Students' ANC Bids," *Washington Post,* September 26, 1996, J1.

[11] Wheeler, "Student's Election Riles Some in Georgetown."

indifference, Sinderbrand observed that "[t]he debate seemed to take place around students, but not including them." [12]

The candidates worked hard to communicate their message to individual voters: Students should be included in decisions such as parking and housing that affect their lives. Sinderbrand and her supporters went door-to-door throughout her ANC district, asking for votes from students and nonstudents alike and placing signs in supporters' yards. But Sinderbrand wanted to do more than just build up her name recognition. She wanted to show that she had specific policy ideas on a number of neighborhood issues, not just those affecting students. As a result Sinderbrand's team produced and distributed a detailed campaign brochure, and she spoke at candidate forums. Those efforts paid off—literally. Despite low individual contribution limits, the campaign found it very difficult to raise money from students. But some local residents, who agreed with Sinderbrand's positions and were disillusioned with the neighborhood activists who opposed her, provided enough resources to help her make it to Election Day.

While the campaigns worked to win a few votes at a time, Campaign Georgetown raised voter awareness of the overall ANC election through the news media. Former Clinton campaign and administration staffer Chad Griffin, who had joined the White House press staff in 1993, when he was only nineteen years old, later matriculated at Georgetown and became one of Campaign Georgetown's leaders. Griffin's experience and media savvy helped to attract coverage from campus newspapers—the Georgetown *Hoya* and *Georgetown Voice*—and national news organizations, including the Associated Press, *Washington Post,* and *Washington Times.* With the onslaught of this mass communication and the contact efforts of the individual campaigns, a voter would have

---

[12] Goodman, "Some Say College Aggravates Area's Decline."

had to work very hard to avoid information about the ANC election.

Registering voters, recruiting strong candidates, raising money, and communicating the message are only part of the battle in a political campaign. If many registered students and other supporters failed to cast their ballots, Fogarty and Sinderbrand would have had little chance of winning. But Campaign Georgetown leaders and volunteers used four strategies of their own design—and one inadvertently handed to them by the opposition—to ensure strong voter participation.

First, Campaign Georgetown cultivated a large number of young student registrants who were excited about voting for the first time.[13] Many, if not most, Georgetown freshmen and sophomores had never cast a ballot in any election, let alone one that would decide a president of the United States and elect ANC commissioners who could affect their lives in very direct ways. Their enthusiasm helped both candidates, but especially Fogarty, whose district included a freshman dormitory. Second, campaign leaders continued to highlight the housing and parking issues that had a direct impact on a large number of student voters. Third, they appealed to students' civic pride. "Some people say students are transient residents and have no stake in the community," Leistikow told a local newspaper. "From our standpoint, if the trash isn't picked up, if there's crime on the streets, if there's traffic, it affects us. We're part of the community and want to be active."[14]

Finally, and perhaps most valuable in practical terms, Campaign Georgetown built an effective voter turnout program. Most campaigns refer to voter turnout operations as their "ground game"—a process at which Campaign Georgetown's leaders and

---

[13] Ibid.

[14] Barrington Salmon, "Georgetown Resident Tried to Keep Students from Voting," *Washington Times,* December 16, 1996, A14.

volunteers were adept. Before Election Day, hundreds of volunteers barnstormed common areas, classrooms, libraries, dormitories, and off-campus student housing to encourage voter turnout. The Election Day effort was especially sophisticated for a student-led campaign. Early in the morning, Campaign Georgetown leaders and volunteers e-mailed and telephoned every registered student with a reminder to vote. Because the ANC had not placed any polling sites on campus, the campaign arranged for shuttle buses that would depart every twenty minutes and provide students with transportation to their precincts. Each of the polling places had a student poll checker who monitored the list of registered voters to determine which students had not voted. Those lists were checked and rechecked throughout the day, and students who had not yet cast ballots were called and e-mailed until they voted.

Opposition leaders worked hard as well, but their messages and tactics often played right into the hands of Campaign Georgetown. Throughout the campaign, some in the opposition continued to question whether students were invested enough in the community to serve effectively or to deserve a say in neighborhood affairs. In late September, one opposition leader suggested that student commissioners would not care about or know how to address everyday challenges, such as sewer problems or tree removals: "The students' concerns are different from the concerns of the people who live here year in and year out." [15] Although these arguments were clearly aimed at nonstudent voters, they helped Campaign Georgetown motivate students to participate at the polls.

Opposition actions on Election Day itself were also motivational, especially for certain nonstudent voters. Throughout the day, opposition leaders maintained a steady presence at the polls to challenge individual student voters as they went to cast ballots. Most if not all of these nearly 400 challenges were rejected, but they caused long delays and angered voters. As one neighborhood

---

[15] Goodman, "Residents Decry Georgetown Students' ANC Bids."

resident described the challenges, "[i]t felt communistic. They singled out young people, looked at their driver's licenses and took their names down." [16] The challenges were so sweeping that even some youthful-looking nonstudents were targeted—which made them more sympathetic to the student commission candidates. One thirty-five-year-old nonstudent voter, who was delayed ninety minutes, described herself as "so angry at the interference that was going on." [17] And, although the challenges could have been devastating had they succeeded, the failed tactic may actually have won votes for Fogarty and Sinderbrand.

The effectiveness of Campaign Georgetown's work was clear on Election Day. When ballots were counted, Fogarty had swamped incumbent commissioner Beverly Jost by a margin of 401–162—giving him more than 70 percent of the vote. Sinderbrand's victory, confirmed nine days later when absentee votes were tallied, was a narrow one over incumbent Patricia Scolaro, 259–256. More than 92 percent of the students Campaign Georgetown had registered had turned out to vote.

A PERMANENT CAMPAIGN

The two new commissioners-elect and their Campaign Georgetown supporters soon learned a difficult lesson about politics and government: Few victories are final, and few losses are irrevocable. In December 2006 the defeated incumbents and another 2E commissioner challenged the results of the election in court. On December 24 the D.C. Court of Appeals stayed the swearing in of Fogarty and Sinderbrand, pending further developments in the challenge. For more than two weeks the two students were in

---

[16] Barrington Salmon, "University Students Questioned at Polls," *Washington Times,* November 8, 1996, C8.

[17] David Montgomery, "Heated Races, Emotions: Local Bids and Ballots Feed Turnout, Tempers," *Washington Post,* November 6, 1996, B13.

limbo and had to watch from afar as the rest of ANC-2E took office on January 2, 1997. But five days later the stay was lifted, and Councilman Jack Evans swore in the new members just hours before their first meeting. Their triumph was official: For the first time in the twenty-year history of this ANC, Georgetown students were serving as commissioners.

The election of Fogarty and Sinderbrand was not the end of Campaign Georgetown. It was only the end of the beginning.[18] Over the next five years, Georgetown students would widen their civic involvement, participation in neighborhood affairs, and influence on the ANC.

In November 1997 the university administration and students, including Commissioners Fogarty and Sinderbrand, persuaded the D.C. Zoning Commission to reject the proposal limiting shared housing to three unrelated residents.[19] One year later, in the 1998 election, Campaign Georgetown helped Matt Payne succeed Fogarty on the ANC. Unlike the situation in 1996, Payne was unopposed and did not face a legal challenge about his right to run or serve. In February 1999 the D.C. Court of Appeals dismissed the challenge of two former commissioners, Beverly Jost and Patricia Scolaro, in the November 1996 ANC election results.

Momentum remained strong in 2000. In the fall of that year Campaign Georgetown convinced more than 750 students to register to vote in the District of Columbia. Co-chair Brian McCabe

---

[18] Speaking in November 1942 after a critical Allied victory in North Africa, British Prime Minister Winston Churchill told his audience, "[N]ow this is not the end. It is not even the beginning of the end. But it is, perhaps, the end of the beginning." www.winstonchurchill.org/i4a/pages/index.cfm?pageid=388#not_the_end.

[19] Government of the District of Columbia, Zoning Commission, http://dcoz.dc.gov/orders/836_96-15.pdf.

attributed the large numbers to continuing student concerns about housing, the ten-year campus plan, and other community issues: "They are excited about voting, and they realize that local politics really does affect them." [20] In November 2000 Justin Kopa and Justin Wagner became the fourth and fifth students elected to serve on the ANC.

From a governmental perspective, 2001 was the year that the continued efforts of Campaign Georgetown had the biggest payback. Ten years earlier the D.C. government had adopted an ANC redistricting plan that attempted to dilute student voters to the point of political nonexistence. Although neither Kopa nor Wagner supported the new plan adopted in 2001 (they had their own plan, which was defeated), Wagner acknowledged that the final product was an improvement over the status quo. The plan effectively guaranteed that students would hold one ANC seat. It also put enough student voters in two other seats to make them reasonably competitive.

But perhaps the strongest sign of how far the ANC had come in a short time occurred at the October 2001 meeting. In a unanimous, 8–0, vote, the ANC enacted a Student Bill of Rights. It proclaimed in part that ANC-2E:

> affirms the right of university students to full participation in community and civic affairs and opposes illegal discrimination against all citizens based upon matriculation status. ANC2E encourages students to inform themselves about the surrounding communities and to actively seek ways to make a positive contribution to the neighborhood.[21]

---

[20] Liz McDonald, "Campaign Georgetown Helps Increase Registration," *The Hoya*, October 13, 2000.

[21] Yasmine Noujaim, "ANC2E Approves Student Bill of Rights," *The Hoya*, October 5, 2001. For the full student Bill of Rights resolution, see www.anc2e.com/minutes/011002 .html.

Just a few years earlier, Campaign Georgetown did not exist and students did not participate in ANC-2E. When they finally began to take part in the process, some ANC members questioned their commitment to community affairs. After Georgetown undergraduates joined the commission, served with distinction, and achieved results, students won respect as neighborhood leaders.

The lesson was clear: Effective citizen participation in democracy makes a difference.

Introduction

In the Arena

"The objects of this primary education ... would be, [t]o give to every citizen the information he needs; ... [t]o understand his duties to his neighbors and country, and to discharge with competence the functions confided to him by either; ... [t]o instruct the mass of our citizens in these, their rights, interests, and duties, as men and citizens."

—President Thomas Jefferson

My tale starts with cold, greasy pizza.

In 1974 I was the chairman of the Florida Senate Education Committee. In preparation for the upcoming spring legislative session, the committee held a series of hearings in public schools throughout the state to hear suggestions for bills we might consider. One such hearing was at Samuel W. Wolfson High School, located in a middle-class area of Jacksonville.

Our practice was to reserve a period of time during each hearing for student comments. In most endeavors, consumers of goods or services know how well their needs are being served—and students are the primary consumers of public education.

On this morning a group of students came to the microphone to tell the committee of a serious school problem and ask for our help. The concern was bad food in the Wolfson cafeteria.

The complaint didn't shock me. As I recalled, the food at Miami Senior High School, from which I had graduated almost twenty years earlier, wasn't very appetizing. But I was surprised that these students, so close to receiving their high school diplomas, thought the Florida Legislature was the place to seek redress.

So I asked if we were the first authority to whom they had taken their concerns. I was relieved to hear that we were the third. But I was distressed when I heard the answer to my next question: Who were the first and second?

The students had first gone to the Jacksonville mayor, who agreed with the students as to the quality of the food but told them it was out of his jurisdiction. Their second request went to the Duval County sheriff, who also sympathized but said that although the food was bad it wasn't criminal. And as I had to inform the students, the Senate didn't control cafeteria menus either.

Less than a month later a group of civics teachers invited me to speak to them in Miami. I related the Wolfson experience and expressed my dismay with the students' lack of knowledge about the roles and responsibilities of government. Perhaps not diplomatically enough, I told the teachers that the students' ignorance was a strong indictment of the quality of civics education in our state.

They reacted with controlled outrage. One teacher in the audience embodied this reaction when she upbraided me. "I am sick to death of you politicians telling us how to do our job better," she seethed. "You don't know what you're talking about. You need to get in the classroom and see what it's really like—prepare the lesson plans that are intended to stimulate disinterested students, make outdated textbooks interesting, deal with all the hassle of paperwork and school bureaucracy, and try to implement politicians' nutty ideas." To deafening applause, she challenged me to come into the classroom and experience public education firsthand.

Figuring that I could afford to give up an afternoon—and reluctant to appear a coward in front of this important constituency—I accepted her challenge. She called three days later: "I have worked it out. You are to come to my school, Miami Carol City Senior High, on the day after Labor Day and report to room 207. I have arranged for you to teach a semester—eighteen weeks—of twelfth grade civics."

Eighteen weeks was far more than I had bargained for. But I felt that I had made a commitment, and I would keep it.

Looking back, I believe the late summer and fall of 1974 transformed my life. Carol City High School assigned me to work with a young, talented, and enthusiastic civics teacher named Donnel Morris. Together we developed a curriculum aimed at students who might face the most formidable obstacles in solving neighborhood problems. The course would center on several questions. How do citizens bend democracy to their will? Is it really possible to fight city hall, the school board, or the employees who run the school cafeteria? How do we organize an effective grassroots campaign for change?

In addition to structuring a curriculum of required knowledge and skills, we taught through hands-on activities. The course exposed our twenty-five students to political practitioners—candidates, officeholders, journalists, civic activists, campaign professionals, and pollsters—so that they would hear firsthand how government could be made to work for them.

On the first day of class, Mr. Morris and I asked the students to organize themselves into groups of three. The students in each group were to select a problem about which they were concerned—and which government at some level could play a role in fixing. They could select any topic. But we added an important caveat: At the end of the semester, one-third of each student's final grade would be based on their effectiveness in solving the problem their group had identified at the outset.

The results were startling. For example, one team tackled the long-standing suspicion that Miami Carol City High School received less funding per student than did a nearby Dade County public high school that was located in a higher-income neighborhood. After the high school's business faculty had given the students an introduction in reading and understanding budgets, the students pored over financial spreadsheets at the county school district headquarters. They proved that the disparity was more than a myth. Thanks to their work, the county schools superintendent recognized the inequity and vowed to correct it in the next budget cycle. That team of students received a very high grade.

I learned a lot about education during the course of the semester: how to teach civics; how to navigate the complex relationship among students, faculty, and parents; and how to understand the workings of a large urban high school. But my most important lesson was that learning by doing is very different from learning by listening. Active learning helps students understand the relevance of a subject to daily life. It provides a deep immersion into reality, not a theoretical laboratory. It contributes to a sense of self-confidence that can last a lifetime. At the end of our semester, Mr. Morris and I could almost hear the students thinking in this new way: "I can do this for myself and my family because I already have done it in the classroom."

When I decided to run for governor in 1978, I needed something to grab the public's attention statewide—something that would help voters identify with me and my campaign, that would convey my concern for the average Floridian, and that would earn free media coverage. During discussions with family, friends, and advisers, I related the lessons I had learned and the joy I had felt in that classroom at Carol City Senior High School. That transformative experience became the catalyst for my campaign strategy of performing 100 "Workdays" around the state before Election Day in November 1978. During these Workdays, I worked full shifts next to real people in typical jobs throughout Florida—everything from construction worker to police officer to bellman. I declared that my job as a civics teacher at Carol City was Workday Number One. For the next twenty-seven years—through two terms as governor and three terms in the U.S. Senate—I worked a total of 408 Workdays, averaging one per month.

In late 2004, as my retirement from the Senate grew near, several Florida newspapers wrote articles looking back over my career. Many of those newspapers offered generous tributes. But the words of praise that affected me most came from someone I had met three decades before. When the *Orlando Sentinel*'s valedictory focused on my Workdays, the story provoked an e-mail to the reporter from one of the Carol City students I had taught. Gary Cohen, now in his forties and a certified public accountant in Orlando, offered the best compliment I received in forty years of public service. He wrote:

> I remember getting a phone call from MCC's [Miami Carol City's] Guidance Department in the summer of 1974, inquiring if I would like to sign up for a class in Honors Contemporary Politics. The description sounded great, especially the involvement of our State Senator, Bob Graham. For the first 18-week semester, Bob came to our classroom on Mondays, Wednesdays and Fridays. We studied units on many topics, including the legislative process, public relations, and campaign advertising. His access to other politicians, staff and business professionals in Miami allowed him to also include other guest speakers in our class. A local television professional and a campaign manager spoke to us. Since it was an election year, he brought several politicians to our classroom. . . . It was a great experience. I have a keen interest in politics, especially at the local level, which touches the citizens most closely. . . . Bob Graham has been one of the 10 most influential persons in my life, though he probably doesn't even know this. The class at Miami Carol City was an amazing experience.[1]

After leaving the Senate in January 2005, I spent the 2005–2006 academic year as a senior fellow at Harvard University's

---

[1] Gary Cohen, e-mail to the *Orlando Sentinel*, December 23, 2004.

Kennedy School of Government. During the fall semester, I led a group of undergraduates in a weekly seminar on the skills of effective citizenship. From those Harvard students, I learned that lessons in participatory democracy also are needed at the college level and into adulthood. Even these highly motivated students had not been exposed to basic skills of citizenship or given the opportunity to apply those skills.

The failure to master the basic skills of participatory citizenship is not limited to students at Carol City or Harvard. Since the 1960s citizenship education has withered in the vineyard of American education. Until that time, the average secondary student had taken three courses in civics. Today, a student is lucky to have taken one. The pace of decline has increased as high-stakes tests, such as those required by the controversial No Child Left Behind law, have pushed civics, as well as history, geography, and the arts out of the curriculum.

What little civics teaching is left only allows students to become better informed spectators—learning names, dates, the three branches of government, and the language of the Constitution and the Bill of Rights. While that knowledge is fundamental, it isn't enough. Our goal should be high school graduates who can pass the Jeffersonian test of discharging citizenship duties with competence and confidence.

Perhaps an analogy better illustrates the mission. Almost any music enrichment course will turn its students into more discerning symphony listeners. But there is a fundamental difference between listening from the audience and playing in the orchestra. Only those students who actually pick up instruments will have the ability and power to change the tune.

There are plenty of institutions in American life that have contributed to the sorry state of citizenship: political parties, elected officials, the media, and various special-interest groups. But the burden to rescue democracy rests primarily on the American educational system. If our elementary schools, secondary schools, community colleges, and four-year colleges and universities do not produce new generations of engaged citizens, our democratic institutions are in peril. As Maynard Hutchins, former president of the University of Chicago, once observed, "The death of democracy is not likely to be an assassination from ambush. It will be a slow extinction from apathy, indifference, and undernourishment." [2]

The excitement surrounding the 2008 presidential election and President Barack Obama's inauguration made American democracy seem healthy. According to the Center for Information and Research on Civic Learning and Engagement (CIRCLE), an estimated 23 million voters under the age of thirty participated in the 2008 election—3.4 million more than had voted in 2004. Between 2000 and 2008 youth turnout grew from 41 percent to 52 percent. The District of Columbia estimates that nearly 2 million people braved freezing cold temperatures in Washington, D.C., on January 20, 2009, to see President Obama and Vice President Joe Biden sworn into office.

But these statistics, while encouraging, are not the entire story. Although young people voted in greater numbers in 2008 than ever before, youth voting was nearly 10 percent less than overall voter turnout. Additionally, CIRCLE reports that in 2008 youth who had never attended college made up 43 percent of the under-thirty population but supplied only 30 percent of the youth vote. In other words, young Americans whose civic education ends in high school are much less likely to engage in the most basic form of citizen participation than are those who attend college. Even more worrisome is the fact that many Americans apparently see voting as the sole form of civic participation. In July 2008 the National Conference on Citizenship surveyed more than 1,000 citizens to produce its 2008 Civic Health Index. Less

---

[2] Robert Maynard Hutchins, *Great Books, the Foundation of a Liberal Education* (New York: Simon and Schuster, 1954), 23.

than 20 percent of those interviewed believed they would talk about campaign issues after the presidential race was over. A mere 14 percent said they would try to change local policies affecting their schools, jobs, or neighborhoods. Less than 10 percent believed they would contact a local official about an issue.

So while the 2008 campaign provided a needed calorie boost, at a much deeper level basic citizenship—our personal commitment to engaging in all aspects of the democratic process—is still starving for sustenance. My goal in writing this book is to provide you with nutrition. I hope that when you have finished reading it, you will have the information and skills you need to do the following:

- Understand and influence the decisions of government. You should be familiar with nuts-and-bolts concepts, such as determining which level of government—local, state, or federal—is responsible for an issue and which specific agency or office at that level can address your concern.

- Achieve a positive experience with government. I strongly believe that young people have lower voting rates than the population as a whole in part because few have had favorable interactions with government. For example, you stood in a long line at the driver's license bureau only to be rewarded for your wait by a desultory clerk. Once you got your license, you got fined for a driving violation within a few months. These are not experiences likely to stimulate you and your peers to see government as an entity that can affect your lives positively.

- Convince your school, college, or university to shift civics teaching from a lecture-based approach that focuses on governmental structure to a dynamic experience that emphasizes personal engagement. Imagine if basketball coaches tried to teach the sport by explaining it to their players, rather than taking them onto the court to play the game. Civics is being taught in just that way, and it is no surprise that many citizens can't play when they step onto the court of democracy.

- Deal with government at the level where you are most likely to experience it—your school, college or university, city hall, county council, local school board, or planning and zoning commission.
- Develop the core personal skills necessary to influence democracy. These include the critical thinking needed to analyze an issue and develop a strategy; the information-gathering aptitude to determine the facts; and the communication skills to persuade the appropriate decision makers.
- Overcome the cynicism that says you can't affect government action and replace it with the confidence that says citizen participation is the lifeblood of democracy.

The worst mistake I could make in writing this book would be to provide the "how to" of active democratic engagement—a lecture on paper—without showing you how citizens have succeeded in making government respond. That's why the book started with the story of the Georgetown University students who attempted to influence their local Advisory Neighborhood Commission in Washington, D.C., and why each of the next ten chapters starts with a real-life case study. The chapters also include numerous other examples and provide hypothetical situations and exercises based on actual events. These studies, examples, scenarios, and exercises should help you understand that civics is not a scientific experiment you can consistently replicate. Civics is exciting precisely because there is no set path to victory. Every citizen campaign is different from the last. As you will see, active civic engagement requires flexibility and the ability to shift tactics quickly. That's the price of a democratic system where human qualities and values—such as ambitions, capabilities, and emotions—affect both decision makers and those attempting to influence decision makers.

Each of the case studies in the ten chapters will introduce a particular citizenship skill. First, you will learn how to identify and articulate the problem that you want to solve—not too narrowly, or too broadly, but just right. Second, you will discover how to gather the facts necessary both to solve the problem and to persuade decision makers to adopt your proposed solution. You are not a parent arguing with a child—"because I said so" will not convince anyone to support you. Third, you will identify the levels of government—local, state, or federal—and the particular agencies or entities within those levels that have the authority to act on your concerns and implement your proposed solutions.

Fourth, you will learn how to determine where members of the public who have an interest in your concern stand on your issue. Put another way, you will know how to put your toe in the water and determine whether and when it is prudent to jump into the pool. Fifth, you will learn how to influence the individual decision makers who have the power to propel your initiative to victory or doom it to defeat. Sixth, you will realize that the calendar on your wall, or even the watch on you wrist, can be your salvation or your undoing. Government decisions come with deadlines, and those decisions are also are affected by cycles and trends.

Seventh, you will appreciate strength in numbers and learn how to find and unite with other individuals and groups who share your concerns. Eighth, you will see that the media can be a powerful ally in sharing your concerns and solutions with both decision makers and the general public to whom those officials are accountable. Ninth, you will learn that civic engagement, like most things in life, has a price. You'll need at least a small amount of financial support to be successful. Tenth, you will recognize that politics is often a zero-sum game: You win or you lose. But winning or losing is not the end of your effort, and you will learn not to snatch defeat from the jaws of victory or surrender at the first obstacle.

While you are reading and absorbing the skill sets of participatory citizenship, I hope you will also be practicing those skills on a subject about which you are passionate—and in the process contributing to a better school, college, community, state, or nation. Nothing is more gratifying than seeing a problem and applying the talents you are mastering to solve it. Once you take those steps, you will have the satisfaction of success and the self-confidence that you can repeat that success throughout your lifetime.

President Teddy Roosevelt said it best in his "Citizenship in a Republic" speech at the Sorbonne, in Paris, on April 23, 1910:

> It is not the critic who counts: not the man who points out how the strong man stumbles or where the doer of deeds could have done better. The credit belongs to the man who is actually in the arena, whose face is marred by dust and sweat and blood, who strives valiantly, who errs and comes up short again and again, because there is no effort without error or shortcoming, but who knows the great enthusiasms, the great devotions, who spends himself for a worthy cause; who, at the best, knows, in the end, the triumph of high achievement, and who, at the worst, if he fails, at least he fails while daring greatly, so that his place shall never be with those cold and timid souls who knew neither victory nor defeat.[3]

---

[3] Theodore Roosevelt Association, "In His Own Words," www.theodoreroosevelt .org/life/quotes.htm.

As you will see over the course of the next ten chapters, active citizenship is flesh and blood, drama and comedy, triumph and tragedy, pleasure and pain. But what those highs and lows ultimately produce is the sublime fulfillment of democracy's promise.

Let the games begin!

1 What's Your Problem?

Defining the Challenge That Active Citizenship Can Solve

"Let's work the problem, people."

—Gene Kranz (Ed Harris) in *Apollo 13*

Case in Point: A Road through the Mountains

For the residents of Jackson County, North Carolina, their area's richest blessing has also turned out to be its worst curse. Wedged between the hills of South Carolina and the heart of the Appalachian Mountain chain, Jackson County is one of the most picturesque locales in the United States. With its green mountains, brilliant autumns, and relatively mild summers, it is little wonder that Scotch-Irish Protestants used to life in the Scottish Highlands founded Jackson County in the 1850s.

For its first century Jackson County was remote and isolated, its stunning beauty known only to residents and a few visitors. That all changed in the 1960s, when Americans discovered the well-kept secret. For the next five decades Jackson County's population kept growing—more than doubling from 17,780 in 1960 to an estimated 36,751 in 2007. When Western Carolina College, in the Jackson County town of Cullowhee, became Western Carolina University in 1964, it had 2,659 students. By 2008 enrollment had skyrocketed to 9,055. But the surge in the number of permanent residents and students is only half the story. It does not account for the multitude of visitors who annually seek temporary refuge in the cool mountain air, crystal clear lakes and streams, and tranquility of mountain life. From April to October towns such as Cashiers in Jackson County and Highlands in nearby Macon County are crawling with travelers from all fifty states.

Growth has brought change to Jackson County. Skeptics need look no further than NC 107, a north–south thoroughfare that mostly parallels the rippling, white-foamed Tuckasegee River. This rural, winding two-lane strip is today lined with the tell-tale signs of urbanization: tourist motels, boat rental shops, gas stations, Wal-Marts, and fast-food franchises. The asphalt is sagging under the increased traffic, which frequently comes to a standstill when parts of the road are closed to accommodate maintenance crews or cleanups after accidents.

In the face of this explosive growth and the resulting strain on the area's infrastructure, Jackson County leaders convened a series of public meetings in 2000 to determine the public's sentiments on possible responses to the population explosion. At these meetings residents voiced overwhelming support for "smart" growth that would enhance their mountain communities and protect the heritage and beauty of the valleys and hilltops.

Some community leaders created a new initiative to give even louder voice to that sentiment. In 2001 the Tuckasegee Community Alliance began meeting to assess growth management in the county. The following year, that effort led to the formation of a new entity with a sharper focus: the Jackson County Smart Roads Alliance (http://wnc.us/smartroads).

At its first meeting, in September 2002, members of the Smart Roads Alliance advocated a comprehensive approach to Jackson County's traffic problems. Their recommendations included transportation planning, which would start with a feasibility study of NC 107; a possible redesign of roadside development; and other initiatives to maintain the community's character and preserve open spaces. This approach took official form in November 2002, when Jackson County and the towns of Sylva and Webster formally requested that the North Carolina Department of Transportation conduct a comprehensive traffic management study of NC 107.

The department complied but only to a point. In the summer of 2003 it released a less-than-comprehensive study on one option: a proposal to build two bypass roads around Sylva, Jackson County's largest town and county seat, to alleviate the congestion on NC 107. According to the plan each segment would consist of a four-lane highway. One of the roads, commonly referred to at the Southern Loop, quickly became a source of great controversy. As designed, the bypass would cause the loss of ninety-four homes and five businesses, and it would have a significant impact on the county's farms, woodlands, and wetlands.

But the greater controversy was the Transportation Department's apparent determination to define the issue with a single choice—whether or not to build both the Northern and the Southern Loops. The department's refusal to consider a more comprehensive set of options ignited the traditionally serene populace of Jackson County. In response, the alliance took steps that would ultimately force all participants to view the debate in broader terms.

First, the Smart Roads Alliance, which was often viewed as a group of outsiders, had the good fortune to find two leaders with local credibility. Harold and Gwen Messer believed in the "cause." Their home, like those of hundreds of other Jackson County families, was in the path of the Southern Loop. The Messers, who are respected general contractors and church members, led the way in getting the larger community involved. When others said the road was a done deal, Herald and Gwen refused to believe it. Both Messers were savvy in shaping the message and in raising money. Together with their friends and allies they raised money from prominent individuals and organized barbeque dinners with donated food from local restaurants. The money raised was spent in ways that broadened the debate—such as paying for critical advertising and retaining a traffic expert and consultant whose opinions brought credibility to the alliance's arguments.

Second, the alliance identified other Jackson County residents who should have been involved earlier but were unaware of their stake in the outcome. A North Carolina law required county governments to advertise the names of all property owners delinquent in their taxes. Jackson County residents had long been so interested in these notices that the local newspaper printed extra copies to meet the demand. Knowing that many people who read the newspaper would be affected by the proposed corridors but were unaware of their significance, the Smart Roads Alliance paid for an advertisement that resembled the property tax notice—but it instead listed all of the residents who would be affected by the proposed highways. When the ad ran in the newspaper, local residents bombarded the Transportation Department with complaints and joined the alliance en masse. Jackson County and the municipalities of Sylva, Webster, and Dillsboro passed resolutions of opposition to the Southern Loop.

Third, the Smart Roads Alliance rested on a broad base of support. Concerns about Jackson County road construction cut across political lines. In keeping with the old adage that politics makes for strange bedfellows, the alliance was a big tent under which conservatives, community activists, environmentalists, preservationists, and even some business leaders opposed the Southern Loop.

Fourth, the alliance targeted specific allies to help frame the debate. It sought advice from the Southern Environmental Law Center in Asheville, North Carolina, and reached out to young people. These new friends brought new skills, such as the best ways to obtain government records, organize and conduct meetings, and turn the alliance into an Internal Revenue Service–approved organization and raise tax-deductible contributions. Even more important, the inclusion of future Jackson County leaders helped to make the debate about more than just roads. Their presence helped the alliance to focus attention on the mountains, rivers, forests, and future generations of the community that the new highways would affect.

Fifth, the Smart Roads Alliance relied on experts whose opinions carried weight with decision makers. Some of the earliest opposition to the Southern Loop came from prominent citizens in Webster, the historical seat of Jackson County. Malcolm Mac-Neill, a local developer, was one of those leaders. MacNeill found Walter Kulash, a nationally known traffic engineer, to advise opponents of the road about possible alternatives to the new four-lane highway. Kulash voiced an expert's opinion to which North Carolina Department of Transportation officials would listen. Additionally, the alliance provided the public with information from experts on alternative transportation. Among them was Dan Burden, a national advocate for "walkable communities." In 2003 the town of Sylva officially incorporated the goal of becoming a walkable community into its long-term planning vision.

Sixth, the Smart Roads Alliance developed reasonable alternatives to the Transportation Department's "build or no build" choice. In this task the alliance was aided mightily by the ingenuity of Jim Aust, Sylva's town planner. In 2003, after carefully studying area traffic patterns, Aust proposed a network of new two-lane roads that would connect preexisting roads to NC 107, thus funneling traffic away from that busy highway. The alliance also recommended the examination of all proposals related to 107 to determine secondary impacts, such as possible pollution of the Tuckasegee River. This switch from defense to offense enabled the alliance to challenge the department's position more effectively. Jackson County Smart Roads avoided the trap into which many citizen initiatives fall: expressing opposition to a proposal without offering a proposal of its own.

The alliance's years-long effort to expand the debate beyond a single construction proposal has made some notable achievements. Jackson County created a transportation task force to study the road issue and appointed two alliance members to the group. A headline in the *Sylva Herald* on December 11, 2008, spoke the loudest about how far the alliance had come: "DOT Officials Say They'll Explore All Options for 107." [1] In the near future, the North Carolina Department of Transportation plans to study alternatives, conduct environmental-impact studies, and collect input from citizens at public hearings and workshops before choosing a course of action in late 2012. Whether the alliance ultimately succeeds in its objectives remains to be seen, but for now to build or not to build is no longer the only question.

HOW TO DEFINE THE PROBLEM

You know the feeling. You're listening to a speaker, watching television news, reading the newspaper, or even talking to friends or family. You may be registering for classes or trying to secure housing for the next academic year. You could be paying for electricity, property taxes, or a doctor's bill that the health insurance you can't afford would have covered. You might even be walking through a neighborhood park, canoeing down a river, or visiting a national park when it hits you. Something isn't right. You feel upset, even angry. Righteous indignation swells within you, and you find yourself saying something like, "There should be a law!" or "If only I were king or queen for a day!"

That feeling is the launching pad for active citizenship. When something you see, hear, read, or experience in your community, state, or nation causes you great anger or worry, and you realize that democratic institutions—the school board, city council, mayor, state legislature, governor, or even the U.S. Congress or president—have the power to address your concern, you are ready to embark on your journey as an active citizen.

---

[1] Stephanie Salmons and Lynn Hotaling, "DOT Officials Say They'll Explore All Options for 107," *Sylva Herald*, December 11, 2008.

A Chinese proverb says that a journey of a thousand miles begins with a single step. Your first step in launching a citizen initiative is to understand and clearly state the problem you want to fix. Be specific and realistic. "I want my community to be a better place to live" is a nice sentiment with which almost everyone can agree, but it is far too broad and vague to be useful. More focused starting points might include the following:

- We don't feel safe because crime has increased in our area.
- Our neighborhood drinking water looks, smells, and tastes odd.
- In the past year my property taxes have doubled.
- My small business is losing workers because I can't afford their health insurance.
- Our daughter is one of thirty-five children in a single kindergarten class.
- The state wants to build a new expressway that would increase the noise level at my house.

Do you see the difference? The statement of the first problem is so nebulous that the democratic process would not be able to address it. On the other hand, the latter statements address particular concerns for which citizen action may produce results.

When you feel anger, concern, or a passionate desire for change rising up inside you, consider whether the source of that feeling could become a political issue. Many people miss the potential for citizen action when they ignore these gut reactions to local issues.

Take this example: At a university's foreign language studies conference, the program director announces that undergraduate foreign language course offerings are being cut. The students in the audience are dismayed. How can they continue their studies with fewer language courses? One faculty member observes that the issue is one of choices: The university has prioritized academic subjects, and languages didn't make the cut. The professor urges the students to organize a plan for citizen action to force a reexamination of the choices made. The students have been confronted with an issue that is vital to their academic and professional careers. This is their moment to exercise active citizenship. With the right definition of the problem, they could begin the process of convincing the university to see foreign language instruction as a vital tool in preparing students to compete in the accelerating global economy. But the students appear unable or unwilling to believe they have the power to reverse the university's decision, and their lack of faith makes the decision that much more final.

Once you have concluded that your concern can be addressed through citizen action, the following five steps will help you define it in the manner most likely to produce a positive result.

1. Look with a Telescope, Not a Microscope

Place the problem you have identified in a larger context. If you do this, you may find that others have the same concern—and that the community faces a collective challenge that requires a democratic response. For example, if you notice that your or your child's chemistry textbook is twenty years out of date, others may have the same concern with other academic texts. Because your local school board or university administration is much more likely to address an across-the-board problem than one that affects only a single student, school, or subject, you can define the problem as inadequate textbooks throughout the entire university or school system—not just in your particular class.

2. Focus the Telescope if Necessary

Politics is the art of the possible, and sometimes it is necessary to narrow the larger context if the wide-angle view presents an outsized target. For example, you may be a local hardware store owner who is concerned that your state's taxation system does not treat small businesses fairly. However, you are even more concerned about the competitive advantage that Internet hardware suppliers enjoy. You are required to collect sales taxes when your customers buy hammers in your store. Because your Internet competitors can escape that requirement, they can sell hammers for less than you do. If you learn that the state is scheduled to explore the issue of sales tax fairness, and you want to present your side of the issue, you will increase your chances of addressing the most important part of the problem if you define and focus it as an Internet sales tax collection issue and leave other perceived tax inequities for future citizen action. As I will discuss more in chapter 6, timing is everything when it comes to influencing policymakers.

3. Define the Problem in Political Terms

Whether you want to improve your neighborhood park or alter U.S.–Middle Eastern relations, your goal is to change policy. Your definition of the problem should either implicitly or explicitly identify the desired outcome. Campaign Georgetown, which was discussed in the prologue, is a perfect example. When the Advisory Neighborhood Commission took steps to prevent students from parking and living in the neighborhoods surrounding Georgetown University, more than 1,000 students suddenly faced serious threats to their transportation and housing. Their problem was the indifference of ANC members to student concerns, and that problem suggested a solution: Elect new ANC members who would listen to students.

4. Define the Problem in Public Terms

Political consultants correctly tell their candidates that voters will usually remember no more than a sentence or two about them. Depending on the size of the electorate and the office being sought, thousands or even millions of dollars are devoted to ensuring that voters remember the right sentence or two when they see a particular candidate's name on the ballot. Similarly, you need to brand your issue in a succinct yet memorable way that drives home your central goal.

One group of motivated and creative citizens did exactly that in persuading voters to put new environmental protections in the Florida Constitution. This coalition was alarmed at the rate of development that was burying the state's coastal areas in condominiums, destroying forest lands, and paving over wetlands; its members wanted to find ways to preserve more land for public use. They sought to persuade the state legislature to put two constitutional amendments on the next general election ballot—each to earmark a portion of the state real estate transfer tax for public land acquisition. The legislature agreed, even though many of those who voted to put the amendments on the ballot secretly believed they had no chance of passage in a state that prided itself on economic growth and individual property rights.

Early in the legislative session the environmental advocates had secured the first and second general election ballot spots for constitutional amendments. They would be pushing Amendments 1 and 2, and they turned that favorable placement into a memorable slogan: 1 + 2 = Lands for You. When Election Day arrived, most voters knew that mantra by heart. The campaign imprinted all of its materials with the catchy label and unveiled two signature images: one, a lake with happy campers in canoes and, two, a pastoral wetlands landscape. A volunteer songwriter penned a 1 + 2 jingle, and the campaign gave donors its two signature images to distribute to other possible supporters. At every rally, press conference, and public appearance, the proponents of Amendments 1 and 2 drove home the point that the preserved lands "would be for you." Voters remembered that when they walked into polling places and overwhelmingly adopted the amendments.

5. Repeat, Repeat, Repeat the Problem

Over the next few chapters, you will learn many skills to help make your citizen initiative a success. But even as you gather information, test the waters of public opinion, build coalitions, and engage the media, your definition of the challenge to be resolved is the North

Star of your efforts. This statement of the problem is your inspiration, and to lose sight of it is to abandon the very concern that motivated you to act in the first place. Summarize your problem in a single sentence, and repeat it to yourself before and during each step in the process outlined in the pages ahead. You won't get lost if you hold tight to your compass.

CHECKLIST FOR ACTION

- ☐ Look with a telescope, not a microscope.
- ☐ Focus the telescope if necessary.
- ☐ Define the problem in political terms.
- ☐ Define the problem in public terms.
- ☐ Repeat, repeat, repeat the problem.

Exercise

YOU HAVE A PROBLEM

Welcome to the exciting world of citizen participation in democracy. When you have finished reading this book, you should have a clear understanding of the skills needed to navigate your campus, local, state, or federal government. But the first step is to select a campus or community problem you want to solve and define it in a focused way. Think carefully about life at your college or university or in your local community or state. Identify a challenge that government at some level is uniquely positioned to address. Select your problem carefully. Throughout this book, it will be the issue on which you practice each of your new citizenship skills. As I noted in the introduction, the class I taught at Miami Carol City High School in 1974 based one-third of the final grade on how effective students were in solving their problem. Be forewarned: Your professor might have a similar performance-based evaluation for you.

2 Just the Facts, Ma'am

Gathering Information to Sway Policymakers

"Facts are stubborn things."

—President John Adams

In 2004 and 2005 the nation watched as one hurricane after another battered the state of Florida. But the driving rains, pounding waves, and destroyed homes and businesses were only the beginning of the problems for many of the state's residents. The storms unleashed an economic crisis that drove groups of Floridians to organize and fight dramatic increases in homeowners' insurance premiums. One such group formed in Monroe County, home to the Florida Keys.

The Florida Keys are a string of low-lying islands as far south as you can go in the continental United States. Given their geographic position near the Gulf Stream and at the entrance to the warm waters of the Gulf of Mexico, the Keys often bear the brunt of violent tropical weather during the annual hurricane season. Yet the Keys were relatively unscathed in the 2004–2005 barrage. Although not left untouched, the property of Keys residents was not damaged—at least not by wind—nearly as much as were homes and businesses in Florida's Panhandle, parts of South Florida, and the inland counties of Central Florida.

All Florida property owners are encouraged or, in many cases, required to carry "windstorm" insurance to cover damages from high winds, such as those in a hurricane. Homeowners and businesses in hardest-hit Central and Northwest Florida could have predicted increases in their insurance premiums. But when residents of Key West started receiving renewals for their windstorm insurance in early 2006, with premiums that in some cases had tripled since the previous bill, they were perplexed. Two Key West residents—Cindy DeRocher and Donna Moody—talked to their neighbors and learned that they were not alone in seeing huge increases in their premiums.

On the evening of February 8, 2006, Fair Insurance Rates in Monroe (FIRM) was born when DeRocher, Moody, and thirty-two neighbors got together and compared notes on their insurance rates. None could understand how the increases could be justified.

The group called its first town hall meeting about a week later. Approximately 120 individuals convened in a local middle school cafeteria. From the outset the leaders asked the group to refrain from anger and focus on constructive solutions to their problem—after all, policymakers were used to hearing residents complain about insurance premiums.

At the meeting FIRM defined its three-part goal:

1. Address the statewide imbalance of insurance rates.
2. Stop a proposed additional increase in rates scheduled for March 2006.
3. Roll back rates to more reasonable and affordable levels.

In addition to defining the problems they wanted to solve, FIRM's members also identified the policymakers with the power to help them. In Florida, insurance companies must receive approval from the state's Office of Insurance Regulation (OIR) to raise or lower policy premiums. The OIR reports to a Cabinet composed of four statewide elected officials: the governor, attorney general, chief financial officer, and commissioner of agriculture. Additionally, because the Florida Legislature provides annual funding for the OIR, legislators exert additional oversight. In order to influence both the unelected regulatory policymakers at the OIR and the elected officials who oversee them, as well as to counter insurance company arguments in favor of the rate increases, FIRM determined that it would need more information on several key issues: the financial impact of skyrocketing rates on Florida Keys homeowners; the insurance rates in Monroe County compared to those in other areas of Florida; the forecasts for future hurricane strikes in Monroe County; and the economics of insurance profits and losses in the Florida Keys.

Financial Impact. As their first step FIRM's leaders asked county residents to provide them with their actual premium statements so that the group could calculate the real dollars associated with increasing rates. Because the OIR, the Cabinet, and the Florida Legislature are used to discussing premium changes in percentage terms, and because Floridians across the state were expressing anger at double- and triple-digit rate increases, FIRM wanted to reframe the debate as a matter of dollars and cents.

This approach to research yielded dramatic results. In one case FIRM discovered that rate increases had produced a $5,000 annual premium on a 900-square-foot home. The owner of a historic property that had weathered storms for more than a century received a $31,000 bill. Even worse, the average homeowner in the Keys was paying $610 per month—more than $7,000 each year—solely for windstorm insurance.

Interviews with real estate companies and employers also revealed that the rate increases were devastating the local workforce. Monroe County was the only county in Florida with a declining population because its police officers, teachers, nurses, and service workers simply could not afford to pay the rising monthly costs of homeowners' insurance.

Monroe County vs. Other Counties. Second, FIRM investigated rates statewide and learned that Monroe County rates were significantly higher than those of other hurricane-prone counties. For instance, rates in the Keys were twice as high as those in Palm Beach County, which had seen the landfall of two hurricanes in 2004 and had suffered more damage in 2005. Rates were nearly three times higher than those of Charlotte County, in Southwest Florida, which Hurricane Charley had devastated in August 2004. Finally, they were four times higher than those of Florida's Panhandle, where Hurricane Ivan wreaked havoc in September 2004 and Tropical Storm Arlene and Hurricane Dennis hit in 2005.

Weather Forecasts. Third, FIRM consulted with experts at the National Weather Service to determine whether windstorm insurance rate increases could be justified by some particular vulnerability of the Keys to hurricane-force winds. As the Monroe County residents suspected from recent experience, the weather experts concluded that the Keys' greatest threat in a hurricane came from water, not wind. And although Monroe has the longest coastline of any county in Florida, the meteorologists denied that it was two, three, or four times more likely to be struck by a hurricane than were other coastal areas—despite what the windstorm rate increases suggested.

Profit and Loss. Fourth, FIRM collected actual insurance claims data for different counties and different hurricanes. The statistics showed that insurance claim payments per policy for storms of equivalent strength were consistently lower in Monroe than in other counties. In other words, insurance companies paid property owners far less for wind damage claims in Monroe County than they did in other parts of the state—but Keys residents were paying significantly more for insurance than were most of their fellow Floridians.

Further, during a meeting with their state representative and insurance company officials, FIRM members received a copy of a spreadsheet showing premiums collected and claims paid for windstorm coverage in Broward (Fort Lauderdale), Miami–Dade, and Monroe Counties. Over the previous four years, Monroe County had produced nearly $250 million in net operating profits from the primary type of wind coverage alone—an 80 percent profit margin. In contrast, the Miami–Dade County profit margin was 46 percent. Broward County's profit margin was 1 percent.

Finally, FIRM investigated whether homes and other buildings in the Keys were structurally more likely to suffer wind damage than those in other areas of the state. In several ways, the answer was "no." Historically, many early Keys homes had been sturdily constructed by shipbuilders who understood the possible ravages of hurricanes. From a regulatory standpoint, architects explained that Monroe County had long utilized stricter building codes for wind resistance than had the state at-large. In terms of design, local building department officials confirmed that standard Keys home-strengthening techniques—such as hurricane straps and shutters—were not practiced in other high-wind coastal areas of the state. Similarly, construction experts and academics confirmed that the metal roofs predominant in the Keys withstood storms better than did the asphalt and shingle roofs that are standard in the Florida Building Code.

Through live presentations, face-to-face conversations, a self-produced DVD, a Web site, phone calls, and e-mails, FIRM took the research it had gathered and shared it with other county residents, reporters, legislators, state insurance regulators, and the Cabinet. In addition to growing the organization—FIRM now has more than 5,000 members—FIRM's investment of time and effort in collecting persuasive data brought welcome results.

In early 2007 the state government rejected the proposed Monroe County rate increases, ordered that rates for the county be rolled back to pre-2005 levels, and passed legislation to address the statewide hurricane insurance crisis. In less than a year all three of FIRM's goals had been achieved. Today, FIRM continues to work on long-term solutions to the insurance problem and now has representatives on several state task forces addressing the issue. FIRM's credibility has helped its leaders gain seats at the policymaking table.

For more on FIRM, see www.fairinsuranceratesinmonroe.com.

THE INFORMATION-GATHERING PROCESS

In the previous chapter, I discussed the foundation of effective citizenship: You cannot solve a problem or successfully confront a challenge unless you have specifically, realistically, and clearly defined it. Once you have defined your problem, you are ready to find the facts that will persuade a decision maker to take on your cause—a process to be described in subsequent chapters.

English statesman and essayist Sir Francis Bacon declared that "knowledge is power." Citizens who have sufficient knowledge of their issue have credibility—and with credibility comes the power to influence other citizens, community leaders, members of the media, and, ultimately, policymakers. An informed citizen who makes persuasive use of facts, figures, and real-life examples is better positioned to sway the city council, county commission, or state legislature than is someone who speaks from ignorance or pure emotion, often claiming without substantiation to be the sole possessor of the truth.

Until the 1990s collecting facts could be cumbersome and time-consuming. Advocates who wanted to gather information in support of their cause spent hours in libraries poring over hard-bound volumes or microfilm copies of old newspapers, magazines, government reports, and academic journals. Even on university campuses, materials were rarely centralized in a single location. Researchers who managed to discover reports or studies from foundations, advocacy organizations, and even some universities or governmental agencies had to request them by mail and then spend weeks awaiting their arrival.

The Internet changed everything. Today the challenge is no longer finding enough information or locating it quickly. Through the Web we have immediate access to nearly unlimited information on any subject, but we face a new but just as daunting challenge: How can we sort through countless resources and find reliable facts that will persuade decision makers? This chapter addresses that challenge.

WHY CONDUCT RESEARCH?

Many first-time issue advocates complain that gathering information is dry or academic. They regard it as not nearly as exciting as campaigning door-to-door, rallying a large crowd of potential supporters, or being interviewed on television or radio—and thus give the research process short shrift. This attitude is a huge mistake that greatly imperils their chances of success. Although research may lack the glitz and glamour of the more public aspects of active citizenship, a cause that is not supported by credible data is in serious jeopardy. On the other hand, taking the time to research a subject thoroughly will pay many dividends, including the following.

Enhance Credibility

The more you know about a subject, the more those you are trying to persuade will respect your opinion. In the 1980s a television commercial for a financial services company proclaimed simply, "When E. F. Hutton speaks, people listen." Strive to be the E. F. Hutton of your issue. If you convince the ultimate decision maker that you know the facts backward and forward, you may get some benefit of the doubt as you argue your position.

In 2003 two students at the University of Florida's Levin College of Law fought to reform the school's grading curve. For years the law school mandated an average grade that was significantly lower than that at other public university law schools across the country, including the University of Michigan, University of North Carolina, and University of Virginia. Florida's relatively low curve made it harder for its law graduates to compete against their counterparts from other schools in critical job markets, such as New York; Washington, D.C.; Atlanta; and Charlotte. The lower grade scale also undermined the Levin College of Law's argument that it could be "just as good as" those higher-profile law schools. However, faculty members were reluctant to make major changes to the grading system.

The two students resolved to turn the tide by developing an encyclopedic knowledge of how other law schools—especially those at the most well regarded public universities—operated their grading systems. Their aim was to take advantage of the great desire on the part of their school's faculty and administration to equal those schools. After months of demonstrating their expertise on grading systems—from the University of Georgia to the University of Texas to the University of California at Los Angeles—the two students convinced enough faculty members that the University of Florida's law school would lag behind other schools if it did not change its system. In May 2003, and then through additional changes in April 2004, the faculty of the Levin College of Law adopted a competitive grading system.

Avoid Redundancy

We're not talking about *Star Trek* here. Chances are good that your goals are not taking you to a place where no one has gone before. In your research, you will likely discover other citizens in your area or elsewhere who have previously fought a similar battle. Were they successful? If so how? If not, why not? What were the decisive moments of their effort that dictated either success or failure? If you have more information about previous efforts similar to yours, you can modify your strategic plan to enhance the chances of success.

Locate Precedent

Those of you who ultimately join the legal profession will learn that every judge in the United States feels more comfortable making a ruling if he or she knows that another judge has made it first. Policy decision makers are no different. It will be harder for the person, panel, or organization you have identified as key to solving your problem to say "no" if others in similar situations have previously said "yes."

For example, let's say that you are concerned about the increasing number of your college classmates who have no health insurance whatsoever. You want the university to provide uninsured students with health insurance. Since this is the kind of financial issue that could determine whether a potential student chooses your college or a rival school, it will benefit your cause if your research shows that many of the rival schools already offer health insurance.

Your effort will receive an even bigger boost if those other decision makers saw good results from their decision to support citizens with goals similar to yours. In this way, effective research helps to identify what many in the business world call "best practices" and allows you to propose specific solutions with positive track records. If you can show a decision maker that your solution has been previously adopted and successfully implemented, you are much likelier to win agreement than if you don't have this information. Going back to the example of student health insurance, you would greatly strengthen your hand if you could show that one of the rival schools not only had provided uninsured students with coverage but had done so in a way that reduced public health problems, stabilized overall health care costs, and improved student morale and productivity.

Achieve Collateral Benefits

In later chapters of this book, we will discuss in more detail the importance of identifying and outperforming your opponents, building strong coalitions to support your cause, and engaging the attention of the media to raise public awareness and influence policymakers. For now, just be aware that effective research is a critical tool in all of those tasks—and that a lack of this collateral research can doom an initiative to failure. Consider these two scenarios:

You have formed a citizens' group to persuade the state legislature to impose limits on how much individual candidates can spend on their campaigns. After defining the problem—that the exploding costs of political campaigns are increasing the public's cynicism about the political process and denying many potential candidates the ability to run—you collect compelling data to support your argument. You present your proposal to the appropriate legislative committee and remain to watch the testimony of the leader of a citizens' group opposed to limits on campaign contributions. She presents several court decisions to demonstrate that your proposal would violate both your state constitution and the U.S. Constitution. Unfortunately, you have not read those decisions and cannot rebut them.

The local government announces plans to widen a street through your neighborhood to accommodate four lanes instead of two. You are concerned that the widened road will increase noise and traffic. In studying the problem, you discover an article about a similar road project in another city that was halted when local parents highlighted the possible dangers to children playing or waiting for the school bus. This information leads you to contact the local parent-teacher association to involve it in the issue.

As you conduct your research, it's easy to become so focused on proving the merits of your cause that you forget the other ways that research can bolster your arguments. If you're not prepared to say why opponents are wrong, or to give possible allies and reporters good reasons to take an interest in your issue, your chances of victory are slim.

EFFECTIVE RESEARCH: A STEP-BY-STEP GUIDE

1. Above All, Stay Credible

From a research standpoint, the biggest danger of the Information Age is the proliferation of unreliable or biased data, particularly data found on the Internet. Remember this cardinal rule of effective citizen participation: If you present a decision maker with information in support of your cause that turns out to be false, misleading, inaccurate, knowingly incomplete, or irrelevant, he or she is unlikely to believe future presentations and just as unlikely to support your position. Be assured that your opponents will look at your research as soon as they see it. If they cannot verify it, or if they can discredit it, their next stop will be the media or the decision maker's office to destroy your credibility.

On the other hand, if you consistently provide reliable data, you will enhance your credibility and the chances that the decision maker will keep an open mind. A checklist to avoid bad information might include the following admonitions.

First, don't rely on outdated information. Work with the most recent data possible. A study from 2008 may in fact use 2000 census information that has been overtaken by more current numbers. If your opponents notice the stale data, they will not hesitate to question its relevance.

Second, don't confine your research to your university or local community. The whole world of ideas does not reside in your zip code. If you're working on a campus issue, for example, look for comparative data to impress whichever administrator you hope to influence. Knowing how other entities similar to yours do the same task puts your issue in perspective. Have other universities or communities dealt with this problem in the past? If so, how did they resolve it? Concentrate on those places that have implemented solutions or that utilize practices similar to those you are proposing. If a collegiate decision maker particularly respects a particular institution, such as one from which she earned a degree, an intercollegiate comparison could be particularly persuasive.

Third, don't use biased sources. Although many foundations, organizations, and academic institutions attempt to be balanced and unbiased, some groups and think tanks produce information that reflects a particular political agenda or ideological viewpoint. For example, data collected from a business advocacy group may not sway a decision maker with close ties to organized labor, and vice versa. Publications from the Center on Budget and Policy Priorities or the Center for American Progress are likely to have a more progressive or liberal bent than those from the American Enterprise Institute. Use of biased sources may cause a decision maker to assume that there is no unbiased or balanced data to support your cause.

Fourth, don't fail to investigate the credentials of your data source. A layperson who posts an Internet article on the environment is less likely to sway policymakers than is the state president of the Nature Conservancy or a distinguished university professor who has multiple degrees and years of experience studying ecosystem management.

Fifth, don't limit your research to traditional, usually secondary, source information. Consider demonstrating support for your cause by presenting decision makers with a signed petition that has been carefully developed and inscribed. Don't let sloppiness thwart your effort. Make sure that every name on the petition is legible, legitimate, and accompanied by accurate contact information. If the organization or person to whom you are presenting the information finds even a single name that is bogus, your credibility will be gone and the petition will be ignored.

After you learn more about polling in chapter 4, you might want to survey a statistically selected portion of the affected population. If you decide to survey without the help of a pollster, your methods must be airtight. If your initiative is on campus, find statistics and communications professors who can help you craft credible survey questions. Accurately identify the group you want to survey so that your responses are meaningful.

Sixth, don't try to bury information that is unfavorable to your cause or pretend that it doesn't exist. Since you found it, you can assume that your opponents have done so as well. Instead, proactively present the "bad facts" and show how the other information you have discovered undermines their significance. Your willingness to admit that your case is less than perfect will boost your credibility and prevent opponents from springing the negative information unexpectedly.

2. Utilize Every Source Possible, but Stay on Target

While one could easily get lost in the vast expanse of the Web and other online search tools, it is easier to navigate these resources if you stay focused on the problem you have defined and the specific questions you need to answer in order to clarify the problem and identify possible solutions. In the 1992 election, when Bill Clinton, then Arkansas governor, was running for president, his campaign posted a sign in the campaign headquarters:

CHANGE VS. MORE OF THE SAME
THE ECONOMY, STUPID
DON'T FORGET HEALTH CARE[1]

In other words, the campaign would be rigorously disciplined about its message. If an issue wasn't directly connected to the previous twelve years of Republican rule, the ailing national economy, or the lack of affordable health care for many Americans, the campaign wasn't going to discuss it. With a laser focus on those three topics, the Clinton team became the first Democratic campaign since 1976 to win a presidential election. As you do your

---

[1] George Stephanopoulos, *All Too Human: A Political Education* (New York: Little, Brown, 1999), 88.

own research, if you can similarly resist the urge to be distracted, the information at your fingertips can greatly strengthen your chances of prevailing in your cause.

In the same way that good research hinges on a clear definition of the problem, it will be much easier to tap into the huge reservoir of information available if you have a good sense of which level of government has jurisdiction over the issue you want to address. Chapter 3 will help you answer the following questions: Is it a campus issue or a local, state, or federal concern? Is there a quasi-public entity that governs the matter, such as the NCAA on intercollegiate athletic issues? In the following paragraphs are roadmaps that will help you locate the data that you will need at each level.

Please note that while the amount of information available today is vast, the tools with which to access that data are relatively finite. Whether your issue is one of campus, local, state, or federal concern, the "hard" research you collect will likely come from one of six sources: the Internet; libraries; official sources, such as university departments or government agencies; organizational sources, such as foundations and think tanks; media sources, such as newspapers, news magazines, and television and radio news; and primary sources, such as interviews and other firsthand accounts. But since effective citizenship is more than just facts and figures, this section also emphasizes everyday people who can help to frame a question in human terms.

Researching on Campus. If your goal is to affect policy on campus, you will be working with college administrators or faculty members and fellow students to solve the challenge you have identified. An effective process for locating information about a campus problem might include the following steps:

- You must first determine which department or office has jurisdiction over the problem you are trying to address. Is there an organizational chart or at least a list of departments or offices in your student handbook or campus phone book, or on the college or university's Web page? If you can't determine the appropriate department or office from these sources, then contact your student government representative to see if he or she can direct you to the right place. If that doesn't work, pick up the phone and start calling departments or offices until you find the right one. The key to identifying the right target is persistence. Make appointments to visit administrators or faculty members who might have knowledge about the issue, either because they have addressed it in the past or because they have some academic expertise on the matter.

• If you attend a public college or university, state law may give you the right to make a public records request for information related to your subject. Once you have identified the appropriate department or office, ask them (in writing) to supply you with any reports, studies, meeting agendas, meeting minutes, or other documents that might shed light on your subject. If you need help to complete a records request, see if your college or university has a student-directed legal-aid program that could assist you.

• Don't reinvent the wheel unless you have no choice. Try to determine if your issue has previously been raised on campus and, if so, how that prior debate was resolved. Go to the main campus library and see if the college or university has published any reports or studies on the issue you want to address. Your campus newspaper may have a way to search back issues, or you can use campus library or electronic resources (for example, the Web, Lexis-Nexis, and Westlaw) to see if past issues are available online. Locate previous issues of the local newspaper (which covers the entire community, including your college or university) to see if it has written on your subject in recent years. You may even want to call and ask the reporter on the higher education beat if he or she can supply any past insights. Finally, consult your student government representatives to see if they have either personal knowledge or archived records that could aid your effort to gain historical perspective on the problem you are trying to solve.

- Determine how other colleges or universities—especially those similar in size or in close proximity to your own—have addressed the issue. For example, if you are concerned that your college or university's grading curve is too low, call around to similarly situated colleges or universities, ask for their respective registrars' offices, and inquire about their curve. They may not reveal it, but you won't know unless you ask.

- Consult relevant periodicals—such as the *Chronicle of Higher Education,* which is widely read and respected by professors, university administrators, and higher education policymakers at the state and local levels—to see if they have written anything on your issue. If they have, those articles may give you new sources to explore at other colleges and universities.

Information Gathering on Federal, State, and Local Issues. If the challenge you are looking to resolve is not exclusively a campus issue, it will almost certainly involve the federal, state, or local government. These levels of government have developed their own resources, and you can use them to do the following:

- Visit the Web site of the federal, state, or local department or agency with jurisdiction over the issue you wish to research. The Web site itself may provide information on the very issue you want to address. At the very least, it will probably tell you with whom you want to speak to gather more information on the subject.

- Determine which legislative bodies—such as Congress, the state legislature, county commission, and city council—publish legislation, bill analyses, and committee information online and in certain designated libraries. Your best first stop would be the Web page of the particular legislative body. For example, congressional information can be found at the Library of Congress's legislative database, known as Thomas, after Thomas Jefferson (http://thomas.loc.gov). Consult the National Conference of State Legislatures (www.ncsl.org) for links to your state legislature. The National Association of Counties (www

.naco.org) and National League of Cities (www.nlc.org) will help you find county and city commissions or councils.

- Take advantage of your powers as a constituent. Contact your city council member, county commissioner, state legislator, member of Congress, or U.S. senator to determine whether they or their staff members know anything about the issue, can help you research it, or can connect you with other citizens who have similar concerns or have experienced problems in your area of interest.

- Locate and make use of the legislative history—in other words, prior testimony, statements, and voting records—of the governmental body you are trying to influence. Some governmental entities keep very detailed records of past proceedings and make them easily available through the Internet. Others require that you find these documents at a designated library. Others still will not keep detailed records or will not make them available. But if you can gain access to legislative history, it will provide invaluable information about what the decision makers in your case have previously voted—and previously said about their legislative intent—on your subject.

- Each level of government has entities that monitor the efficiency and productivity of individual agencies. The federal government relies on the Government Accountability Office (www.gao.gov). States and localities have similar watchdog agencies. For example, in Florida the Office of Program Policy Analysis and Government Accountability (www.oppaga.state.fl.us) performs this function. When you find the local or state agency that performs this function in your area, visit its Web site or contact officials by telephone to determine whether they have previously analyzed the problem you want to solve.

- For problems at the state and local level, take advantage of umbrella organizations of policymakers that focus on larger issues of universal state and local concern. For state-level governance, these include (among others) the Council of State Governments (www.csg.org), National Governors Association (www.nga.org), and the previously mentioned National Conference of State Legislators. Uniquely local concerns are the province of the U.S. Conference of Mayors (www.usmayors.org), as well as the previously cited National Association of Counties and National League of Cities. These organizations provide a high-level, summary view of issues and potential solutions and direct you to research worth exploring in greater detail. Additionally, they have staff members who specialize in various issue areas ranging from criminal justice to early childhood education to urban renewal.

- National organizations also exist for specific policy issues at the federal, state, and local levels. Although there is no shortage of policy-oriented entities focused on Congress and the White House, make sure to determine which ones are most credible before you rely on research obtained from them. Organizations that concentrate on state and local policy concerns include the Education Commission of the States (www.ecs.org), National Association of Insurance Commissioners (www.naic.org), National Association of State Budget Officers (www.nasbo.org), and Environmental Council of the States (www.ecos.org). These organizations also have research arms and conference proceedings that can be valuable in finding information on specific state and local issues.

- Think tanks such as the Brookings Institution and the Heritage Foundation also produce extensive research on public policy issues, but as mentioned earlier, you should be mindful of potential biases. For a list and description of major political science think tanks, visit the University of Michigan's Documents Center (www.lib.umich.edu/govdocs/psthink.html).

- Many colleges and universities have think tanks, public policy centers, or special institutes. Examine universities and colleges in your state or locality to determine if any are studying your area of concern. If so, make contact with the faculty member in charge of that specific field of research.

- Check out various nonpartisan foundations such as the Pew Charitable Trusts and the Ford, Gates, or MacArthur Foundations to see if they have funded research relevant to your problem. This information should be available on their respective Web sites, but you may need to call and speak to specific scholars directly.

- Use the Web to identify sources of information such as newspaper, magazine, and online articles. If you can't access articles through the Web, try a public or university library in your area. They may have full access to online news services and will have back issues of many publications.

3. Harness the Power of Real People

An old adage says, "A picture is worth a thousand words." Similarly, though information is important, a powerful human story is more compelling than a thousand statistics in persuading decision makers as to the rightness of a cause. Consider the following pieces of research:

> Example A: Your town backs up to a forested area. On the other side of the woods is a small manufacturing plant that is rumored to have dumped toxic chemical wastes in the forest for many years. You find several complex scientific studies showing that your town's groundwater supply may have higher than normal rates of the chemicals used in or discharged from the plant.

> Example B: Over the past five years the family whose house is closest to the wooded area has lost three children to a kind of leukemia often caused by the linked chemicals used by the plant. The parents had another child in hopes of finding a bone marrow match for the older children, but he has recently shown signs of leukemia.[2]

---

[2] The examples are inspired by Jonathan Harr, *A Civil Action* (New York: Random House, 1995).

Both examples suggest that something is amiss with the local environmental conditions, but the latter is far more likely to draw media coverage and persuade regulators to investigate the plant than is the first example. It isn't hard to see why. Although collecting research studies, statistical data, and other facts on paper is critical to building a compelling case, human beings are creatures of both intellect and emotion. The best citizen initiatives take a two-pronged approach, using cold, hard facts to establish credibility and warm-blooded people to humanize an issue and build popular support. This does not mean that successful citizen advocacy requires a tragedy like the one described in Example B. But it does require the involvement of everyday people because their opinions, comments, and stories are far more memorable than numbers on spreadsheets.

Finding the real people who can influence a public policy issue is not an easy task. It requires effective planning, persistence, and communication. But there are proven ways to gather information from real people in support of a cause:

First, revisit the problem you want to solve. Who else in the community might have a stake in your issue? Whether these stakeholders are neighbors, store owners, volunteer agencies, organizations, or even your classmates, get together with them in person, by phone, or by e-mail, and find out what they know and believe about the issue.

Second, use technology to your benefit. Most communities have Web logs, or blogs, that track local issues and offer users the opportunity to post comments and exchange ideas. Visit YouTube (www.youtube.com) to see if you can find anyone who has weighed in on your subject, or post a video there to solicit comments.

Third, organize discussions, town meetings, and other gatherings to collect information and various viewpoints on your issue. These conversations may generate the personal anecdotes that are so powerful in persuading decision makers or even produce possible solutions.

Fourth, newspaper and television reporters—including those at your campus newspaper or television station—are likely consumers of any "real life" perspectives you can add to a public policy issue. But these media representatives can also *produce* this kind of information. If you build relationships with reporters and provide them with valuable research that informs their stories, you will encourage them to use their superior resources to dig deeper and uproot new sources and information that you could not find on your own. The deeper they dig, and the more they uncover, the more it will force a decision maker to pay attention.

FINAL THOUGHTS

Cynics claim that effective citizenship is more about who you know than what you know. In truth, what one knows is usually the key to shaping debate and determining the final outcome of public policy controversies.

In his autobiography, former Chrysler chairman Lee Iacocca demonstrated this principle in action. In 1979 the Chrysler Corporation was reeling financially from a weak national economy, poor management, and increased competition from the Japanese automotive industry. Desperate to stay afloat, Chrysler asked Congress to guarantee more than $1 billion in loans that the company needed to finance a turnaround plan.

At first, the proposed loan guarantees had little support in Congress. Members worried that U.S. taxpayers—their constituents—would be left holding the bag if Chrysler defaulted on its loans. Alarmed at this lack of support, Iacocca, then the new chairman of Chrysler, rallied his troops to change the nature of the debate—"to force the congressmen to think of the loan guarantees in real human terms instead of ideology." After gathering the facts to show how each House district would be affected economically if Chrysler went out of business, Iacocca and his legislative team went to work presenting their targeted research to every member of Congress. They "delivered to each representative a computer printout of all of the suppliers and dealers in his district who did business with us . . . and outlined exactly what the consequences for that district would be if Chrysler went under." Douglas Fraser, president of the United Auto Workers, simultaneously lobbied individual representatives and senators about the devastating effects that a Chrysler bankruptcy would have on automobile industry employees.

Chrysler's list hit home. With the national economy already in turmoil, few members of Congress wanted more businesses and jobs to be lost in their districts if Chrysler went bankrupt. In the end, Congress passed the Chrysler loan guarantees by a sizeable margin.[3]

In this Information Age, a citizen need not be the chair of a major corporation to use research effectively in a public policy debate. City council members, county commissioners, state legislators, and members of Congress rarely have the time or staff resources to research problems comprehensively on their own. A citizen who effectively informs them is much more likely to earn their support than one who does not.

Bacon's statement that "knowledge is power" is true—but only if those with the knowledge know how to use it effectively in advancing toward their goals. To lead a successful civic action, you must use the knowledge you have gained to build a coalition of allies, rebut the arguments of those who may oppose you, enlist the media to help you win broad support for your aims, fashion polls and other tools to help you gauge public opinion, and otherwise convince decision makers that your position should become theirs. The coming chapters will help you transform the raw knowledge you gain into a powerful tool for changing the way your college, locality, state, or federal government handles your issue.

---

[3] Lee Iacocca, *Iacocca: An Autobiography* (New York: Bantam Books, 1984), 224–225.

CHECKLIST FOR ACTION

- ☐ Above all, stay credible.
  - Work with the most recent data possible.
  - Don't confine your research to your university or local community.
  - Use unbiased resources.
  - Investigate the credentials of your data source.
  - Use more than secondary sources.
  - Admit unfavorable information.
- ☐ Utilize every source possible, but stay on target.
  - Research on campus.
  - Gather information on federal, state, and local issues.
- ☐ Harness the power of real people.
  - Find other community members who might have a stake in your issue.
  - Use modern technology to locate examples.
  - Organize discussions, town hall meetings, and other gatherings to hear various viewpoints on your issue and collect anecdotes.
  - Build relationships with journalists.

Exercise

USING RESEARCH TOOLS

Is the problem you identified in chapter 1 a campus, local, state, or federal issue or a combination? Use the resources suggested in this chapter to develop more information on your problem. Be prepared to discuss what you found. How will the data you found help you argue your case? What types of information are most likely to sway decision makers? What types of information will help you recruit allies or media attention? If you face opposition, which arguments are your opponents likely to make? What data do you need to rebut them?

The Buck Stops Where?

Identifying Who in Government Can Fix Your Problem

"I'm in control here."

> —Secretary of State Alexander Haig,
> statement to the media, March 1981,
> after President Ronald Reagan was shot

Case in Point: Putting the "Be" in South Beach

Ask your friends and neighbors what they know about South Beach, and expect to receive a wide range of answers. Pop culture history buffs will recall undercover cops Sonny Crockett and Rico Tubbs speeding down Ocean Drive or across Biscayne Bay. Celebrity watchers know it as the home-away-from home for Robert De Niro and numerous other stars. Fashion mavens flock there to honor the late Gianni Versace, who died there in 1997. Partygoers celebrate the world-famous restaurants and nightclubs. Real estate experts think of multimillion-dollar condominiums. Movie fans laugh at memorable lines from *The Birdcage*. Seafood lovers flock to Joe's Stone Crabs. Architects marvel at the Art Deco structures.

None of the people you ask are likely to know the name of the person most responsible for making South Beach what it is today. Barbara Capitman did not have Don Johnson's fame or Versace's following. But she did have a deep love and appreciation for South Miami Beach's unique architectural style, the determination to preserve that distinct look, and a keen understanding of those government agencies and programs that could help her safeguard this treasured piece of South Florida history and culture. Those qualities proved to be more than enough to overwhelm better funded forces that would have consigned Miami Beach's Art Deco district to the dustbin of history.

For the fifty years after the end of World War I, Miami Beach was a haven for both millionaires and middle-class families using it as a vacation spot, winter retreat, or year-around home. Jackie Gleason taped his television show there in the 1960s. It became the center of the political universe in 1968, when Republicans held their presidential nominating convention there, and again in 1972, when both the Democrats and the Republicans met there. But by the mid-1970s South Beach had fallen on hard times. The economy was in recession, and tourism had slowed to a trickle. Many of the famous Art Deco hotels had become rundown apartments for fixed-income retirees. Others sat empty and deteriorated. Drug traffickers used the area as a base of operations.

In short, South Miami Beach was primed for a takeover—and local developers made the first move. In 1969 the Florida Legislature enacted the Community Redevelopment Act, legislation that authorized the creation of special districts to encourage economic development in blighted areas. The Miami Beach Redevelopment Agency (RDA) was created in 1973. Three years later, on July 26, 1976, it proudly released its plans for a new Miami Beach. The RDA proposed to demolish all structures on the southernmost portion of the island and replace them with new luxury hotels, condominiums, restaurants, and shops. Conventional wisdom held that the RDA plan was actually the first step in a more ambitious redevelopment that would eventually encompass all of historic South Beach and wipe out its Art Deco heritage.

But the RDA had not counted on Barbara Capitman. Born Barbara Baer, Capitman was part of a family that had helped to pioneer the Art Deco boom of the 1930s and 1940s. She had grown up surrounded by the mixture of industrial design and regional architecture that was the essence of Art Deco. Barbara married a man who was himself a pioneer in visual design and marketing. In 1976, at age fifty-six and recently widowed, she possessed the knowledge, passion, and skills to match the political and economic power of the Miami Beach establishment.

The same month that the RDA announced its plan, Capitman led the creation of the Miami Design Preservation League (MDPL). Not lacking in marketing savvy, Capitman realized that Vietnam and Watergate had taken a huge toll on the nation, and that Americans might respond favorably to cultural reminders of a time before the turmoil of the late 1960s and early 1970s. Powering memories of the celebrities and other "beautiful people" who had entertained and vacationed there, the Art Deco structures embodied a romance and sophistication that might be more valuable than the planned redevelopment.

But even more important, Capitman discerned that a confusing labyrinth of governmental, quasi-governmental, and private entities would play a key role in deciding South Beach's future. She was determined to understand and successfully negotiate that maze—with the goal of designating South Beach as a historic district and thus frustrate the RDA's plans to turn the island into another garden-variety tourist destination.

Capitman's immediate goal was to persuade the U.S. Department of the Interior to include South Beach on its National Register of Historic Places. But she also knew that other government agencies would have to get involved first, and so she engaged federal, state, and local entities in a variety of ways. Because no private developer would fund her admittedly risky plan, Capitman would need federal assistance to secure the required financing. After Congress passed the 1976 tax reform, the modernization of existing low-income housing was one of the few viable tax shelters. Working with her son, Andrew, a Yale University economics graduate with a master's degree from the University of Miami's Graduate School of Business, Capitman learned how the U.S. Department of Housing and Urban Development (HUD) and the National Trust for Historic Preservation administered those benefits. The mother-and-son team helped to demystify these arcane tax provisions for other investors. They also obtained funds from the federal Community Development Block Grant (CDBG) program to plan and design the restoration.

Although the federal government would decide South Beach's historical status, Capitman realized that she would probably not succeed in her goal if the City of Miami Beach opposed her efforts. In October 1977 the MDPL endorsed and campaigned for Dr. Leonard Haber, a Miami Beach mayoral candidate who was an Art Deco restoration supporter. When Haber won the race, he carried into office a slate of like-minded city commission candidates.

Capitman's support of the Haber slate paid off immediately. Shortly after he was sworn in, Mayor Haber led the media on a walk through the Art Deco district and proclaimed that "there is a broad and deep national interest in this area and it looks like preservation and restoration can be the economic turning point for Miami Beach." Even more significantly, the city made MDPL a planning partner. In the early 1970s Gov. Reubin Askew had persuaded the Florida Legislature to adopt sweeping new growth-management legislation to govern land and water use. The plan required local governments to develop comprehensive land and water development plans with enforcement mechanisms. As the City of Miami Beach drafted its plan, it granted MDPL a contract to draft the portion of the plan encompassing the historic areas of South Miami Beach.

In early 1978, with the city's support seemingly secured, the MDPL turned full-time to the task of placing South Beach on the National Register of Historic Places. That spring, Capitman led a steady stream of federal and state officials—all of whose approval would be necessary to secure historic status—on tours of Miami Beach. Many were effusive in their praise of the Art Deco district. It seemed that restoration had the momentum it needed to succeed.

But a funny thing happened on the way to apparent success: The MDPL did its best to snatch defeat from the jaws of victory. Given the opportunity to shape Miami Beach's comprehensive plan, the MDPL submitted a historic district report that professional planners found confusing and unorganized and never took seriously. When the city updated its state-required comprehensive plan in June 1978, the proposal did not include historic preservation. Then, rather than attempting to work out their differences with the city, the MDPL sought to reverse the omission through sympathetic local newspapers. Miami Beach leaders saw this media strategy as an end run designed to embarrass them, and they reacted angrily. This was a grave development. The MDPL would need the city's cooperation and support to implement historic preservation in South Beach. Less than six months before, that cooperation had seemed assured. Now it was in serious peril.

Into this breach stepped Barbara Capitman, aptly described as a leader "who is able to leap short and tall commissioners with a single bound, jumble city brass and red tape, never take no for an answer, leave the most poised and sophisticated politicians exasperated and scratching their heads in wonderment." Capitman refused to give up. In October 1978 she coordinated an "Art Deco Week in Old Miami Beach" in conjunction with the national convention of the National Recreation and Park Association. The two events combined to showcase the historic district idea to influential national visitors and unconvinced local residents.

Capitman's double whammy had the desired effect of bringing the city around and influencing key officials throughout government. During the Art Deco Week, the city of Miami Beach invited federal, state, and local officials to a workshop where they could learn more about the Art Deco district. The timing was perfect. Soon thereafter developers were blocked from razing historic motion picture houses, the post office, and certain hotels after Capitman and the MDPL staged dramatic demonstrations and challenged the reconstruction building permit.

In September 1978 the MDPL submitted its application for historic designation to Florida's state historic preservation officer, Robert Williams. Williams refused to accept the application after determining that it contained incorrect information and lacked a statement of significance. After two weeks of frenzied work, the MDPL eliminated those deficiencies, and Florida accepted the submission.

Barbara Capitman understood the critical importance of interacting with decision makers at every level of the process. Throughout the campaign, she had personally made contact with relevant officials from various levels of government, including the U.S. Departments of the Interior and Housing and Urban Development, the state of Florida, the city of Miami Beach, and Dade County. She wasn't about to let up now. Capitman made almost daily calls to Williams, his staff, and members of the review board to reiterate the importance of expediting a favorable review. As one MDPL member put it: "It was her baby, and she intended to have a healthy, on-time delivery."

The Florida Historic Preservation Board met on February 8, 1979, at the University of Florida in Gainesville. Expecting fierce opposition to its plan, the MDPL assembled a team of fifteen experts and residents for the meeting. Following their presentations, the review board chairman admitted that he didn't "know a damn about Art Deco . . . but it does represent a distinct era of history." His colleagues agreed, and the board voted unanimously to approve the district.

The state forwarded its approval to the National Register of Historic Places in Washington, D.C. The agency gave affected Miami Beach property owners thirty days to comment. Federal officials made field visits. Finally, on May 14, 1979—two years, ten months, and nineteen days after the Miami Beach Redevelopment Agency announced plans to demolish the Art Deco area— the National Register officially designated a one-square-mile area of Miami Beach as a national historic district.

Over the next two decades, what we now think of as South Beach rose and flourished because Barbara Capitman and her allies clearly defined their challenge and then identified the governmental entities they needed to drive toward a solution. Their target wasn't cut and dried. Although only the National Register of Historic Places could ultimately grant a historical designation, the MDPL required approval and assistance from agencies and officials scattered throughout local, state, and federal government before they could even reach the point of consideration by the National Register. Capitman's mastery of this spider's web of governmental involvement enabled her to recruit investors, block demolition permits, draft land-use rules, defeat opponents with substantially greater financial resources—and rescue a neighborhood.

The MDPL won a critical triumph with the National Register designation. But, as is frequently the case with citizen initiatives, one victory was not all that was needed to protect historic South Beach. Although the National Register's designation gave South Beach recognition and tax benefits for its rehabilitation, the substance of preservation would be in local ordinances, codes, and enforcement. The continuing nature of the struggle was clear within months of the National Register's listing, when four landmarks—El Chico Restaurant, the Boulevard Hotel, the New Yorker Hotel, and the Senator Hotel—were reduced to rubble.

The battlefield shifted back to local government. Although Dade County had adopted a historic preservation ordinance by July 1981, the city of Miami Beach steadfastly resisted. When the Miami Beach City Commission finally passed its own ordinance—under threat of losing all authority in this area to the county government—preservationist attorneys described it as the weakest one in the nation.

Two years later Barbara Capitman ran for a city commission seat in the 1983 city elections. Her confrontational style, which had been effective in securing the national designation, was equally ineffective in the election campaign. In a five-candidate field, she finished last. Two years later Abe Resnick, a prominent Miami Beach developer who had tangled with Capitman over the demolition of the New Yorker Hotel, won a city commission seat. He quickly became the strongest and most assertive elected voice against South Beach preservation.

But these setbacks were temporary and against the tide of history. Continuing her work as a private citizen, Capitman expanded her coalition of allies, including sympathetic members of the city commission. It also helped that conditions on the ground were changing dramatically. South Beach was emerging as a new international destination for celebrities, show business personalities, supermodels and their photographers, arts and culture aficionados, and the gay community. South Beach's makeover was highlighted in *Miami Vice,* one of the most popular television series of the mid-1980s. The show introduced hundreds of millions of American and international television viewers to South Beach and depicted it as a neon paradise, filled with excitement, tinged with danger, and populated by beautiful people. *Travel and Leisure* magazine described South Beach as the "hippest hangout on earth." This notoriety brought booming economic advantages, and many Miami Beach power brokers who previously had opposed preservation became supporters.

This new support produced tangible results. Between 1986 and 1990 Miami Beach created three preservation districts:

Espanola Way, Collins Avenue, and Flamingo Park. These new safe havens combined to preserve 85 percent of the South Beach historic district. Unfortunately, these were the last triumphs in which Capitman would share. On the eve of her seventieth birthday, she fell ill, was hospitalized, and died on March 29, 1990. The city commission recognized her contribution by naming one block in the historic district after her: Barbara Capitman Way. Abe Resnick was the only commission member to vote no.

Capitman's death meant that she was not there to witness the climactic year—1992—in the preservation of South Beach. The year began with preservationists reaching a painful compromise with developers; they would allow a convention-scale hotel to be built in South Beach provided that historic oceanfront hotels in the northeastern sector of the district were incorporated into the design. In August, Hurricane Andrew ravaged Dade County but largely spared the historic buildings.

Finally, in October, the National Trust for Historic Preservation held its national conference in Miami. As Capitman had done fifteen years before, preservationists used the attention from this event to press the city commission for a final vote that would extend a protective ordinance to the entire South Beach historic district. On October 24, with Resnick absent, the commission approved the extension unanimously. Seventeen years after the Miami Design Preservation League was founded, and thirteen years after national designation, the one-square-mile South Beach historic district was complete.[1]

---

[1] Two distinguished South Floridians and three books provided the background for this case study. Arva Parks and Ruth Shack shared their extensive knowledge and memories of Miami-Dade County history. The three books were Michael H. Roley, Linda G. Polansky, and Aristides J. Millas, *Old Miami Beach, A Case Study in Historic Preservation, July 1976–July 1980* (Miami Beach: Miami Design Preservation League, 1994); M. Barron Stofik, *Saving South Beach* (Gainesville: University Press of Florida, 2005); and Bill Wisser, *South Beach: America's Riviera, Miami Beach, Florida* (New York: Arcade Publishing, 1995).

YOU KNOW THE PROBLEM—WHO HAS THE SOLUTION?

You should now have a better grasp on what it is to formulate a problem for which governmental action can provide a solution—and in the terms that will be most advantageous to your cause. But even a well-defined problem cannot be solved until you determine which government agency has the power to address your problem. Is it a local problem or a challenge that requires statewide or even national attention? Does your proposed solution require legislative, executive, or judicial approval, or some combination of all three? Which specific government agency has the power to make or break your initiative or, alternatively, has the most influence to determine its fate? The answers to these questions will light your path to the decision makers who can turn your vision into reality.

The identification of the appropriate decision makers is the source of some of the worst misconceptions in the entire citizen advocacy process. In the introduction to this book, I shared the story of my visit to Samuel W. Wolfson High School in Jacksonville, Florida, when I was a member of the Florida Legislature in the early 1970s. During that visit, students complained about the food in the school cafeteria, forcing me to explain that Tallahassee legislators had no say over local school district menus. When I asked who else they had consulted about their problem, they told me they had approached Jacksonville's mayor and sheriff, both to no avail because neither of those officeholders had any power to order changes in school cafeteria cuisine. The officials who could do something about it—the cafeteria manager, principal, school superintendant, and school board—had been let off the hook.

My purpose in sharing this story is not to criticize either Wolfson High School or those individual students. Wolfson has produced many outstanding graduates, and I'm sure that the students with whom I spoke are now productive members of their respective communities. But the story shows that even citizens with reasonable concerns and the best intentions can meet with failure if they don't take time to find out who can solve their problem and determine how that person or persons can be persuaded.

AIMING AT THE RIGHT TARGET

All of the time you spend formulating your problem into a cogent, specific challenge will be for nothing if you waste your research and advocacy time on the wrong decision makers. If your concern is campus security, you don't want to spend time trying to enlist the U.S. Army or call in the Federal Bureau of Investigation. Your local council member may feel great sympathy when you complain that public colleges and universities are underfunded, but he or she can't do anything about it. On campus, the English Department would show understandable puzzlement if you asked it to do something about poor water pressure in dormitory bathrooms. Fortunately, the task of picking the right decision maker is intuitive if you follow several simple steps:

1. Determine Which Level of Government Is Involved

As you have learned in your school courses, the American constitutional system provides for two sources of governmental power: state governments and the federal government. For the ten years following the Declaration of Independence, in 1776, the United States was essentially a confederation of loosely affiliated independent states. Our first governing document, the Articles of Confederation, vested political authority in state governments and left the national government virtually unable to act without state consent. Because the new nation had many challenges that transcended individual state boundaries and required unified action, the states soon found the confederated arrangement to be unwieldy and ineffective.

When the Framers began drafting what would become the U.S. Constitution in the mid-1780s, they decided to take a different approach. Instead of subjecting central government actions to case-by-case state consent, the states would instead delegate certain powers to the national (federal) government so that it could act without prior approval. Articles I, II, and III of the Constitution, as well as the twenty-seven amendments to the Constitution, define the federal government's powers. The states retain all powers not delegated to the federal government and are sovereign in their exercise of those powers. You can find the relevant sections of the Constitution at the end of this chapter.

At both the state and federal levels government is divided into three branches: the executive (U.S. president and state governors), legislative (U.S. Congress and state legislatures), and judicial (federal and state courts). States also have the authority to delegate their powers to local subunits, such as counties, cities, towns, and other municipal entities. In addition, many states have created special-purpose districts that have boundaries which may or may not coincide with units of general government. For example, depending on how your state organizes the administration of public education, one county may have multiple school districts or be limited to one. Many states have set up multicounty environmental districts to govern the use of water bodies, such as lakes, rivers, and aquifers, and those districts track the water bodies' boundaries rather than the boundaries of local governments.

These levels and branches constitute "government" in the traditional sense. But plenty of institutions that have no connection to Washington, D.C., the state capital, or the county seat govern in other ways. Your college or university has rules and administrators that govern campus affairs and your life as a student. If you are an intercollegiate athlete, the National Collegiate Athletic Association (NCAA) governs how you are recruited, the time of year you practice and play your games, and your relationships with university administrators, faculty members, coaches, alumni, and other athletes. Even in your dormitory or apartment complex, a resident adviser or landlord governs how you occupy your living space.

The key is determining which entity controls the particular problem you aim to solve. Although the answer to this question can be complicated, there are some hard and fast rules that can help you narrow the possibilities.

College Administration. If the problem you want to solve is limited in scope to your campus, university administrators may have the power to address it. If they don't have the power (or if they have the power but won't use it), you may need to lobby higher authorities. Many colleges and universities, including community colleges, report to individual boards of trustees, a statewide board of regents or governors, and ultimately the state governor or legislature.

State or Local Government. Unlike now-defunct entities such as the Roman Empire and the Soviet Union, which centralized government to the point that officials in Rome or Moscow were involved in purely regional or even local matters, our states delegated some power to the federal government and retained the rest to manage their own particular affairs. But although state and local governmental actions have the most direct impact on our everyday lives, many—if not most—Americans know much more about what happens in the U.S. Capitol than in their own state house or county seat. (For information about contacting your local government, see "Tips from the Pros: Contacting Local Governments.")

Tips from the Pros: Contacting Local Governments
ALYCE ROBERTSON

Local government actions (or inactions) have the biggest potential to affect citizens' everyday lives. If you need to flex your citizenship muscles at the city or county levels, here are some suggestions.

- Find information on the Internet. The quality of information and ease of Web site navigation varies by jurisdiction, but most government agencies have an Internet presence of some kind. You can "Google" the name of the city or county government to direct you to the right Web site. Make sure you get the correct URL, since nongovernmental entities may use similar handles. For example, Miami-Dade County's Web site is miamidade.gov. If you mistakenly omit the "gov" and visit miamidade.com, you will find a commercial Web site.

- Some government Web sites organize information by department, while others arrange content by the service you need performed. Many localities now provide Web listings of services available over the Internet and also provide links to other government agencies. For example, you may be able to search property records, pay taxes and fines, or set a traffic court hearing online.

- If you don't have a computer, check the local library for free Internet services.

- Government agencies change names frequently—especially when newly elected officials want to put their own mark on local government, or if a scandal prompts the rebranding of an affected entity. Keep your eyes on the Web site and the newspaper so that you don't lose track of renamed agencies.

- Many local governments take the alphabet soup approach and refer to agencies by acronyms (for example, FDOT for Florida Department of Transportation and BART for Bay Area Rapid Transit). If you're not sure what an acronym means, ask.

- Most governments have general-information telephone lines to direct you to the right agency. Consult your local telephone book to see if it has a special section (sometimes called the "blue pages") that provides government telephone numbers. Check to see if your local government is using the easy-to-remember 311 prefix to provide citizens with information.

• Both public television (your local PBS station) and public-access television (found on your local cable system) sometimes offer informational programming to educate citizens about the services that agencies provide. Consult your local television listings or the stations' Web sites.

• Government agencies also provide printed materials. For example, during Miami–Dade County's Adopt-a-Tree events, county officials teach people how to plant a tree and also give them a community forestry booklet in case they forget the details.

• Invite key government officials to your civic, homeowners, condominium, or apartment association meetings to explain what their agency does and how you can report problems. Start with priority problems that are of interest to your neighborhood, such as police and fire services, traffic control, and park maintenance.

• Some communities have established programs to educate local residents about government services. Take advantage of these programs.

• Show resilience and persistence in seeking the right agency to address your problem. As Ralph Waldo Emerson said, "Patience and fortitude conquer all things."

• Remember the old maxim that you can catch more flies with honey than with vinegar. No matter how frustrating your search becomes, maintain a friendly and polite attitude. If you approach government officials with anger, you will discourage them from providing further assistance.

The Pothole Scenario

You drive onto your street one morning and see one of the most common citizen complaints: a pothole. How do you get it fixed? Follow this step-by-step approach:

1. If there is an immediate life safety or health concern—for example, the pothole has exposed underground electrical cables—call 911 to report an emergency.

2. Otherwise, decide which level of government is responsible for fixing the pothole. If you live on a small, two-lane road, your town, city, or county is probably in charge. But if you live on a four-lane boulevard or expressway, the state department of transportation or public works may have the responsibility of fixing the pothole.

3. Assuming the pothole is a local responsibility, call 311 or another central government phone number to report the problem. (Some Web sites also accept citizen complaints). On the telephone, ask the operator which department will handle the assignment. Ask for the operator's name, and note the date and time you reported the problem. Request an estimated time frame for fixing the problem and a return call or e-mail when the repair has been completed.

4. Don't get frustrated if the person who answers the phone does not know every detail involved in solving the problem. Your goal is to find the agency that will know those details, and the public servant on the other end of the phone can help you more readily if you are patient and respectful.

5. If the problem is not corrected within the specified time frame, call back for a status update. If you don't get a satisfactory response, ask to speak with a supervisor, or e-mail your concerns to the person in charge. Keep track of your conversations and e-mails. If all else fails, contact your town council member, city commissioner, or other elected official. Provide details of the nature and location of the problem and when and to whom you reported it.

Alyce Robertson is executive director of the Miami Downtown Development Agency (MDDA). A 30-year veteran of Miami-Dade County, she started as a management trainee in 1979 and served in increasingly responsible positions during her tenure. Before joining the MDDA in 2008, she served as the Miami-Dade County community image manager.

Thanks to unprecedented advances in telecommunications technology, more and more Americans get their news on satellite and cable television (CNN, MSNBC, and Fox News) or the Internet rather than through local sources, such as a city newspaper or a local television news affiliate. Additionally, we live in an era of mass media consolidation, where ownership of newspapers, networks, and television and radio stations is becoming concentrated in the hands of a few large corporations. The combined effect of these phenomena is that media coverage of the White House, Congress, and other federal governmental entities has crowded out local stories. At the end of any given day, you may know that the president has held a Rose Garden press conference, but you probably won't know that your local school board has decided to change graduation requirements or school boundaries.

State governments are sovereign, and they typically delegate authority to local governments to regulate purely parochial matters, such as local road maintenance, parks and recreational facilities, trash collection, sports stadiums, zoning changes, approval of new commercial or residential developments, fire and police service, and other matters that are confined within the city or county limits. When an issue goes beyond the city limits or county lines, however, states maintain and exercise authority. For example, it is not uncommon for states to govern public universities, issue licenses to drivers and businesses, maintain prisons, regulate power companies, protect sensitive lands and waters, run the state lottery, oversee at-risk children through adoption and foster-parenting agencies, prepare for and respond to natural disasters, collect sales taxes, and mediate intercounty disputes.

Federal Government. For the most part, problems that affect individual localities or states exclusively do not rise to the level of federal concern. In determining whether your issue is a matter of federal interest, ask yourself whether the problem crosses state boundaries and has an effect on citizens throughout the nation.

For example, the federal government exerts exclusive or primary jurisdiction over the U.S. military, international relations and trade, foreign intelligence gathering, Social Security, Medicare, national parks and monuments, interstate commerce, the national economy and the Federal Reserve (banking) system, and other matters that affect Americans whether they live in Seattle, St. Louis, or St. Petersburg.

Blurred Lines of Authority. Despite those clearly labeled descriptions of the levels of government, here's the rub: Issues sometimes do not fit neatly into just one category. Your initiative may cross jurisdictional lines. An example is law enforcement. While colleges provide training for police officers, and local governments largely fund and administer their police forces, state governments determine the criminal laws that police are charged with enforcing. They also regulate training, licensure, and pension and other retirement issues for law enforcement officers. The federal government has the smallest role in police protection, but it retains influence through grants that have assisted local law enforcement agencies in hiring new officers, training police, conducting joint operations, and making equipment purchases.

Environmental matters are another example. Local governments usually control their own land-use decisions. States determine water quality standards under state law and offer the first line of defense for environmentally sensitive lands and waters. The federal government identifies and protects threatened or endangered species and regulates interstate environmental issues, such as the use and protection of navigable waters. Additionally, through enactments such as the Clean Air and Clean Water Acts, federal policymakers establish national standards in air, soil, and water quality and then give states the opportunity to administer and enforce the standards. Conflict often arises when a state wants to set more stringent standards than those of the federal government. It took a presidential election to resolve California's effort to set automobile-emission limitations greater than those established in Washington. President George W. Bush had repeatedly denied California's request. One of Barack Obama's first actions as president was to grant it.

In the area of public education, state governments retain the ultimate control of schools and often directly set curriculum standards, approve textbooks, certify teachers, and provide significant funding. States delegate other responsibilities to local school districts, which manage the schools; hire principals, teachers, and other personnel; and provide funding for school operations and facilities, usually by levying property taxes.

The federal government has almost no formal authority over education. However, particularly since the passage of the G.I. Bill in 1944 for returning World War II veterans, Washington has played a role in providing universities with financial support through student grants and loans, assistance with construction of facilities, and scientific research. The federal government also protects civil rights throughout the educational system. It provides help to economically disadvantaged students and children with disabilities or special needs. And it maintains data and funds research on educational issues.

In addition to situations like those noted, in which different levels of government exercise discrete forms of authority on broad policy issues, the federal and state governments sometimes share responsibility for particular programs or initiatives. Perhaps the best example is Medicaid, which helps to provide a national health care system for low-income Americans. Medicaid is "federal" in the sense that Congress established the program, and the federal government sets general guidelines and appropriates about 60 percent of the cost. But Medicaid is also a "state" program in that state health care agencies help to determine eligibility for individuals who need care, administer the delivery of health care, enhance benefits consistent with federal guidelines, and provide the nonfederal balance of funding.

Joint federal–state initiatives to address region-specific challenges also exist. For example, the federal government and affected states have agreed to share the costs and responsibilities involved in restoring the health of America's Everglades, the Chesapeake Bay, and other threatened environmental treasures.

Your job is to determine the authority that each level of government exercises over your issue—and then to address each level to achieve your goal. Start at the level of government closest to you and work upward. Let's say that your goal is to expand the State Children's Health Insurance Program (SCHIP), a joint program much like Medicaid, so that more children will have access to health insurance. Check with the state health care administration agency. Are all eligible children in your state currently covered? If not, there is work to do in your own backyard. But if all eligible children are covered, and if you believe that even more children should have access to the program, you will have to persuade the federal government to expand eligibility, and then persuade officials in Washington *and* your state capital to increase funding so that the newly eligible kids can be included.

Nobody ever said that federalism was simple or for the weak of heart. Our uniquely American multilayered system of government is complex—a condition befitting a nation of our large size, political history, varied geography, and rich diversity. Don't be frightened by this complexity, but master it. Those citizens who recognize and understand the nuances of our federal system are the ones most likely to transform their initiative into action.

2. Pinpoint Your Specific Targets within the Proper Level of Government

Determining whether a problem is local, state, federal, or nongovernmental in nature is only the first step. You must also determine which entities at different levels have the power to solve your problem. Note the use of the plural. In our system of government, sole decision-making authority is a rare occurrence.

The Almanac of American Politics once described my friend and former Senate colleague, the late Daniel Patrick Moynihan of New York, as "the nation's best thinker among politicians since Lincoln and its best politician among thinkers since Jefferson." [2] Senator Moynihan observed that our form of government was the first one created with the deliberate goal of having it not work. Having rebelled against the monarchical rule of King George III, the Framers did not want a government that could easily deprive citizens of life, liberty, or property. They addressed this concern through the U.S. Constitution's intricate system of checks and balances and the subsequent adoption of the Bill of Rights. For the most part, individual states have used the same model. The practical consequence of the Framers' design is that our democracy has established multiple checkpoints on the road of governmental decision making.

Imagine you learn that a new expressway has been proposed through your city, but the suggested route will require clearing 500 acres of forest that host unique species of plant and animal life. You are determined to stop what you see as unnecessary destruction of the community's natural treasures. But where do you begin? The first step is to determine who has the power to halt the new expressway. Think carefully about the governmental or administrative bodies that affect your life. If you are a student, your college or university's administration probably won't be able to help directly because it oversees only what occurs on campus. Assume for the sake of this scenario that the new expressway will not be limited to your local community but will instead connect several counties. Through the process of elimination, you

---

[2] *The Almanac of American Politics 1998*, ed. Michael Barone (Washington, D.C.: National Journal, 1997), 962–963.

determine that your concerns will be addressed at either or both the state and federal levels of government. But how do you determine which local, state, and/or federal entities have any say over the problem? Here are the steps:

• At the state level, consult your state's main Web site (you can find it at www.usa.gov/Agencies/State_and_Territories. shtml). Study the information on each of the state agencies to determine which ones can help you. The goal should be to find the *enabling* departments or agencies that will plan and execute the proposed highway and the *regulating* departments or agencies that will ensure the project is planned, constructed, used, and maintained consistent with other public priorities, such as environmental protection, safety, and growth management. With the information gathered from the Web site, you should be able to determine the department or agency that is responsible for state road and highway construction and maintenance, as well as the departments or agencies with jurisdiction over natural resources, highway safety, and land use planning.

Assume for the sake of this example that the state department of transportation oversees approved road construction projects and that the state department of environmental protection governs potentially sensitive lands, waters, and species.

• Visit the Web site of your state's department of transportation (find yours at www.fhwa.dot.gov/webstate.htm). Determine whether the department has an office or an official who oversees state road construction and maintenance in general. Some state transportation departments may take a different approach and delegate all road and highway matters to regional offices placed throughout the state. Yours may give you the opportunity to review road projects and provide feedback to a regional officer. Regardless of which approach your state takes, you should be able to locate the name and phone number or e-mail address of an official who can answer your questions. It will be your responsibility to decide what to do with the answer.

- Follow the same process to locate your state's department of environmental protection (consult www.epa.gov/epahome/state.htm). In most states the agency that regulates environmental matters is required to study proposed projects that threaten natural resources and issue permits before any work can begin. You will derail the proposed expressway if you can convince regulators to deny permitting.

- Don't forget that environmental issues often invoke multilevel jurisdiction. At the federal level the Environmental Protection Agency (www.epa.gov), Forest Service (www.fs.fed.us), Fish and Wildlife Service (www.fws.gov), or Army Corps of Engineers (www.usace.army.mil) may well have the authority to examine the environmental impacts of the proposed highway and halt construction if the project falls short of federal standards for the protection of air, water, wildlife, vegetation, and wetlands.

- Take advantage of representative democracy. The United States is rare in that its elected legislative representatives provide constituent services that range from assisting you in replacing a lost passport to helping you communicate with government agencies. This service does not exist in most parliamentary democracies outside the United States.

Unless you live in Nebraska, the only state to have a one-house, or unicameral, legislature, you have at least one state senator and one lower house member who were elected to represent your interests in state government. Two U.S. senators and a congressperson serve you in the federal government. Find out who your elected representatives are and contact their offices to make known your concerns.

Remember that legislative staff members play a critical role in shaping policy. Most state legislators have at least some staff. U.S. representatives and senators typically will have staff assigned to specific areas of governmental authority, such as transportation or the environment. Determine the appropriate staff members and work with them to leverage your influence with the legislator.

It is possible that the legislator may both exercise direct oversight of transportation and the environment and, especially at the state level, play a role in approving and appropriating funds for the proposed project. Furthermore, because other legislators are likely to defer to the elected representative whose district or state will host the proposed new road, you will go a long way toward killing a project if you can convince your legislators and their staff that the highway is a bad idea.

- Finally, be sure to keep one eye on the clock at all times. As you will read in chapter 6, timing is everything. All of the processes, reviews, and decisions described here occur in specific time frames and are subject to strict deadlines. You may have a winning defense, but if you don't get it on the field in time, you will lose.

CHECKLIST FOR ACTION

☐ Determine which level of government is involved.
☐ Pinpoint your specific targets within the proper level of government.
- Consult your state's main Web site.
- Don't forget that environmental issues often invoke multilevel jurisdiction.
- Take advantage of representative democracy.
- Keep an eye on the clock.

Exercises

LOCAL COVERAGE OF LOCAL NEWS

Most government decisions that affect our everyday lives are made at the local or state level, but media outlets increasingly focus on Washington. Over the next week, read your local newspaper each morning and watch at least one local television news show each evening. Carefully note the percentage of newspaper stories devoted to state and local issues, and calculate how many minutes the television station spent covering state and local news during each half-hour broadcast. Compare and contrast the two types of media coverage for their accuracy and comprehensiveness in reporting state and local stories.

TARGETING THE DECISION MAKER

Take the problem you have defined and use the methods outlined in this chapter to identify the level of government responsible for solving your problem. Once you have defined the level of government, pinpoint the specific office or official(s) best situated to handle your problem. If you are concerned about campus safety, have you checked with the university police department? If your worry is the pollution of a nearby lake or river, have you located the office in your state's environmental protection agency with jurisdiction over that problem? How could your elected legislator help?

Constitutional Sources of State and Federal Authority

I. Article I (Legislative Power)

Section 8. The Congress shall have power to lay and collect taxes, duties, imposts and excises, to pay the debts and provide for the common defense and general welfare of the United States; but all duties, imposts and excises shall be uniform throughout the United States;

To borrow money on the credit of the United States;

To regulate commerce with foreign nations, and among the several states, and with the Indian tribes;

To establish a uniform rule of naturalization, and uniform laws on the subject of bankruptcies throughout the United States;

To coin money, regulate the value thereof, and of foreign coin, and fix the standard of weights and measures;

To provide for the punishment of counterfeiting the securities and current coin of the United States;

To establish post offices and post roads;

To promote the progress of science and useful arts, by securing for limited times to authors and inventors the exclusive right to their respective writings and discoveries;

To constitute tribunals inferior to the Supreme Court;

To define and punish piracies and felonies committed on the high seas, and offenses against the law of nations;

To declare war, grant letters of manqué and reprisal, and make rules concerning captures on land and water;

To raise and support armies, but no appropriation of money to that use shall be for a longer term than two years;

To provide and maintain a navy;

To make rules for the government and regulation of the land and naval forces;

To provide for calling forth the militia to execute the laws of the union, suppress insurrections and repel invasions;

To provide for organizing, arming, and disciplining, the militia, and for governing such part of them as may be employed in the service of the United States, reserving to the states respectively, the appointment of the officers, and the authority of training the militia according to the discipline prescribed by Congress;

To exercise exclusive legislation in all cases whatsoever, over such District (not exceeding ten miles square) as may, by cession of particular states, and the acceptance of Congress, become the seat of the government of the United States, and to exercise like authority over all places purchased by the consent of the legislature of the state in which the same shall be, for the erection of forts, magazines, arsenals, dockyards, and other needful buildings;—And

To make all laws which shall be necessary and proper for carrying into execution the foregoing powers, and all other powers vested by this Constitution in the government of the United States, or in any department or officer thereof.

Section 9. The migration or importation of such persons as any of the states now existing shall think proper to admit, shall not be prohibited by the Congress prior to the year one thousand eight hundred and eight, but a tax or duty may be imposed on such importation, not exceeding ten dollars for each person.

The privilege of the writ of habeas corpus shall not be suspended, unless when in cases of rebellion or invasion the public safety may require it.

No bill of attainder or ex post facto Law shall be passed.

No capitation, or other direct, tax shall be laid, unless in proportion to the census or enumeration herein before directed to be taken *(amended by Sixteenth Amendment)*.

No tax or duty shall be laid on articles exported from any state.

No preference shall be given by any regulation of commerce or revenue to the ports of one state over those of another: nor shall vessels bound to, or from, one state, be obliged to enter, clear or pay duties in another.

No money shall be drawn from the treasury, but in consequence of appropriations made by law; and a regular statement and account of receipts and expenditures of all public money shall be published from time to time.

No title of nobility shall be granted by the United States: and no person holding any office of profit or trust under them, shall, without the consent of the Congress, accept of any present, emolument, office, or title, of any kind whatever, from any king, prince, or foreign state.

Section 10. No state shall enter into any treaty, alliance, or confederation; grant letters of manqué and reprisal; coin money; emit bills of credit; make anything but gold and silver coin a tender in payment of debts; pass any bill of attainder, ex post facto law, or law impairing the obligation of contracts, or grant any title of nobility.

No state shall, without the consent of the Congress, lay any imposts or duties on imports or exports, except what may be absolutely necessary for executing it's [stet] inspection laws: and the net produce of all duties and imposts, laid by any state on imports or exports, shall be for the use of the treasury of the United States; and all such laws shall be subject to the revision and control of the Congress.

No state shall, without the consent of Congress, lay any duty of tonnage, keep troops, or ships of war in time of peace, enter into any agreement or compact with another state, or with a foreign power, or engage in war, unless actually invaded, or in such imminent danger as will not admit of delay.

II. Article II (Executive Power)

Section 2. The President shall be commander in chief of the Army and Navy of the United States, and of the militia of the several states, when called into the actual service of the United States; he may require the opinion, in writing, of the principal officer in each of the executive departments, upon any subject relating to the duties of their respective offices, and he shall have power to grant reprieves and pardons for offenses against the United States, except in cases of impeachment.

He shall have power, by and with the advice and consent of the Senate, to make treaties, provided two thirds of the Senators present concur; and he shall nominate, and by and with the advice and consent of the Senate, shall appoint ambassadors, other public ministers and consuls, judges of the Supreme Court, and all other officers of the United States, whose appointments are not herein otherwise provided for, and which shall be established by law: but the Congress may by law vest the appointment of such inferior officers, as they think proper, in the President alone, in the courts of law, or in the heads of departments.

The President shall have power to fill up all vacancies that may happen during the recess of the Senate, by granting commissions which shall expire at the end of their next session.

Section 3. He shall from time to time give to the Congress information of the state of the union, and recommend to their consideration such measures as he shall judge necessary and expedient; he may, on extraordinary occasions, convene both Houses, or either of them, and in case of disagreement between them, with respect to the time of adjournment, he may adjourn them to such time as he shall think proper; he shall receive ambassadors and other public ministers; he shall take care that the laws be faithfully executed, and shall commission all the officers of the United States.

Section 4. The President, Vice President and all civil officers of the United States, shall be removed from office on impeachment for, and conviction of, treason, bribery, or other high crimes and misdemeanors.

III. Article III (Judicial Power)

Section 1. The judicial power of the United States shall be vested in one Supreme Court, and in such inferior courts as the Congress may from time to time ordain and establish. The judges, both of the supreme and inferior courts, shall hold their offices during good behaviour, and shall, at stated times, receive for their services, a compensation, which shall not be diminished during their continuance in office.

Section 2. The judicial power shall extend to all cases, in law and equity, arising under this Constitution, the laws of the United States, and treaties made, or which shall be made, under their authority;—to all cases affecting ambassadors, other public ministers and consuls;—to all cases of admiralty and maritime jurisdiction; to controversies to which the United States shall be a party; to controversies between two or more states; between a state and citizens of another state (*amended by Eleventh Amendment*); between citizens of different states; between citizens of the same state claiming lands under grants of different states, and between a state, or the citizens thereof, and foreign states, citizens or subjects.

In all cases affecting ambassadors, other public ministers and consuls, and those in which a state shall be party, the Supreme Court shall have original jurisdiction. In all the other cases before mentioned, the Supreme Court shall have appellate jurisdiction, both as to law and fact, with such exceptions, and under such regulations as the Congress shall make.

The trial of all crimes, except in cases of impeachment, shall be by jury; and such trial shall be held in the state where the said crimes shall have been committed; but when not committed within any state, the trial shall be at such place or places as the Congress may by law have directed.

Section 3. Treason against the United States, shall consist only in levying war against them, or in adhering to their enemies, giving them aid and comfort. No person shall be convicted of treason unless on the testimony of two witnesses to the same overt act, or on confession in open court.

The Congress shall have power to declare the punishment of treason, but no attainder of treason shall work corruption of blood, or forfeiture except during the life of the person attainted.

IV. Tenth Amendment

The powers not delegated to the United States by the Constitution, nor prohibited by it to the states, are reserved to the states respectively, or to the people.

Source: U.S. Constitution.

4 Testing the Waters

Gauging and Building Public Support for Your Cause

"In the modern world the intelligence of public opinion
is the one indispensable condition for social progress."

—Charles W. Eliot

Case in Point: Reversal of Fortune in Steamboat Springs

High in the mountains west of Denver is the majestic valley and beautiful ski resort of Steamboat Springs, Colorado. A Rocky Mountain community blessed with magnificent vistas, Steamboat Springs surged in population in the 1970s and 1980s as the Colorado skiing industry boomed. In 1970 Steamboat Springs had 2,340 residents. Ten years later that number had more than doubled to 5,098. By 1990 the population was 6,695.

This huge growth greatly affected the community's public schools. In 1970 voters had approved a $5 million bond issue for new school construction. But two decades later, with student enrollment growing at the rate of 4 percent annually, elementary and secondary schools were bulging at the seams. Steamboat Springs High School, built in 1964 to hold 434 students, now had 528 pupils to accommodate. In the short term, school officials managed the overflow through unpopular split sessions and portable classrooms. But that was triage at a time when the town really needed a cure.

Responding to community pressures, the school board placed a $41.8 million school bond issue on the November 7, 1995, ballot. An advisory question also asked citizens where they wanted the new high school to be located: in town, out of town, or no preference. It was not until October 25 that citizens learned that the question about location was rhetorical—the school board had already tentatively selected a site just south of town in a known flood plain.

On Election Day voters spoke loudly against the bond issue, defeating it by the surprisingly wide margin of 70 percent to 30 percent. The morning after the election one of the principle opponents of the bond issue—Bob Maddox, a highly regarded business and civic leader—sent a two-page letter to the superintendent of schools, Dr. Cyndy Simms. Stunned at the results of the election, Simms didn't open the letter for two days. When she did read it, she saw that Maddox had provided a detailed analysis of the reasons the bond issue failed.

Simms called Maddox on the Friday after Election Day. They met for lunch and had a three-hour conversation about their different views of the schools. Simms stressed the strong results on standardized tests and the success rate of graduates in their subsequent college and university educations. Maddox recounted the concerns of many citizens and parents about the high school and what he felt was the school district's tone deafness to those concerns.

During the lunch Maddox and Simms agreed to organize a citizen committee for which he would select five bond issue opponents while she selected five proponents. With the two of them also participating, the group would be known by its number: the 10 Plus 2.

The twelve participants represented a cross-section of the Steamboat Springs community, including a local hotel manager, a contractor, a third-generation woman civic activist, and the new principal of the high school. All were considered to be people "of good heart" and genuinely interested in what was best for the town and its future.

The initial meeting of the twelve was limited to a discussion of concerns—such as why bond issue proponents felt a new high school was necessary and why opponents disagreed. The meeting went well enough that the dozen decided to open the process to the entire Steamboat community. They organized a forum to be held in the ballroom of the Sheraton Hotel and selected other community leaders to serve as facilitators to keep the meeting moving in a productive direction.

Two hundred citizens attended the forum, gathering around dining room tables in the conference center to discuss their concerns. During the course of the evening, it became clear that voters rejected the new high school for reasons having little to do with the pros and cons of school construction. Instead, they were angry because they felt that the school district was not open to citizen input and feedback on educational matters. Parents of the brightest students had urged the high school to provide gifted programs, such as advanced placement. Parents of struggling students felt their children were not receiving appropriate supplemental services. Still others were concerned that the cohesion of the town would be threatened if the school district relocated the high school from its downtown site to a place outside town. Many bond opponents saw the advisory committee that had supported the new high school as nothing but a rubber stamp for the school district and felt it did not represent a variety of community perspectives.

The level of skepticism toward the school district led the 10 Plus 2 to take detailed minutes of each table discussion and send copies to all 200 participants. This transcription and mass distribution ensured that every participant would receive the same factual information about the concerns expressed. The school board stood back, recognizing that it was perceived as part of the problem by many Steamboat residents.

After this successful community forum, the 10 Plus 2 followed up with a second forum, inviting every resident who had attended the first. Two hundred new citizen participants attended as well. The third and fourth community forums transitioned from expressing concerns to discussing and compiling possible solutions.

It was now the fall of 1996, almost a year before the 1997 election during which the 10 Plus 2 wanted to place a school construction bond issue on the ballot. In November the group received some positive foreshadowing. In 1993 voters in Steamboat Springs had approved a half-cent sales tax for schools. Three years later they renewed the sales tax by a wide margin, 60 percent to 40 percent. Community leaders saw passage of the extension as a reaffirmation of the town's essential support for public education.

The 10 Plus 2 reviewed and organized the recommendations from the final community forums, grouping the suggestions under six categories: Curriculum, Finance, Facilities, Communication, Innovative Concepts, and Accountability. The 10 Plus 2 then established action task forces comprising twelve to eighteen persons for each of the six categories. Each action task force was led by co-chairs—one who had supported the bond issue, the other who had opposed it. The membership of each task force was equally divided between "yes" and "no" voters on the failed 1995 bond issue.

For two months these task forces met, with co-chairs holding monthly meetings with the 10 Plus 2 to facilitate information flow among the six groups. By the spring of 1997 the 10 Plus 2 had received the task force reports. After refining and integrating the reports, the 10 Plus 2 was prepared to submit a series of recommendations to the school board for its consideration and submission to the voters.

The 10 Plus 2 was not the only entity promoting a spirit of change. The school board had previously dismissed the architect who designed the 1995 high school and the bond underwriter who would have procured the financing. The new bond underwriters agreed to provide the funding for a professional pollster to assess public opinion before the bond issue was finalized. They recommended a Houston academic and political pollster, Dr. David Hill.

Hill arrived in Steamboat Springs in early June 1997. Through a series of face-to-face meetings and conference-call discussions, Hill gained perspective on the schools from a diverse set of community members. Aware that the school board had the final say as to whether and how a bond issue would appear on the 1997 ballot, Hill was especially attentive to board members' questions.

By late August 1997 Hill was ready to go into the field. He and his survey research team conducted 304 telephone interviews with local voters who had been selected to represent the diversity of the community (see excerpt of the poll in the Appendix at the end of this chapter). Hill described the effort as one of assessment rather than persuasion. His goal was to determine voter attitudes on the bond issue and use that information to refine the campaign message. The results were illuminating and encouraging:

- Overall, voters were inclined to support the bond issue by a margin of 62 percent to 26 percent.
- The two groups that most influenced community opinions on the bond issue were local school teachers (39 percent of those surveyed listed them as most influential) and students currently enrolled in Steamboat schools (30 percent rated them as most persuasive).
- Of the 47 percent of Steamboat voters who were familiar with the work of 10 Plus 2, two-thirds evaluated its work as open, fair, and complete.
- Fifty-seven percent thought the level of local and school taxes was "about right."
- Steamboat Springs schools received a grade of A or B from 53 percent of the respondents; only 6 percent rated them D or F.
- Sixty-six percent thought most local public schools in Steamboat were overcrowded, and 47 percent thought school maintenance was insufficient.

- Two-thirds believed that the school board had been more responsive to parents and taxpayers following the 1995 bond issue defeat.
- A massive majority—85 percent—stated that striving for educational excellence was a high priority. Two-thirds ranked giving teachers the tools and space to be effective instructors as a critical goal.
- Of those surveyed, 78 percent gave as a reason to support the bond issue the new architect's provision of facilities for the visual arts and music.

Armed with these data, the 10 Plus 2 worked feverishly to turn public opinion into actual votes. On November 4, 2007, Steamboat Springs saw a record turnout of voters. When the votes were counted, the bond issue had passed, 77 percent to 23 percent. Looking back at the events that led to victory, Jim Gill, one of the school board members, summed them up as follows: "The defeat of the 1995 bond issue was a train wreck. But it took a train wreck to help us get back on the right track. The train wreck was a blessing in disguise."

WHY DOES PUBLIC OPINION MATTER?

As you have no doubt noticed, none of the skills presented in these chapters is alone sufficient to turn your well-intentioned initiative into governmental reality. Instead, you will have to use these skills in combination with others if you want to persuade decision makers to embrace your cause. The court of public opinion is the place where your efforts find synergy. If you have your finger on the pulse of popular thinking, you can more effectively define your problem, focus your research, determine your optimal coalition partners, engage reporters, raise money, and apply all of the other tools presented in this book.

This is not to say that you should simply determine public opinion and design your initiative to follow it blindly. The act of telling people just what they want to hear is not leadership. But if you know where people stand at the start of your campaign, and keep a close watch on their ever-shifting feelings and impressions, you will have a strong sense of what arguments will persuade them to adopt your position. Once you have the public on your side, your chances of convincing the officials accountable to them will increase immeasurably.

Put another way, you will know how to connect with the decision makers (voters, government officials, or university administrators) or with the people who heavily influence them (voters, citizens, or, on a college campus, alumni, faculty, and students). In order to connect, you need to know where your targets stand now—and what data or arguments will move them to a position of support.

In addition to gaining these strategic benefits, you will also enjoy tactical advantages if you stay abreast of public opinion. Your initiative is no place to fly blind or utilize a one-size-fits-all approach. If you thoroughly analyze relevant public opinion from the outset, and continue to update the analysis throughout your campaign, you will be able to take the following steps that will help you reach your ultimate goal.

1. Determine the Level of Support

The first step is to determine whether you have strong public support at the beginning or whether you will need to convince people to support you. This is a critical step that you should not take lightly. More than one campaign has foundered because its advocates were convinced of the rightness of their cause, and they assumed that decision makers would do the right thing and support them without question. In his autobiography former Speaker of the House Thomas P. "Tip" O'Neill of Massachusetts discusses the four years that Jimmy Carter served as president. In April 1977 Carter gave a nationally televised address from the Oval Office in which he discussed his plan to make the United States energy independent. The nation had recently suffered through several international oil embargoes that had driven gasoline prices to then all-time highs and had subjected U.S. motorists to long lines at gas stations. Carter hoped that both the general public and Congress would embrace his initiative with enthusiasm.

O'Neill attended Carter's speech. When the president had finished and the cameras had stopped rolling, O'Neill walked over to Carter, congratulated him on his remarks, and handed him a list of representatives to call to press them to support the plan. According to O'Neill, Carter refused the list and said that the merits of his initiative were enough to win public support and congressional backing. The president learned how wrong that notion was when Congress passed a watered-down bill that barely resembled his ambitious vision for a national energy policy.[1]

Carter made the fatal mistake of assuming that Congress would simply fall in line because his plan was just and his arguments defensible. From O'Neill's perspective the president didn't take the time to determine whether members of Congress matched his fervor or would need to be coaxed into supporting his plan. Even if your initiative is as seemingly noncontroversial as curing cancer, cleaning up a local lake, or making your campus walkways safe, don't assume that you have an automatic reservoir of support with the decision maker or with the general public that influences the decision maker. Make the effort to know for sure.

2. Identify the Arguments Most Likely to Resonate with the Public

You almost certainly have your own reasons for wanting the relevant decision makers to embrace your cause, but others may have different reasons, even if they support the same goal. When you test public opinion, you can identify which arguments are appealing and which are not so effective. For example, assume

---

[1] Thomas P. "Tip" O'Neill with William Novak, *Man of the House: The Life and Political Memoirs of Speaker Tip O'Neill* (New York: Random House, 1987).

that you want your local town council to install a traffic light at a busy intersection near your home. Your motivation is simple: A light will better regulate traffic flow, ease congestion, and make it easier for you to drive in your own neighborhood. But your neighbors and others positioned to sway the council may have other concerns. Residents who have children or pets may be concerned about safety. Others may see the traffic light as an improvement that increases neighborhood property values. If you take the time to learn all of the reasons that other people might have for supporting your idea, you will discover multiple arguments that can be used to persuade the decision maker.

3. "Micro-Target" Specific Groups of Persuadable Officials or Citizens

Whether you are running a candidate for office or supporting an issue initiative for voters' approval, the same argument won't necessarily appeal to every member of the electorate. In any election different groups of voters may have different interests and be open to different methods of persuasion. This is why public surveys always ask a wide range of demographic questions (age, race, gender, occupation, geographical location, income, and political party membership and identification). Once armed with that information, you can tailor your campaign's message for a particular group.

But although demographic distinctions are extremely helpful in targeting segments of the public, other distinctions also matter. If you are trying to change policy at your college or university, you may determine that one method will best persuade alumni, another will influence faculty, yet another will appeal to administrators, and still another will attract students' interest. The point is to know various segments of the public so well that you can communicate effectively with all of them, regardless of their differences.

My home state of Florida provided a telling example of effective micro-targeting in the 1974 race for the U.S. Senate. At that time Florida still employed a system in which no candidate could receive the party's nomination for office unless he or she received an electoral majority (50 percent plus one vote). If no candidate received a majority during the first primary election, the top two vote getters advanced to a second primary election. The candidate who won this runoff would become the party's nominee and compete in the November general election.

In 1974 eleven Democrats ran for the U.S. Senate nomination. Two emerged from the pack: front runner and U.S. representative Bill Gunter, a Central Floridian, and Florida's secretary of state, Dick Stone, a Miamian who would become the first directly elected Jewish senator from a southern state if he won in November. Gunter had won a convincing victory in the first primary, but he did not achieve an electoral majority. On the other hand, Stone finished a distant second and barely edged out the third-place candidate. While it was assumed that Stone would run well in South Florida, most political observers believed that Gunter would capture large margins in Central and North Florida, where his southern accent and folksy manner would be decisive factors in winning votes.

But Stone had refused to concede any territory. He showed a folksy side of his own by playing the harmonica and spoons on campaign stops in North Florida and criticized what he saw as excessive federal government spending. His parochial appeals and conservative message paid off. On the day of the runoff, Stone won strong support at home in South Florida and added enough votes in North Florida to win statewide by a narrow margin, 51 percent to 49 percent. One month later Stone won the general election and became a U.S. senator.[2]

---

[2] Jack Bass and Walter De Vries, *The Transformation of Southern Politics* (Athens: University of Georgia Press, 1995), 125; Alan Abramowitz and Jeffrey Alan Segal, *Senate Elections* (Ann Arbor: University of Michigan Press, 1992), 79; Michael Barone and Grant Ujifusa and Douglas Matthews. *The Almanac of American Politics 1976* (New York: Dutton, 1975), 161–162.

Once you have identified the distinct segments of the public and have determined which arguments are most likely to persuade each of them, you will find that each of the citizen advocacy tasks identified in the other chapters will come into better focus. For example, to use a slightly modified example of the traffic problem mentioned earlier, let's assume that you are concerned about uncontrolled speeding on a street in your neighborhood, and your goal is to have the local government install new traffic safety devices (lights, stop signs, or traffic-calming circles). Effective public opinion analysis may show which members of your coalition are more likely to persuade elected officials (city commissioners or council members), key appointed officials (police and traffic planners), and different types of voters who influence both groups. Once you have assigned various coalition members to take responsibility for individual groups of decision makers or segments of the general public, the coalition members can tailor their appeals appropriately. For example, the coalition partner assigned to a legislator whose district includes a state university might visit the campus newspaper to argue your case and ask for an editorial endorsement or appeal to members of the university administration, faculty, or student body who have influence with the legislator. Another group may win over traffic planners by compiling accurate and compelling data demonstrating the benefits of calming devices.

Regardless of whether your campaign or initiative is at the campus, local, state, or federal level, you can still build public support across the spectrum of the citizenry. Although diversity is one of the strengths of our democracy, it also complicates the tasks of gauging and shaping overall public opinion. Micro-targeting helps to organize the members of the public into persuadable parts.

4. Get the Most Bang for Your Campaign Buck

Any campaign or citizen initiative that fails to allocate its main resources efficiently is probably doomed to failure. Public opinion research is critical to ensure that time, money, and energy are spent wisely. Successful advocacy efforts don't waste significant resources trying to persuade either true believers or lost causes. If your analysis demonstrates that people in Group A strongly support your cause, make sure that they vote or register their opinion with the decision maker—don't waste time trying to convince them. If those in Group B strongly oppose your initiative, don't waste energy trying to convert them. Instead, focus your persuasion campaign on Group C, whose members are predominantly undecided and may break your way if you communicate with them frequently and effectively.

HOW DO I DETERMINE WHAT PUBLIC OPINION IS?

In many respects, politics is an art rather than a science. Although my goal in this book is to provide you with the basic skills and insights you need to be an effective citizen advocate, you'll find that political success involves lots of improvisation, learning by experience, and good fortune. However, the accurate determination of public opinion is one aspect of the political process that often relies on scientific principles. This analysis can take many forms.

Polling

Polling is the most effective way to accurately gauge public opinion. Political candidates and issue campaigns subject to voter approval use it most often for many reasons: to measure support for their candidacies, to gauge their opponents' support, and to determine where voters stand on a variety of issues. Polling is useful in determining how prospective voters will react to potential policy proposals, as well as to positive or negative information about a candidate or an issue—and opponents of the candidate or issue. In American politics today, nearly every candidate—from citizens running for city council and state legislative seats to those seeking to win the presidential nomination—use polling as their roadmap to victory. (See "Tips from the Pros: Why Polling Matters.")

Tips from the Pros: Why Polling Matters
TOM ELDON

Polling is one of the most misunderstood tools in political campaigns. Polls are frequently cited in the news media. Seemingly everyone has a poll on nearly every subject. But how can polls help you in your effort?

The first thing to realize is that polls come in all different sizes. Some ask a few questions and give you only the narrowest of information. Others probe issues from a myriad of directions and test various messages. Not all polls provide the demographic minutiae you see on TV. Most polls will never find out if the person interviewed is a soccer mom or a NASCAR dad.

When polls are brief, it is almost always for one reason: cost. Every question asked makes the poll longer and more expensive. Every person you interview costs more money. Campaigns on small budgets simply cannot afford the same level of research available to a statewide gubernatorial or Senate campaign.

This is not to say that small campaigns should avoid polling. The Steamboat Springs High School bond issue is a classic example of the perils of not polling. The proponents of building a new school ended up having to run the campaign twice because they failed to assess the mood of the electorate before the first election. Instead of determining the mood of the public, they ran a campaign based on faulty assumptions and lost.

The question is what kind of poll could have helped avoid the setback in Steamboat Springs? A community the size of Steamboat Springs could easily have been measured by conducting 300 interviews. In most cases, 300 interviews is the minimum number that you would want to consider for a poll. With a margin of error of 5.6 percent, that size poll provides enough statistical confidence for the general sample as well as the larger subgroups.

Your poll should measure the basic elements critical to the campaign. In a campaign for city council, for example, it should measure a candidate's performance. If the goal is educational reform, measure the quality of schooling. If your concern is crime, assess the quality of crime prevention, law enforcement, and public safety.

Elections are about affirmation or rejection. Knowing how the voting public feels about your issue will (or a least should) define your approach to a race.

Polls can change a campaign's assumptions about how the public feels about an issue. Campaigns that identify false assumptions through polling are far more likely to regain their footing in time to achieve victory than are those that wait for voters to set them straight on Election Day.

Tom Eldon is the managing officer of the public opinion research and strategic consulting firm Schroth Eldon & Associates (www.sea-poll.com). He has more than two decades of experience assisting grassroots, legislative, and statewide campaigns across the United States.

Polling has become popular because it maximizes limited resources. In any kind of campaign, it is virtually impossible to contact every potential voter, or every individual who might be affected by the outcome of an initiative, to determine where they stand on the candidates or the issues. In statewide efforts, this could mean making contact with millions of individuals. Even on a college campus, it could mean touching base with tens of thousands of students. The cost of such an effort, in terms of both time and money spent, would be prohibitive.

Pollsters employ a shortcut. They analyze the group in which you are interested to determine certain key demographic statistics (such as age, sex, party affiliation, ethnic background, and geographic location). Using that data, they poll not the entire target population but instead a representative sample that mimics the demographic characteristics of the whole population. For example, let's say your goal is to pass an amendment to the county charter that would sharply restrict the construction of billboards along local roadways. Since voters must approve the measure, and a poll would be worthless without a representative sample that accurately mimics the electorate, your pollster will need to know that your county's registered voters are 43 percent Republican, 43 percent Democratic, and 14 percent third-party or unaffiliated. The pollster will need to know that 52 percent of the county citizens registered to vote are female and 48 percent are male. Similar statistics about age, race, and other demographic categories will ensure that the polling sample is a microcosm of the entire voting-eligible population.

Once a pollster has set the sample characteristics, he or she conducts telephone interviews with anywhere from 200 to 1,000 people to determine how they feel about candidates, issues, and other subjects. The number of interviews conducted is significant because it affects the poll's margin of error. Simply put, the margin of error is the numerical amount by which the poll results could be off in either direction. For example, a poll that completes 200 interviews usually has a margin of error of plus or minus 7 percent. In other words, if the poll results show that Candidate A has 43 percent support and Candidate B has 36 percent, Candidate A's lead could be as much as 14 percent or there could be no lead at all. Candidate A's advantage is said to be "within the margin of error," and a race within the margin of error is too close to predict a result with any certainty.

Most pollsters contend that 200–300 interviews are the minimum number needed to generate meaningful public opinion data. Each additional interview beyond 200–300 reduces the error rate but also adds to the expense of the poll. In determining the size of the sample, you must know the size of the target universe. If you are hoping to determine statewide public opinion in a large state such as Florida, California, New York, or Texas, you will probably need from 600 to 1,000 interviews to secure a statistically valid result.

This polling method generally produces accurate results indicating what the entire target population is thinking about a candidate or an issue. Rather than having to spend the enormous energy and time necessary to communicate individually with, say, 100,000 people, you can obtain virtually the same data after talking to less than 1 percent of that population. But there is a problem with polling: It can be extremely expensive. Depending on the sample size and complexity of the questionnaire, pollsters charge thousands or tens of thousands of dollars to design the poll, hire call centers where professionals conduct telephone interviews with voters, and compile and analyze the results.

Other Methods of Measuring Public Opinion

If your issue has national, statewide, multicounty, or countywide significance, you are well advised to hire a pollster to conduct your public opinion research. But if your campaign budget and the scale of the population to be sampled are small, professional polling is not the only way to take the public's temperature on a candidate or an issue. Lower cost methods also exist.

Explore pro bono polling. Although it won't be easy to convince a pollster to offer services for free, it doesn't hurt for you to ask. If a pollster believes in your cause, he or she may be willing to provide you with some resources at no or little cost.

Use a focus group. Professional pollsters and corporate market researchers often convene focus groups to test candidate or product profiles, concepts, and arguments on potential voters or consumers. A focus group usually consists of a small gathering of individuals who represent the audience targeted by a campaign. Focus group leaders engage the participants in conversation, show them advertisements, and use other interactive techniques to assess how a particular candidate, issue, or product should be presented to the public at large.

If it's beyond your means to hire a firm to conduct a focus group, you can organize your own. (See "Tips from the Pros: The Dos and Don'ts of Focus Groups.")

Tips from the Pros: The Dos and Don'ts of Focus Groups
GEOFF GARIN

Focus groups are a good way to elicit opinions about your candidate or issue and help you shape your campaign message. If you want to organize an effective focus group, here are ten steps to follow.

1. Invite ten to twelve people you don't know who are representative of the people you will have to win over in your campaign or other initiative. As much as possible, make sure the group represents a cross-section of the targeted community—not just the people who are likely to agree with you.

2. Give participants some incentive to show up at the focus group. Common inducements are checks or gift certificates—but sometimes a free meal will do the trick. Use your best judgment depending on whom you hope to recruit to the focus group.

3. Hold the focus group in a relaxed environment. Your goal is to engage the participants in conversation and encourage them to voice opinions and answer questions candidly. People are much less likely to cooperate if the room feels like Antarctica in winter or the Sahara in summer or if the chairs are so uncomfortable that they want to stand up every few minutes.

4. If it is economically feasible, hold the focus group in a room with a one-way window. This will allow you and other advocates—such as the campaign manager or communications director in a political race or various coalition leaders in an issue campaign—to listen to the participants without distracting them or intruding on their thoughts. You must tell participants they are being observed, but assure them that their names and responses will be kept confidential—and keep that promise.

5. Carefully select your focus group moderator. The best facilitators are even-tempered but have warm, engaging personalities well suited to drawing out reluctant or shy participants. They

must also be able to politely control any participant who tries to dominate the group. Moderators must avoid steering responses to a particular outcome. Your goal is to learn from the participants, and leading questions will interfere with your achieving that goal.

6. Don't dive straight into your topic. The focus group guide should move from the general to the specific. Include some warm-up questions, and try to understand the broader context before you get into the details.

7. Use handouts and other visual aids to stimulate the discussion and give participants ideas to which they can react. For example, a newspaper article that discusses your issue may be a useful way to present the kind of information that might be heard during a campaign. You might ask people to react to a page with arguments in favor of your position so that you can identify the most persuasive ones. Don't forget to have participants react to arguments from the other side as well.

8. Include the moderator in your preparation of questions for the focus group. If the moderator fully understands the questions in advance, he or she is more likely to ask them in an informal way that elicits honest answers from the participants and will know when to ask probing follow-up questions.

9. Engage the participants in conversation for no more than ninety minutes about the subjects on which you are trying to measure public opinion.

10. Record the session so that you can go back and review what people said and the words they used to express their ideas— but make sure to let participants know you are recording the session for this purpose.

Geoff Garin has been president of Peter D. Hart Research Associates since 1984. For more than three decades, he has brought his skill, insight, and innovative approaches as a researcher and strategist to a wide variety of fields—including social and economic policy, consumer marketing, and politics. His clients have included the Bill and Melinda Gates Foundation, the Pew Charitable Trusts, the U.S. Fund for UNICEF, MTV, and many leading Democratic members of the U.S. Senate.

Conduct a town hall meeting. If all else fails, this method, which many elected officials use to gather constituent feedback, can also help you test public opinion. Although town hall meetings provide a less controlled environment than do focus groups, they can generate even more reactions. The process is straight-forward. Set a public meeting in a central and easily accessible location and invite any people who are interested in your issue to attend. It should be a neutral site. For example, the school board conference room would probably not be the best location to discuss a controversial matter related to local education.

As is the case with focus groups, you will boost attendance if you can give members of the public an added incentive—free food or a small gift certificate—to attend. Present your initiative, and invite legitimate questions and feedback from the audience. Many elected officeholders and political candidates who have held town hall meetings have made the mistake of screening questions in advance or planting friendly questions with sup-porters in the audience. Those tactics cheapen the meeting and insult citizens who took time out of their busy schedules to attend. A better methodology is the one that Sen. John McCain of Ari-zona used in his 2000 and 2008 presidential campaigns, which he described in his memoir: "We didn't pick or screen the audience. We didn't plant questions. We took them as they came. Nor would I use every question to nod my head in agreement and compli-ment the questioner's intelligence. When I disagreed with some-one I said so." [3]

Since town hall meetings allow for give-and-take exchanges, see if you can engage audience members in a way that elicits all of their reactions to your issue.

---

[3] John McCain with Mark Salter, *Worth the Fighting For: A Memoir* (New York: Random House, 2002), 370–371.

Use the Internet for targeted public opinion analysis. As a way of testing the waters of general public opinion about a candidate, initiative, or issue, however, use of the Internet has significant limitations. The "digital divide" means that Internet users tend to be more affluent, younger, and more politically aware than the population at large; these demographics compromise the Internet's ability to produce a representative public opinion sample. However, the Internet is an extremely powerful opinion-gathering tool among certain audiences—especially college students. The use of social networking Web sites such as Facebook (www.facebook.com), Twitter (http://twitter.com), and My Space (www.myspace.com), which allow users to share photographs, profiles, and other information online, has become phenomenally popular both on college and university campuses and in the community at large. A University of Texas poll, in March 2008, concluded that more than 80 percent of Texas undergraduates had Facebook accounts.[4]

One month after the Texas poll the *South Florida Sun–Sentinel* reported that a University of Florida senior who was concerned about proposed changes to the state's main undergraduate scholarship program created a Facebook group named Protect Your Bright Futures. The student, twenty-one-year-old Will Anderson of Plant City, Florida, invited 200 of his peers to join the group and encouraged them to forward the invitation to other collegiate friends. Less than two weeks later, Protect Your Bright Futures had 20,000 members statewide, prompting the state legislator

---

[4] In February 2009 Facebook stated that it had more than 150 million members and that users collectively spent more than 3 billion minutes on Facebook each day. Facebook's founder, Mark Zuckerberg, has noted that if Facebook were a country, it would be the eighth most populated nation in the world—bigger than Japan or Russia. (www.facebook.com/press/info.php?statistics#/press/info.php?statistics). The University of Texas report is from a story by Wunmi Bakare, "Facebook Is Top Daily Web Stop for Students," *On Campus*, April 3, 2008, www.utexas.edu/oncampus/2008/04/03/web-feature.

who suggested the scholarship changes to withdraw his proposal. Sen. Jeremy Ring explained his change of heart: "You can't ignore 20,000 people." [5]

If you are a student who wants to test campus opinion on an issue, determine which social networking sites are popular at your college or university and take advantage of their information-gathering resources, as Anderson did at the University of Florida. If you are not a student, search legitimate social networking sites for organized groups or pages that may reveal potentially interested citizens. Within a very short period of time, you should know whether your idea enjoys a groundswell of support or needs more work.

Try the old-fashioned way. Before there were scientific techniques to measure public thinking, politicians and citizens simply walked around and asked questions. Their experience told them which people in their school, local community, state, or even nation were reliable barometers of more general opinion. Speaker O'Neill didn't take a poll to determine which members of Congress President Carter should lobby on the energy bill. He took the time to walk around the House chamber and get to know his colleagues and their concerns.

As you begin your citizen campaign, try the old-fashioned approach. If the problem you defined is a campus issue, visit the student union, student center, or dormitory dining hall during lunch and ask a few of your peers what they think. Post your idea on campus blogs and message boards and seek feedback. Write an op-ed piece for the college newspaper—make sure to include your phone number or e-mail address in the byline—and see if readers respond. Seek permission to address key student organizations during their regular meetings and ask members to react. Your efforts will not only help you determine where students stand on your issue

---

[5] Josh Hafenbrack, "Online Political Action Can Spark Offline Change," *South Florida Sun–Sentinel*, April 6, 2008.

but will also lay the foundation for a coalition in support of the initiative. (Look for more on developing that skill in chapter 7.)

CONCLUSION: PUTTING PUBLIC OPINION DATA TO GOOD USE

As you now understand all too well, the process of gathering information on where the public stands on your candidate, issue, or cause is laborious and time-consuming. But the roadmap that results from your efforts will make your hard work worthwhile. Now that you have a better idea as to which arguments will persuade undecided citizens to support your initiative, you can craft your plan to convince decision makers to take on your cause (see chapter 5) and engage the media's attention (chapter 8). Your success in attracting media coverage will disseminate those strong arguments to decision makers as well as to a wide range of potential supporters. Decision makers will be impressed with both statistical and anecdotal data showing support for your position.

The data you have collected on specific groups gives you a unique opportunity to engage them, through their representative organizations, as coalition partners. Conversely, you now have a better idea of how to convince groups that are undecided to join you or to persuade those who oppose you to change their minds. Asking questions has given new momentum to your cause, but public opinion is an ever-shifting phenomenon that requires regular testing. As Albert Einstein observed, "The important thing is not to stop questioning."

CHECKLIST FOR ACTION

☐ Set public opinion research goals.
  • Determine your level of support.
  • Identify your strongest arguments.

- Micro-target specific groups.
- Use resources wisely.

☐ Select strategies to gauge public opinion.
- Polling
- Focus groups
- Town hall meetings
- Internet and social networking sites
- Traditional methods

Exercises

WHAT DO YOU WANT TO KNOW?

As in every other aspect of citizen advocacy, don't start the public opinion analysis of your defined problem without a plan. Remember that you have two goals: first, to collect data that will help you determine which of your arguments are most likely to influence persuadable voters and decision makers, and, second, to learn which claims by the opposition are likely to resonate among listeners so that you can effectively challenge those statements.

What are the four best arguments in favor of your initiative? Which four arguments are most likely to be offered in opposition to your position?

If you were going to conduct a poll or use another survey research tool, which characteristics about the people being interviewed are important to your particular micro-targeting efforts? Keep in mind that micro-targeting strategies vary depending on the size and scope of your campaign and the nature of your decision maker.

GO INTO THE FIELD

Now that you have identified the public opinion data you need, it is time to go into the field and collect it. Use one or more of the methods identified in this chapter to test public support for your initiative. Keep the following questions in mind as you perfect your data-collection technique and answer them after you have gathered responses:

The Big Picture. What do the findings say about public awareness of the issue you are championing? Will you have to educate citizens about the issue *and* your position? What is your current level of support? For those who support the initiative, what arguments appeal to them most? If there is opposition, what are the apparent sources of opposition and reasons for it?

Micro-targeting. Do your data suggest support or opposition from any specific and easily identifiable groups (for example, students, faculty, or alumni; men or women; Democrats, Republicans, or Independents; whites, African Americans, or Hispanics)? For the specific groups that support the initiative, what arguments appeal to them most? If there are particular groups in opposition, what are the apparent sources of their opposition and reasons for it?

APPENDIX

Steamboat Springs Schools Survey

HILL RESEARCH CONSULTANTS
25025 I-45 North, Suite 380
The Woodlands, Texas 77380
281-363-3840

VER A: Final draft; #CODB0871; n=300LV; Field 8/25-27/97

Hello, this is _____ calling for Hill Research Consultants, a public opinion polling firm. We are calling people like yourself throughout Steamboat Springs seeking the opinions of registered voters about important issues facing your community and its public schools today.

May I speak with_____.

1. __ Is anyone in your household an elected state or local government officeholder, or an employee of a news organization?

YES .... THANK & TERMINATE
NO .... CONTINUE

2. __ <u>VERSION A:</u> The Steamboat Springs School District Board of Education may recommend a bond issue of $24.2 million. With principal and interest over the next 20 years, the bond program will cost taxpayers $48.4 million dollars. Annual taxes on the typical $200,000 home would be increased about $146. Over the next 3 years, the bonds would pay for renovation and expansion of the existing High School, the Strawberry Park Campus and the Soda Creek Elementary Campus If the election were held today, and you had to decide, would you vote for or against this $24.2 million school bond proposal?

VOTE FOR THE BOND PROPOSAL 1
VOTE AGAINST THE BOND PROPOSAL 2
UNSURE 8
REFUSED 9

> **IF DECIDED (FOR OR AGAINST) ABOVE, ASK THIS Q; OTHERWISE, SKIP THIS Q**

2.1. And would you describe your feelings about this issue as strong nor not-so-strong?

STRONG 1
NOT-SO-STRONG 2
UNSURE 8
REFUSED 9

> **ASK EVERYONE**

Now, I'll read you the names of several individuals, organizations, and publications that are sometimes active in Steamboat Springs political or civic affairs. Please tell me how influential each might be in helping you make up

your mind about a school bond proposal. Will they be very influential, somewhat influential, only a little, or not at all influential on you?
ROTATE ORDER

	VERY	SOME WHAT	ONLY LITTLE	NOT AT ALL	UNS	RF
3. __ Local school teachers (<u>PROMPT:</u> Will they be very influential, somewhat influential, only a little, or not at all influential on your views?)	1	2	3	4	8	9
4. __ Members of the Steamboat Springs School District Board of Education	1	2	3	4	8	9
5. __ The Steamboat Springs Chamber Resort Association	1	2	3	4	8	9
6. __ The P.I.C. or Principal's Information Committee	1	2	3	4	8	9
7. __ S.A.C., The Schools Accountability Committee	1	2	3	4	8	9
8. __ The Steamboat Pilot	1	2	3	4	8	9
9. __ Students currently enrolled in Steamboat Springs schools	1	2	3	4	8	9
10. _ School Superintendent Cyndy Simms	1	2	3	4	8	9
11. _ Your own friends and neighbors	1	2	3	4	8	9

END ROTATION

	VERY	SOME WHAT	ONLY LITTLE	NOT AT ALL	UNS	RF
12. _ Members of the 10 Plus 2 Committee	1	2	3	4	8	9

13. _ As you may recall, the 10 Plus 2 Committee is a group of concerned local citizens, some who favored the last school bond proposal and some who opposed it, who have organized and lead a community-wide exploration of attitudes and opinions toward facility needs as well as other issues facing Steamboat Schools. Would you say that you are very familiar, somewhat familiar, or not very familiar with actions of the 10 Plus 2 Committee?

VERY FAMILIAR 1
SOMEWHAT FAMILIAR 2
NOT VERY FAMILIAR/NOT AT ALL FAMILIAR 3
UNSURE 8
REFUSED 9

IF NOT VERY FAMILIAR/UNSURE/REFUSED, SKIP NEXT TWO QUESTIONS

13.1. And would you say that you participated directly in any of the activities or meetings organized by the 10 Plus 2 Committee, or did you not?

PARTICIPATED DIRECTLY 1
[DO NOT READ] UNSURE..2
DID NOT PARTICIPATE DIRECTLY 3
REFUSED 9

13.2. From all that you may have read, heard, seen, or experienced directly, would you say that 10 Plus 2 Committee has generally been open, fair, and complete in its hearing of issues and positions on school facilities and policies, or would you not say that?

WOULD SAY OPEN, FAIR 1
[DO NOT READ] UNSURE..2
WOULD NOT SAY THAT...3
REFUSED 9

13.3. Besides studying school facility needs, the 10 Plus 2 Committee and its task forces have studied other matters including curricula, school accountability, communications, and other important topics. Would you say that you generally approve or disapprove of the way in which the committees has handled these matters?

APPROVE 1
UNSURE 2
DISAPPROVE 3
REFUSED 9

14._ Before now, how much have you read or heard about the possible $24.2 bond proposal to finance Steamboat Schools facilities renovation and expansion? Have you read or heard a lot, some, just a little, or absolutely nothing about this matter?

A LOT 1
SOME..2
JUST A LITTLE 3
ABSOLUTELY NOTHING 4
UNSURE 8
REFUSED 9

15._ In 1995, Steamboat Springs voters resoundingly rejected a $41.8 million school bond proposal by a vote of 61% to 39%. Do you happen to recall whether you voted for or against that bond proposal in 1995?

DON'T RECALL/DIDN'T VOTE/WASN'T HERE 0
VOTED FOR BOND PROPOSAL [SKIP NEXT Q]....................................1
VOTED AGAINST BOND PROPOSAL 2
UNSURE 8
REFUSED 9

IF 'VOTED FOR' THEN SKIP THIS Q

15.1. Given that the 10 Plus 2 committee and the school board may agree to a new bond proposal of only $24.2 million, much less than the bond proposal that was rejected two years ago, and for different projects, are you much more likely to vote for the new proposal, somewhat more likely to vote for it, or are you no more likely to vote for this proposal?

MUCH MORE LIKELY	1
SOMEWHAT MORE LIKELY	2
NO MORE LIKELY	3
UNSURE	8
REFUSED	9

16._ Overall, how satisfied are you with the level of communication you receive from or about the Steamboat Springs school district? Are you very satisfied, somewhat satisfied, or not very satisfied?

VERY SATISFIED	1
SOMEWHAT SATISFIED	2
NOT VERY SATISFIED	3
UNSURE	8
REFUSED	9

17._ Do you feel that your combined local and school taxes today are much too high, a little too high, about right, a little too low, or much too low?

MUCH TOO HIGH	1
LITTLE TOO HIGH	2
ABOUT RIGHT	3
LITTLE TOO LOW	4
MUCH TOO LOW	5
UNSURE	8
REFUSED	9

18._ How concerned are you about the impact of the proposed school bond issue on your own home or residential property taxes? Are you extremely concerned, very concerned, somewhat concerned, not very concerned, or not at all concerned?

EXTREMELY	1
VERY	2
SOMEWHAT	3
NOT VERY	4
NOT AT ALL	5
UNSURE	8
REFUSED	9

19._ And how concerned are you about the impact of the proposed school bond issue on business or commercial property taxes? Are you extremely concerned, very concerned, somewhat concerned, not very concerned, or not at all concerned?

EXTREMELY	1
VERY	2
SOMEWHAT	3
NOT VERY	4
NOT AT ALL	5
UNSURE	8
REFUSED	9

Thinking about local Steamboat Springs public schools...

20._ Students are often given the grades A,B,C,D, and FAIL to rate the quality of their work at school. Suppose the public schools themselves were graded in the same way. What grade would you give the public schools as a whole in the Steamboat Springs School District?

A	1
B	2
C	3
D	4
FAIL	5
UNSURE	8
REFUSED	9

21._ Regarding the facilities of your local public schools, which one of the following do you believe is the most pressing need today?
<u>READ LIST AND ROTATE OPTIONS</u>

USING SPLIT-SESSIONS OR YEAR-ROUND SCHOOL TO RELIEVE OVERCROWDING	1
RENOVATING OR UPDATING OLDER SCHOOL FACILITIES	2
EXPANDING EXISTING SCHOOLS TO RELIEVE OVERCROWDING	3
BUILDING NEW SCHOOLS TO RELIEVE OVERCROWDING	3

[DO NOT READ]
NONE PRESSING 6
ALL PRESSING 7
UNSURE 8
REFUSED 9

Now I am going to read you some opinions that other Steamboat residents have expressed about your local schools. Obviously, some of these are opinions and may not be true in your view. Please tell me if you agree strongly, agree somewhat, disagree somewhat or disagree strongly with each statement.
<u>ROTATE ORDER</u>

	STRG AGREE	SOME AGREE	SOME DIS	STRG DIS	UNS DIS	REF
22._ The use of more split sessions and a year-round calendar could comfortably delay the need for expanding local school facilities.	1	2	3	4	8	9
23._ My local school district spends its money wisely.	1	2	3	4	8	9
24._ School officials need to reconsider the configuration of grades assigned to each school. Some grades should be sent to different schools.	1	2	3	4	8	9
25._ Most public schools in Steamboat Springs are overcrowded.	1	2	3	4	8	9
26._ Most public schools in Steamboat Springs are in good repair with few pressing maintenance needs.	1	2	3	4	8	9

5 Winning Friends and Influencing People

How to Persuade the Decision Maker

"Example is not the main thing in influencing others.
It is the only thing."

—Albert Schweitzer

Case in Point: Getting MADD at Drunk Drivers

Cari Lightner should have spent her fourteenth birthday celebrating with family and friends and looking forward to future successes—starting high school, attending the prom, walking across the stage at commencement, going to college, pursuing a career, getting married, and raising a family. But in May 1980, four months short of that birthday, a repeat drunk driver with a blood alcohol level twice the legal limit killed Cari as she walked on the sidewalk in her suburban Sacramento neighborhood on the way to a church carnival. She left behind her parents and two sisters, one of them her twin.

It would have been easy for Cari to become just another statistic. After all, more than 27,000 Americans died in 1980 because of alcohol-related traffic crashes. But Cari's mother, Candy Lightner, wanted her daughter's death to be more than another senseless tragedy. So on the day that Cari should have been celebrating her birthday, Candy channeled her grief into what would soon become a national movement to change attitudes and laws on drunk driving.

On September 5, 1980, Lightner, along with a group of women sitting around a table, founded Mothers Against Drunk Driving (MADD). The gender designation was purposeful. Their initiative was a statement of feminine and maternal anger against a primarily male perpetrated offense, one that primarily male police officers, prosecutors, and judges often trivialized. Popular culture mimicked these attitudes, with movies frequently depicting drunk drivers as comical figures rather than public safety threats. MADD aimed to persuade policymakers that driving while intoxicated was no laughing matter but rather an action fraught with potentially devastating consequences for families.

MADD started as a neighborhood organization on the same street where Cari died. Within five years, hundreds of local MADD chapters had been located nationwide. Knowing that policy change would alter society's view of drunk driving, these advocates persuaded decision makers in Washington, D.C., all fifty state capitals, and countless municipalities to raise the drinking age from eighteen to twenty-one, establish stringent breath and blood alcohol standards, require mandatory sentences for violations of those standards, and improve police procedures for targeting motorists suspected of driving under the influence of alcohol. How did MADD act so fast and so effectively? The answer is that MADD's organizers understood the skills and techniques needed to influence officials at every level of government.

These insights took several forms. First, MADD understood the "follow the leader" effect. In other words, MADD leaders realized that certain elected officials are powerful not only in their authority to make decisions but also in their ability to galvanize the public and generate action. If MADD could persuade that special breed of political leader, then with that support the organization could start an avalanche of publicity that would attract more allies in other communities across the state and nation.

Fortunately for MADD, one the nation's most visible and influential public officials also lived in Sacramento: California Governor Jerry Brown. Within weeks of founding MADD, Lightner convinced Brown to establish a state task force on drunk driving. Brown appointed MADD leaders to the task force. Less than two years later, California became the first state to increase its legal drinking age from eighteen to twenty-one—a policy change that has saved hundreds of thousands of lives across the nation.

After persuading Brown to support the cause, MADD set its sights on Brown's gubernatorial predecessor: Ronald Reagan, who was then serving as president of the United States and had more influence on public opinion and power to set the domestic agenda than any governmental official at any level. Reagan was not a natural ally. He won the presidency on a platform deeply suspicious of the federal government's role in anything other than national defense, and he professed a strong belief in states' rights on policy matters. In his first inaugural address, on January 20, 1981, Reagan famously observed that "government is not the solution to our problems; government is the problem." When MADD began clamoring for the federal government to persuade all states to increase the drinking age, Reagan seemed the least likely president to impose a top-down solution from Washington.

But MADD's second skill was its ability to read and understand individual decision makers. As much as Reagan resisted large-scale government action, he was by his own admission very sympathetic to hard-luck stories. In his chronicle of the Reagan presidency, *President Reagan: The Role of a Lifetime,* Lou Cannon writes that Reagan's aides "tried to limit the number of letters he received from people undergoing hardships, to which the president would often respond with advice and a small personal check." [1] By this time, MADD had collected many heartbreaking

---

[1] Lou Cannon, *President Reagan: The Role of a Lifetime* (New York: Simon and Schuster, 1991), 118.

stories of families who had lost loved ones to accidents caused by drunk drivers but were determined to find triumph in tragedy— exactly the kind of emotional evidence that could override Reagan's antigovernment instincts.

For Reagan, the issue had come down to a simple question he posed to Elizabeth Dole, then transportation secretary, in an Oval Office meeting: "Doesn't this help save kids' lives?" Dole replied in the affirmative. In 1984, at Reagan's urging, Congress voted to condition the granting of federal highway funds to state governments on an increase in the drinking age from eighteen to twenty-one. Any state that did not comply would lose tens or even hundreds of millions of dollars in federal bridge and road funds. All fifty states eventually met the age twenty-one standard.

Third, MADD was effective because it employed an organized and streamlined system of member advocacy. The organization provided helpful instructional manuals and trained its members in classroom-like settings, giving MADD the ability to screen for unpredictable individuals who might hurt the cause. When MADD spokeswomen appeared before executive or legislative bodies, they were armed with research supporting their positions.

Fourth, MADD avoided a one-size-fits-all approach to advocacy. Although Lightner's grief inspired her to found MADD, the organization's advocates did not rely solely on emotional arguments. Instead, MADD struck a balance between facts and emotions—explaining the large number of traffic fatalities, but speaking of them as daughters, sons, husbands, wives, and friends who had been killed by a preventable crime. MADD also put a price tag on the problem. In addition to emphasizing how drunk driving took innocent lives, MADD also cited the economic consequences—lost wages, declining productivity, and increased health care costs.

Fifth, MADD chose its battles carefully. It concentrated on four goals: raising public awareness about drunk driving; supporting victims of drunk driving; increasing the legal drinking age from eighteen to twenty-one; and establishing .08 (80 milligrams of alcohol in 100 milliliters of blood) as the blood alcohol threshold across the nation. MADD resisted entreaties to be involved in other anti-alcohol crusades that might have undermined its core mission. If MADD was not certain that a proposed policy idea had clear factual support, it did not risk its credibility.

Sixth, MADD used its feminine origins to shape public opinion. The compelling facts and figures against drunk driving may have been enough to sway the public, but the marriage of that data to the emotions of motherhood gave MADD almost unparalleled credibility. Even if numbers don't lie, it was much easier for policymakers to ignore statistics than grieving mothers who had lost children or other loved ones to drunk driving. This powerful combination also helped to draw coalition partners, such as General Motors, Chrysler, Allstate, Nationwide, State Farm, Coca-Cola, and Avis.

Seventh, MADD understood how powerful the media could be in influencing policymakers. On October 1, 1980, Lightner and Cindy Lamb, a Maryland woman whose five-year-old daughter became the nation's youngest paraplegic because of a drunk driver, held a dramatic press conference on Capitol Hill to announce MADD's formation. Their story appeared on television screens and in newspapers across the country. In 1983 the NBC television network produced and aired a made-for-TV movie, *MADD: Mothers Against Drunk Drivers,* starring well-known character actor Mariette Hartley as Lightner. Other celebrities, including Connie Sellecca, Stevie Wonder and Aretha Franklin, made public-service spots and personal appearances on MADD's behalf.

Five years later, MADD was once again in the national spotlight and drew more public attention to the cause. This after the nation's deadliest drunk-driving incident, in which a repeat drunk driver with a high blood alcohol level killed twenty-seven people and injured thirty-four more in a bus crash on May 18, 1988, in Carrolton, Kentucky. In recent years, performers such as country music star Brad Paisley and television host Kelly Ripa have helped to sustain public awareness by serving as MADD celebrity spokespersons.

Finally, MADD never stopped trying to persuade decision makers. Even after it had won monumental national victories on raising the legal drinking age in the 1980s and setting the .08 blood alcohol standard in the 1990s, MADD targeted law-enforcement officials charged with enforcing the new standards. The organization worked with police and prosecutors to prepare officers to testify against drunk drivers in court. It held special-recognition ceremonies for those who distinguished themselves in enforcing DUI charges.

The combined effects of MADD's persuasive skills have been nothing short of amazing. Over nearly three decades the organization can claim the following accomplishments from its grassroots efforts:

- Starting with one member in September 1980, MADD had 650,000 members in forty-seven states by 1985, and it had inspired the founding of a Canadian organization with similar goals: People to Reduce Impaired Driving Everywhere (PRIDE).
- In 1984 Congress induced states to increase their drinking age from eighteen to twenty-one. By 1988 all states had complied.
- The *Chronicle of Philanthropy* declared in 1994 that MADD was the most popular charitable organization in America.
- In 1995 Congress persuaded states to make it illegal for anyone younger than twenty-one to drive with any alcohol in their system.
- By 1998 MADD had chapters in all fifty states.
- MADD coined the phrase "designated driver."
- In 2000, when MADD celebrated its twentieth anniversary, 97 percent of the public recognized its name.

- By 2005, under threat of losing federal highway funding, all fifty states had set .08 as the legally intoxicated blood alcohol content (BAC) for drivers twenty-one and older.
- Annual alcohol-related deaths in the United States have dropped more than 55 percent since MADD's founding—from 30,000 in 1980 to fewer than 13,000 in 2007.

That record of success is not the product of good fortune or happenstance. Before MADD's emergence, drunk driving had long been a serious problem without a serious effort to solve it. But the grassroots movement that was MADD determined how to motivate policymakers and produce solutions. The lesson is that no matter how intractable a problem may appear, you can find ways to make it a priority on a decision maker's agenda.[2]

INFLUENCING AND PERSUADING THE DECISION MAKER

If you have correctly identified and familiarized yourself with the person or persons who have the power to solve your problem, the next step is to persuade the decision maker to support—and, if possible, advocate for—your position. MADD's organizers were masterful in that task, and if you learn from their example and follow the steps outlined below, you will increase your chances of turning a policymaker into an ally.

---

[2] Two sources were particularly critical to the development of the MADD case study. The first was Karolyn Nunnallee, who served as MADD president from 1998–1999 and generously shared her insights. The other was Laurie Davies's piece, "Twenty-Five Years of Saving Lives," *Driven*, Fall 2005, www.madd.org/getattachment/48e81e1b-df43-4-f31-b9a1-d94d5b940e62/MADD-25-Years-of-Saving-Lives.aspx.

1. Define the Relationship with the Decision Maker before You Create It

The type of relationship you need to build with a decision maker will dictate how you first approach him or her. If your interaction with an official is likely to be short-term—that is, you want help on a single problem—your "relationship" will consist of educating the decision maker on the specific challenge and how it might be solved. On the other hand, if your goals have a long-term focus, you will need to build an actual relationship through frequent contacts over time. Consider the following situations and determine which kind of relationship is most applicable to the problem you want to solve:

A specific, singular situation that requires relatively immediate attention. In some cases you may need to apply your political skills to public officials only once. For instance, if your local school board is considering a boundary change to balance shifting student populations, you may want to intervene if you believe the changes being considered would be disadvantageous to your child or would adversely affect your property values. Your goal would be to persuade your specific school board member and his or her colleagues on this single boundary change.

A policy issue that requires continuing interest and activism. Sometimes your goal can't be achieved in one fell swoop. You may need to win many small battles before you can claim ultimate victory. For example, the effort to restore the health of America's Everglades or, on a smaller scale, an attempt to clean up a polluted lake or river, requires policymakers to make multiple decisions incrementally over the years. These types of challenges require you to build long-term relationships of trust and confidence with a few elected legislators and some elected but mostly appointed executive officials who are responsible for your specific area of concern.

During my career, I found Florida's chiropractors to be very effective at building these lasting political–policy relationships.

Chiropractors are highly motivated because government decisions substantially influence the success of their practice, including such matters as whether health insurance carriers are required to recognize chiropractic services for reimbursement. In Florida the chiropractors' association assigned a member to each state legislator to keep the legislator well informed on chiropractic issues. The association designed this effort, which included a meeting at the local office of the state representative or senator, to foster personal friendships between chiropractors and legislators. When a busy representative or senator had to decide which telephone calls to return first, the chiropractor was generally at or near the top of the list.

A continuing concern that never changes with specific issues that often change. Some groups have broad interests that remain constant over time, but those interests are advanced through a constantly shifting series of issues. For example, although a state Chamber of Commerce's general interest is the protection and advancement of the business community, that interest may be asserted in tax policy one year, government regulation the next, and immigration the next. In this or a similar case, you will want to be close to officials who can influence a broad array of matters—such as the House Speaker, Senate president, and governor.

Once you have decided which type of relationship you need to form, determine whether the decision maker is singular—for example, a college president or a strong mayor—or plural—a board of trustees or a city council. If you are trying to persuade a collegial group, such as a school board, determine which of the members has the greatest commitment to your position and is most able to persuade his or her colleagues. Ask that individual to be your advocate in chief.

2. Follow the Chain of Command

Your initial contact should be with the individual closest to the problem for which you are seeking a solution. If a neighborhood park is poorly maintained, start with the superintendent of that park. The condition of the park is the superintendent's responsibility, and you must give her a chance to discharge the obligation. If you don't get results, you can then go to the director of the city or county parks system. When you start with the person closest to the problem, you maximize the chance of an expedited resolution. And if you give people a chance to do their jobs, and they are unable or unwilling to help because they have different priorities, they are less likely to become an obstacle if you have to go over their heads—and their boss orders a solution.

3. Respect Professional Staff

Remember that behind most decision makers is a staff person or persons who also need to be persuaded. Given the sheer number and complexity of policy issues that both executive and legislative officials must address as part of their duties, staff members play a vital role in helping to prioritize issues and counsel decision makers on their relative merits or demerits. At the same time you approach a college administrator, mayor, county commissioner, state legislator, or another decision maker, make sure you take the time to engage and educate staff members. Give them your respect and gratitude. They can help you gain access to the decision maker and likely will provide input into the deliberations on your issue. Ignore them at your peril. Elected officials come and go. Staff members remain and remember.

4. Know the Decision Maker before You Begin to Lobby

You wouldn't build a home without examining the record of the prospective contractor. You wouldn't send a child to a day care center without thoroughly investigating that facility's administration and teachers. For similar reasons, you shouldn't approach decision makers without knowing who they are, what they believe, and why they believe it.

First of all, know the decision maker's name and be able to pick him or her out of a lineup. Many citizen advocates do not take the time to put a name and face together. When I joined the U.S. Senate in 1987, one of my classmates was John Breaux from Louisiana. He had come to the Senate after fourteen years in the House of Representatives, which he joined at the age of twenty-eight. On January 24, 2007, in the op-ed "When They No Longer Call You Senator," Breaux told readers of *The Hill* this story from his early days in the House:

> A senior chairman of a major maritime company came down with several lawyers in tow to lobby me on an issue of great concern to him. After several minutes of looking directly at me and explaining his problem, he asked, to the gasps of his lobbyist lawyers, "When do you think the congressman can come in?" It was certain he was paying his legal team a lot of money to explain how he should present his case to members of Congress, and they hadn't even bothered to tell him who the congressman was!

Second, know what interests or values motivate the decision maker. If you are lobbying an elected officeholder, you can be sure that a key interest is the desire to advance policy initiatives that benefit constituents and ensure voters' goodwill in the next election. Your job is to show the decision maker that adopting your position is both good policy and good politics. Be able to provide specific instances of the benefits to be gained if your proposal is adopted. Provide letters of support from constituents and statistics on its positive impact.

But don't stop at that superficial level. All citizen advocates worth their salt know to portray their issue as a challenge that, if solved, will confer great economic, social, or other benefits on the elected official's constituency and thus electoral benefits on the official. You can distinguish yourself by digging deeper into the decision maker's biography and public record and finding other ways to show the merits of your position.

Use the Internet, past newspaper stories, previous television reports, and any of the other research tools we discussed in chapter 2 to discover the following information about your decision maker:

- Places of birth and upbringing
- Undergraduate and graduate alma maters
- Marital status and number of children and grandchildren
- Professional history before entering politics
- Other appointed or elected offices held
- Priority issues in current or former offices
- Past public service awards or honors received
- Previous bills introduced (particularly in your area of interest)
- Prior positions on similar issues

Although this list is not exhaustive, you'll be surprised how far this kind of information can go in helping you to persuade an elected decision maker. For example, if you have studied her past positions as a candidate and elected official, you may be able to show that support for your initiative is consistent with her previous stances. That kind of consistency will make it easier for her to support your position. Even more important, you need to know if you are asking the decision maker to deviate from past positions so that you can be ready with a suggested rationale for change.

Third, realize that most decision makers are not elected. Most have been appointed to their jobs by elected officials or higher level appointees. At Wolfson High School in the early 1970s, the decision maker on food quality could have been the school cafeteria manager, the principal who appointed the cafeteria manager, or the county superintendent of schools or school board who appointed the principal. But the analysis you need to do is the same as it is with elected officials: If you know how the person came to his position of responsibility, and what personal values and professional interests influence his behavior, you will have a much easier time persuading him to take up your cause.

If your decision maker is the local public health officer, and he was given the job because of his professional competence, you will likely influence him through well-researched and effectively presented data. If he won his job through political connections, you will need to understand those relationships and determine how to use them to your advantage. If he has a chip on his shoulder, don't hesitate to make use of it. For example, pretend that your community's highly respected school superintendent has retired after many years of service. The school board selects a new leader who is intimidated by the reputation of his predecessor and reluctant to take new initiatives. If you want to persuade the new superintendent to support your cause, convince him that the previous one would have handled it as you suggest.

5. Understand Internal Politics and Dynamics

In a collegial setting—such as your student council, town commission, school board, or state legislature—it is not enough to know the decision maker's resume and relevant personal characteristics. You need to know the interplay among the members. Do certain officials band together on every issue and form a bloc? If so, you may be able to secure multiple votes for your position if you can win over just one or two policymakers in the bloc. Conversely, you will go down to defeat if one or two members of the bloc are persuaded to vote against you and bring their allies along for the ride. Unrelated internal animosities within many groups can inflict serious collateral damage on your goals. For example, has the member you selected to sponsor your bill recently voted against or offended the key committee chair? In that event, you may need to find a new advocate. The more awareness you have of these intangible factors, the better your chances of maneuvering around them in support of your initiative.

6. Do Your Homework—Always Be Credible

It is essential to know your decision maker, but all the knowledge in the world won't make much difference if you can't provide him with critical information on the issue for which you seek his help. There is no substitute for adequate preparation. At the very least, you should know the topic better than the decision maker. Ideally, you will know it better than anyone else.

But don't let your superior knowledge get the best of you. Never overstate or misstate. When confronted with other people's assertions, my father applied the "China standard." Dad was a mining engineer by training, but he spent most of his adult life in the dairy business. If a person was speaking on a subject Dad knew little about—such as China—he gave the speaker the presumption of accuracy. But if the speaker wandered into a discussion of mining or cows and misrepresented what Dad knew to be the facts, the speaker was summarily dismissed on the subjects of mines, cows, *and* China. The late Daniel Patrick Moynihan of New York, another Senate colleague of mine, attributed this line to former Federal Reserve chair Alan Greenspan: "Everyone is entitled to their own opinions, but no one is entitled to their own facts." Remember that bit of wisdom as you argue your case.

When I was serving in the Senate, I had a China reaction when I read an issue paper about the Medicare program. In one section, the paper misrepresented an arcane policy on Medicare physician reimbursement for drugs administered to cancer patients outside a hospital. That blunder caused me to question the accuracy of the balance of the paper, which covered subjects less familiar to me. Even worse for the citizens who wanted my support on a proposed Medicare change, I questioned the credibility of their organization and its advocates.

Since the decision maker will likely press you to explain why you are right and your policy opponents are wrong, you should know your adversaries and their arguments. The research you conducted in chapter 2 should help you prepare convincing answers to a decision maker's questions. Show respect when you discuss the opposition, but know how to counter your opponents' assertions on the issue you are advocating.

7. Maximize Your Face-to-Face Opportunities with the Decision Maker

It has finally arrived: the big day when you will meet the decision maker in person and try to convince her to solve your problem. Since the course of that meeting may well determine whether you succeed in your initiative, it is important that you choose the right venue and prepare a concise, effective presentation that will leave the decision maker inclined to support you. In addition to the detailed expert advice provided in "Tips from the Pros: Getting in the Door," remember five key principles in your quest for a successful meeting.

First, as to location, many citizen activists wrongly assume that the best place to meet is in the decision maker's office in the court house, city hall, state house, or U.S. Capitol. Often the office is not the best place. In an official setting the decision maker is on a tight schedule with frequent appointments and interruptions, especially if it is the bell announcing a floor vote is underway. A priority for most legislators is to maintain as close to a 100 percent voting record as possible. Your meeting may be affected by stressful time constraints. The decision maker has probably already had several meetings that day with several more to follow after you. Actions generated from those earlier meetings or mental preparations for the later ones will distract her attention from your presentation. Staff will be in and out of the meeting to manage the day's busy schedule. If the decision maker is a legislator, I recommend that you have the meeting in her home district, either at an office or at a more informal off-campus site. If the person you are trying to persuade is an appointed official, ask people who know the official and the area to recommend a location that would facilitate a successful meeting.

Tips from the Pros: Getting in the Door
MARK BLOCK

Persuading the decision maker often requires direct communication. How do you get in the door to make your case? Here are four keys to the door.

1. Do your research.

- Know the names and correct spellings and pronunciations of the official and the staff members with whom you will be meeting.

- Recognize the potential impact that this decision maker might have on your issue. For example, does he or she chair a committee that will consider your proposal? Does the official represent constituents or interests that will be affected by your proposal? Don't waste the decision maker's time asking for an action beyond his or her authority to deliver.

- Identify individuals who are close to the official and ask them to identify any personal or political background, protocol, or other idiosyncrasies that might affect the official's receptivity to your efforts.

2. Initiate your scheduling request with candor and specificity.

- Bring to the meeting only those participants necessary to the discussion, and don't add to your contingent at the last moment. Staff members responsible for managing an official's time don't like surprises, and no decision maker wants to meet with a cast of thousands in his office.

- Request only the least amount of time that you need to present the problem you want to solve, possible solutions, and reasons why the official should support your proposal. Strictly enforce that time limit during the meeting. If you fail to respect the time limitations for the meeting, the decision maker and his staff may take a dim view of your issue and any future meeting requests.

- Stay focused on the agenda. With limited time, the last thing you want to do is distract from the purpose of the meeting. Stick to your points and do not raise extraneous and unexpected items. Additionally, avoid time consuming personal requests such as photographs with the official unless you have previously arranged them with staff members.

- Don't bring gifts. You may have the best of intentions in delivering a tangible gesture of thanks and respect, but your gift will put the official in an awkward position and leave the inappropriate impression that you are attempting to buy his support.

3. Impress at the meeting.

- Manage expectations of your group in advance of the meeting time. It is not uncommon for the meeting to be delayed or even cancelled because of last-minute demands on the official. As a result, the formal meeting that was scheduled in her office may become a brief courtesy meeting followed by a more detailed discussion with staff. In some cases, a meeting may become a "walk and talk" as you and your associates join the official in moving to her next commitment. Do not interpret these changes as snubs—they simply reflect the realities of a busy official's uncertain schedule.

- As close as possible to the meeting, determine if there have been any late-breaking developments affecting your issue. The official will expect you to have the most current information. If you haven't scanned relevant newspapers or conducted a last-minute Internet search on your issue prior to the meeting, you are not ready.

- Minimize the use of handouts and other materials. You can give them to staff, but don't add to the clutter on the official's desk.

- Use concise, well-considered, and written talking points. Before the meeting, determine which members of your group will cover which points and establish strict time limits. If the meeting is cut short or runs beyond the time allocated, the written talking points can be left behind to ensure that the official fully understands your case.

4. Follow up after the meeting.

- Send hand-written thank you notes—one to the official and others to any staff members who attended or assisted with the meeting. Your notes to the staff should include an additional typewritten page that summarizes your arguments, provides your contact information, and supplies the names and points of contact for anyone who accompanied you to the meeting.

- Respond quickly if the official or members of the staff request additional information during or subsequent to the meeting. If you don't answer their questions in a timely fashion, they may receive answers from other citizens or groups who don't share your interests or values.

- Keep staff members regularly updated on your issue with brief, factual communications. When the official takes an action that indicates receptivity to your cause, call, write, or e-mail with recognition and appreciation.

Mark Block lives in New York City and is the director of external relations for *Newsweek*. For nearly fifteen years he worked for Sen. Bob Graham in Florida and Washington, D.C., where his staff positions included scheduler, campaign scheduler, and deputy chief of staff.

Second, when you are presenting your case, focus on a short list of relevant points. Show consideration for the official's time—you are important, but so are others that she is scheduled to meet that day. Know precisely and state clearly what you want the decision maker to do—open an American Studies Department on campus, deny a permit application to construct a cement plant near a pristine spring, or vote for a precise amount of dollars to put a certain number of additional police officers on the streets. Be specific as to your purpose, and be prepared to present a specific amount or at least a range of costs if your initiative will require public expenditure.

Third, stay abreast of new developments. Political issues can change daily. Keep tabs on the latest lay of the land and revise your request, if necessary, to be timely and relevant.

Fourth, and particularly important if any of the decision maker's staff members attend the meeting, establish an ongoing dialogue with the aides. Make sure to get their names and pronunciations of their names correctly. In most cases, these staff members will be your points of contact with the decision maker.

Fifth, don't lose sight of the need for aggressive follow-up. After the meeting, write the decision maker, express appreciation for her attendance, and clearly state any commitments that she made. Keep the decision maker informed of new developments through her staff members.

8. Don't Assume that the Final Decision Maker Is the Right Target

At times, citizens have to persuade third parties to use their influence with policymakers to produce positive results. Consider the case of Northern Ireland. When Ireland gained its independence from Britain in 1921, six Irish counties in Northern Ireland—the province known as Ulster—remained under British control. Unlike the rest of Ireland, which was predominantly Roman Catholic, Ulster had then and continues to have a Protestant majority. For much of the next seventy years, Northern Irish Catholics suffered under a second-class status that grew worse in the 1960s and 1970s. Cities were segregated along sectarian lines, with Protestants and Catholics living in distinct neighborhoods. Catholic citizens often found it hard to find jobs and homes.

Despite increased media attention and pressure from international human rights organizations in the 1970s and 1980s, the British government repeatedly failed to enact meaningful reforms to prohibit discrimination against Ulster Catholics in housing, employment, and education. When the U.S. government proved unwilling or unable to exert pressure on Britain, its closest ally, Irish American activists took their case to state and local governments that bought goods from invested pension funds in American companies operating in Northern Ireland. States and localities used their economic power to persuade companies to adopt the MacBride Principles, a corporate code of conduct created in 1984 meant to prevent anti-Catholic workplace practices. Since then, the British Parliament has adopted new antidiscrimination measures, and more than ninety U.S. and Canadian companies in Northern Ireland now follow fair employment practices and submit to independent monitoring of their compliance.

The effective use of third parties to advance an initiative is not limited to sweeping problems such as anti-Catholic discrimination in Northern Ireland. You can make use of this kind of influence to address almost any challenge. For example, in the expressway dilemma cited in chapter 3, we said that your college or university administration would probably not have direct control over the fate of the new highway. But it might have indirect influence. Colleges are important institutions in states and local communities because they generate economic activity, educate students who will become business employees, and provide research into state and local issues.

If you can convince the college president, student government, or an academic expert to speak against the expressway project, you may slow its progress considerably. Unlike typical legislators, who are considered available to constituents at all times, most college administrators distinguish between their official and private lives and hold set office hours. Visit with your president during her office hours and engage her on the subject. Raise the issue at the next student government meeting, ask your elected representatives to pass a resolution opposing the project, and make sure the campus newspaper knows about it. If your college or university has a public policy department or an engineering school, try to find a professor with expertise on highway projects and enlist his help in building a case against the new road.

Once you have defined the problem that you want to solve, consider all of the people who may be positioned to fix the problem. Usually, your target will be the decision maker himself, but be prepared to focus on intermediaries who might be more effective in making your case than your original target would be.

9. Don't Let the Perfect Be the Enemy of the Good

Some citizen activists define success as achieving 100 percent of their agenda—and they almost always end up disappointed. Don't make that mistake. The ideal result is rarely the actual result. Be prepared with fall-back options if the decision maker can't or won't give you all of what you want. The official may be constrained by time, fiscal limitations, or other political or policy considerations. Your effort to persuade the decision maker is a negotiation of sorts. Keep an open mind and consider alternatives as you work to secure your vital interests.

CHECKLIST FOR ACTION

- ☐ Define the relationship with the decision maker before you create it.
- ☐ Follow the chain of command.
- ☐ Respect professional staff.
- ☐ Know the decision maker before you begin to lobby.
- ☐ Understand internal politics and dynamics.
- ☐ Do your homework—always be credible.
- ☐ Maximize your face-to-face opportunities with the decision maker.
- ☐ Don't assume that the final decision maker is the right target.
- ☐ Don't let the perfect be the enemy of the good.

Exercises

CONNECTING WITH THE DECISION MAKER

Using the information provided in this chapter and data that you obtain through research, analyze the background and public record of one of the officials who might be able to solve your problem. Identify at least five innovative ways in which you might use the information you have gained to enlist the decision maker's help. Think creatively. Did you attend the same undergraduate or graduate institution as the person you have targeted? Does the decision maker's resume provide any special opportunities for common ground?

PLAYING THE DECISION MAKER

Choose three students in your class to play the role of active citizens and one to serve as the decision maker. The citizens should state their issue, explain how they prepared for the meeting with the decision maker, and then meet with that individual to present their request. The decision maker will evaluate the citizens' effectiveness and then render judgment on the issue they raised and the request they made.

6 Timing Is Everything

Using the Calendar to Achieve Your Goals

"For everything there is a season, and a time for every matter under heaven."

—Ecclesiastes 3:1

Case in Point: A Lesson from the U.S. Senate

It was September 19. With only eleven days left in the federal government's fiscal year, we faced a major crunch time in the congressional calendar. The budget and appropriations process that had started a year earlier was rapidly coming to a close, and I had a problem: A Floridian I knew and respected needed funding for a worthy cause, but he was out of time.

The federal government's fiscal year begins on October 1 of each year, but it is labeled by the year in which the budget will conclude. Thus the budget year that begins on October 1, 2009, will be known as fiscal year (FY) 2010. The federal budget is actually the compilation of individual appropriations bills for the thirteen major components of the federal government, such as defense, transportation, environment, and health. My staff and I were closely monitoring scores of items we had advocated throughout the year to make sure they would be included in the final budget negotiation.

These efforts were critical to Floridians and required my year-round attention and vigilance. Some were titanic struggles with national implications, such as the battle for federal funds to restore the environmental health of America's Everglades. With a twenty-five-year window to complete this large and complex project, it was imperative that Congress appropriate funds to keep the restoration on schedule. Others had statewide significance, such as road construction grants to the Florida Department of Transportation. Others still were community-specific projects, including beach restoration, cancer research at a state university, and expansion of a national wildlife refuge. All spending items, regardless of size, are politically important to members of Congress. Appropriations usually create economic activity, which typically means profits and jobs. Members of Congress who don't care about creating jobs at home probably won't keep their own jobs in Washington for very long.

In the midst of this annual budget pandemonium, a venerable Florida university professor asked to meet with me. During this period of the year I tried to keep office meetings to a minimum so that I could focus on the inevitable appropriations emergencies. But the professor was an exception. I had been his student four decades earlier. I had great respect for his contributions to urban planning and land use, and I enjoyed his company. To the consternation of the harried staff members responsible for my schedule and our appropriations agenda, I told them to make room in that day's schedule for the professor.

The professor was describing an urban housing program he had initiated at a Florida university—a program for which he was seeking a federal grant through a congressional earmark. Earmarks are specific projects inserted in the appropriations legislation, generally to benefit a constituent or supporter. In recent years earmarks have become the subject of great controversy. For example, the Democratic Party's 2006 recapture of the House of

Representatives is attributed in part to furor over the "Bridge to Nowhere," a nearly $400 million project linking the Alaskan city of Ketchikan to a small island with an airport and fewer than 100 residents. Two years later Sen. John McCain made earmarks a centerpiece of his presidential campaign. But while reform is definitely needed, earmarks remain part of the appropriations process.

Although I generally resisted earmark requests, I was willing to listen when the initiative was worthwhile and the advocate was credible. The professor's project passed both tests. Every element was in place for congressional support but one: the clock. As I explained to him, "The federal fiscal year begins on October 1. Congress is in the eleventh hour of its budget negotiations. If I were a senior member of the Senate Appropriations Committee, I might have a slim chance of getting your idea in the budget, but I am not. You are a year too late."

The professor was obviously deflated, but I continued to explain. "My advice is to identify the federal agency with the greatest interest in your initiative—probably HUD, the Department of Housing and Urban Development. With your reputation and that of the university, you might persuade HUD to include your proposal in the departmental budget. HUD will submit its budget to the White House Office of Planning and Budget in December. The president will then submit a proposed federal budget to Congress, which will start its annual appropriations process. With the support of the HUD secretary, your idea may well be included in the president's budget. You will be riding with the budget tide rather than swimming upstream. That is your best path to get the program in the budget for the fiscal year that starts 376 days from now."

Still disappointed, but chastened and informed of the realities of the governmental hourglass, the professor left with a promise to give it a try. He contacted HUD and was greeted with interest in his proposal. Although he is still working to have his initiative included in the HUD budget, his chances of success have greatly increased because he is now making the clock his friend. Understanding the calendar will do the same for you in your citizen advocacy.

MANAGE THE CLOCK

All college and professional football fans know the pain of watching their teams try to come from behind as time is running out. Anxiety builds every time the quarterback seems to take too long behind center. Spectators hurl curses at every play that fails to gain significant yards or at least stop the clock. Anger rains down on any player who loses time. And when the clock expires before your team can make the winning touchdown or field goal, the resulting feeling is one of emptiness and demoralization.

It is no less painful to watch your citizen initiative go down to defeat because you didn't manage the clock correctly. The good news is that you can dramatically increase your ability to make time an ally rather than an enemy by following a few pointers.

1. Be Aware of Fixed Deadlines—and Start Long in Advance

There is almost always an optimum time for citizens to intervene in government decisions. But some government timelines are set in stone, and failure to honor them can spell death to your initiative. Probably the best examples come from the legislative process. If you have identified a problem that requires the passage of legislation, be aware that every bill has a built-in expiration date: the end of the legislative session.

In Washington, D.C., congressional sessions run for two years, from January of one odd-numbered year to January of the next odd-numbered year. Thus the 111th Congress, which began January 3, 2009, will end January 3, 2011. Any bill introduced in a Congress that is not passed before the Congress ends automatically dies—meaning that any work that has been done on that bill must be started from scratch during the next two-year Congress. When you consider the extensive work that is required to pass legislation—finding a sponsor or sponsors in both the Senate and the House who will champion the bill, helping them build support among their colleagues, heading off opponents' efforts to kill the bill, convincing the relevant congressional committees to endorse the bill, securing initial passage, reconciling any Senate and House differences in a conference committee, passing consensus legislation in both houses of Congress, and then securing the signature of the president or finding enough votes to override a presidential veto—it is obvious that a late start will increase the chances of your bill dying at the hands of the two-year clock.

Other legislative bodies have similar rules. Like Congress, most state legislatures operate on a two-year clock, but some have additional restrictions that make early action imperative. For example, in Florida, legislators are limited in the number of bills they can introduce during each legislative session. If you want a state senator or representative to sponsor your bill, you're out of luck if the officeholder has already reached the limit for that session. But you can increase your luck by being first in line when your legislator begins to consider what should be on his or her legislative agenda. County and municipal legislators (council members and commissioners) often have even tighter restrictions than do their state and federal counterparts. Depending on which level of government controls your issue, check to see which rules apply so that you can plan appropriately.

Of course, do-or-die deadlines exist even in situations where a citizen initiative doesn't depend on the passage of legislation. If you are a student, let's assume that you have identified problems with the way your university assigns housing for the next academic year. If you want to change that system, the time to start is not two weeks before the Housing Department holds "room draw," or whatever the process is called on your campus. Weeks or even months of planning go into making room assignments. You would be wise to start your lobbying efforts as soon as one year's room draw has ended so that you have time to lobby for a change for the following year. The same is true if you want to add new courses to the curriculum. Because the university will need time to find professors to teach the courses, add them to the schedule, and ensure that meeting rooms are available, start your campaign as early as possible.

2. Study the Budget

As my professor friend learned on his visit to Washington, no area of governmental policymaking is more fraught with time constraints than is the budgetary process. The work of enacting the annual budget has three main parts:

1. Agencies and departments submit their individual budget requests to the budget and planning office of the chief executive (president, governor, county chairperson, or mayor).
2. After reviewing the individual requests and merging them into a single, integrated budget, the chief executive presents a proposed budget to the legislative branch (Congress, state legislature, county commission, or city council).
3. The legislative branch reviews, revises, and approves the budget and sends it to the chief executive for his or her final signature.

Time is short at each stage in this process. The agencies and departments have a deadline to submit their budget requests to the chief executive's office of budget and planning. Chief executives usually have a statutory deadline to submit their proposed budget to the legislative branch. And legislators are required to pass a budget that the chief executive will sign before the end of the fiscal year (usually June 30, September 30, or December 31, depending on the calendar used). If your citizen initiative requires governmental spending and you miss any of these deadlines, your chances of success will be severely diminished.

Several guidelines will help you negotiate the key first step of the tricky budgetary process. First, give the person closest to the problem the chance to provide the solution to the problem. Whether you are dealing with a rural village with an annual budget of $10,000 or the Pentagon with its hundreds of billions in annual appropriations, determine the person responsible for your issue of concern. If you are well prepared, and make a good presentation, you stand a good chance of convincing that decision maker to favor your proposal for inclusion in the annual budget.

Second, as the saying goes, if at first you don't succeed, try, try again. Government agencies are often and accurately accused of being bureaucratic. Bureaucracy, however, gives you multiple chances to sell your idea. The people who occupy the lowest rungs of the ladder are usually long-serving, steady, and reliable but not always visionary or receptive to new ideas. You might well find someone farther up the chain of command who will take a more open view on your proposal and say "yes" to it.

Third, look for someone who can help you demystify the often-baffling budget process. At the local level, this could be someone in the chief executive's office of budget and planning. But it could also include other citizens who have successfully dealt with your target agency in the past. Legislative aides—staffers who assist members of Congress, state legislators, county commissioners, or city councilors on budget matters—can also help to shine the light of understanding on an often dark and murky enterprise. Depending on your issue, you may be able to seek advice from a like-minded advocacy organization. If your goal is to increase funding for grants that support new business ventures, for example, consult with the legislative affairs staff at an entity like the National Federation of Independent Business (NFIB). If your aim is to create a new veterans health care clinic in your community, the American

Legion, AMVETS, or another veterans association may have experts who can help. Finally, if you have sufficient financial resources, you can hire a governmental affairs consultant—also known as a lobbyist—with expertise in the budget process.

Fourth, aspire to become an expert in the unique role that legislators play in the budget process. In your past civics courses you probably learned that Congress has the power of the purse in our federal government. Most states give the same power to their legislatures. Congress and many state legislatures—and frequently local legislative commissions or councils—employ a two-step process for budget approval. Once the president, governor, or mayor has presented a proposed budget, these legislative bodies must authorize the proposed spending. For example, let's say the president has proposed $100 million to fund a new federal highway bridge over the Willamette River in Oregon. Both the House and the Senate are required to give permission for the funds to be spent in that manner—to approve the president's policy goal. But that is only half the battle. If Congress merely authorizes the bridge, the bridge won't be built. Before construction can begin, the House and the Senate must also appropriate the necessary funds. That is, they must open up the national wallet and provide the $100 million to the U.S. Department of Transportation—or more likely to the state of Oregon.

Fifth, present your ideas in strategic terms. In well-run budget offices, the annual allocation of public funds is a means of implementing goals that will guide the government over a five- or ten-year cycle. Convince budget planners that your proposal is consistent with their long-term priorities, and they are more likely to accept it.

3. Think in Terms of "Best Time" to Achieve Your Goal

Although the governmental decision-making process has plenty of time constraints that require you to start early in order to achieve success, you must also pay attention to the optimal time to convince the decision maker to take on your initiative. For deadline-dependent issues, such as the budget, you will have little discretionary time: The legislature will appropriate money when it is legally required to do so. But for other initiatives, it is critical to think about how the timing of the ultimate decision may affect the decision maker and thus your prospects for success.

Examples of this need to pay attention to timing abound at every level of governmental decision making, especially for issues tinged with any controversy. For example, if a college administrator needs to make a decision that could raise the ire of the student body, he is much more likely to do so in the summer when few students are paying attention. In local, state, and federal governments, elected officials are much more likely to make tough decisions in years that don't end with an election, or in lame duck sessions that take place after an election has passed but before the legislative session expires. Conversely, they love to deliver good news—such as appropriations for their districts—in election years when such actions could increase their standing among the voting public.

Your dealings with agency and departmental officials will be more successful if you apply the same insights. If a state or local government is experiencing a budget crunch and looking for ways to reduce its size, don't ask an official to take action that may draw negative attention. She may soon find herself out of a job. On the other hand, many ambitious government officials are looking for opportunities to make a name for themselves. If presented at the right time, your initiative may be the star to which they will hitch their wagon.

TAKE ADVANTAGE OF TRENDS, CYCLES, AND DEADLINES

If you think timing matters only in the short term, think again. If you are interested in influencing decisions over a long period of time, or achieving permanent change at the collegiate, local, state, or federal level, you will have to monitor the tide of history, which is governed by the ebbs and flows of trends and cycles.

Trends are a function of historical momentum—events evolving over time to form a pattern that influences the fate of various policy matters. Trends may involve population growth or decline, demographic changes, economic growth or stagnation, partisan realignment, subtle shifts in public perceptions about issues, or other factors.

To give two examples, the post–World War II migration of African Americans from rural southern states to industrial Midwestern cities was a trend. The more recent overall shift in population from northeastern states to the Sun Belt is also a trend. Both had significant impacts over time. Nicholas Lemann describes how the Great Migration changed the political character of cities like Detroit, Chicago, and Cleveland to the point that each of these elected African American mayors in the 1970s and 1980s.[1]

The movement to the Sun Belt also had monumental effects on both policy and politics. Presidential politics changed as southern and western states picked up electoral votes at the expense of the Northeast and the Midwest. The same was true of the U.S. House of Representatives, where the allocation of seats is based on the populations of states. In 1950 Pennsylvania had thirty House members; Florida had eight. Today, the numbers are starkly different—the 2000 Census left Pennsylvania with nineteen members, while Florida now has twenty-five. As Americans have moved from one part of the country to another, the federal government has had to change the formulas it uses to distribute veterans' benefits, highway funding, and other types of spending. State and local governments in the Sun Belt have gained residents that generate tax income, but increases in population have also placed more demands on their budgets.

---

[1] Nicholas Lemann, *The Promised Land: The Great Black Migration and How It Changed America* (New York: Vintage Books, 1991).

Because of Florida's explosive growth in the sixty years after World War II, it offers many examples of how trends can powerfully reshape the political and policy landscape. Here's one: Before the 1960s Floridians strongly resisted state interference with their private rights over land and water. In 1939, when Florida gave municipalities the authority to enact zoning ordinances, it was the forty-eighth state to extend that power to cities and towns. Thirty years later it was the last state in the nation to give counties general zoning power. This reluctance to let government play a role in determining how lands and waters were used affected a number of policy areas, but none more so than efforts to safeguard and preserve Florida's environmental treasures.

During the 1960s a combination of trends resulted in the fastest reversal of state environmental policy in U.S. history. Florida's population was expanding at a massive rate, largely fueled by new residents moving from other states. The mild climate and environmental quality were major draws for these newcomers. These new Floridians shared a deep desire to preserve Florida as it was when they crossed the state line for the first time. A small but influential group of these new residents consisted of affluent citizens who had been national environmental movement leaders. Additionally, the new population and the resulting reapportionment of the Florida Legislature transformed the state's political scene. While rural interests and Democrats once dominated the agenda, urban areas and Republicans now had a much greater say. Finally, Florida was in what would prove to be a thirty-year period of lessened rainfall.

This critical mass of trends generated a new trend: greater state participation in matters affecting the natural environment. Environmental leaders saw and understood Florida's demographic and meteorological trends and had the political skills to make those developments work in their favor. Starting at the local level, they enacted some of the most aggressive environmental legislation and policies in the nation.

Many of the environmental leaders' initial successes were defensive. Their insight that Florida was changing helped them reverse or prevent government actions that could have severely damaged certain natural habitats. These triumphs included saving the brown pelican from near-certain extinction, blocking the construction of a large commercial airport in America's Everglades, and halting construction of the controversial Cross-Florida Barge Canal.

Those defensive stands gave environmental advocates the energy and momentum to play offense and push for systematic policy changes that have provided long-term benefits for the state as a whole. The successful transition from defense to offense led Florida policymakers to embrace a number of monumental reforms, including:

- Establishing state control over areas of critical concern, such as the Florida Keys
- Building a statewide network of regional water-management agencies
- Persuading the state to purchase extensive amounts of sensitive lands
- Initiating an ongoing effort to save America's Everglades

College campuses have also been significantly affected by trends. Sixty years ago a significant number of colleges and universities still restricted their enrollment to men. Some of your grandfathers and fathers probably did not attend class with women. But the positive national trend in favor of granting women equal access and prohibiting gender-based discrimination has reshaped campuses across the United States. Today, men and women apply to college, live in university housing, attend classes, earn degrees, win scholarships and fellowships, and take advantage of other academic offerings on relatively equal terms. The trend in favor of equal gender opportunity also led Congress to pass legislation in 1972 (Title IX) that requires universities to provide women with equal opportunities for athletic participation.

Trends represent long-term, or even permanent, changes, while cycles are recurring phenomena that influence the timing and impact of trends. Republican control of the White House for all but four years from 1969 to 1993 was a cycle that was not broken until Bill Clinton won the presidency in 1992. Conversely, Republicans ended a forty-year cycle of Democratic control of the House of Representatives with their November 1994 sweep of congressional elections. Democrats returned the favor in November 2006.

Cycles take different forms, each offering challenges and opportunities to the participating citizen. For example, with policy cycles, it is important to remember that most government policy decisions are based on a yearly cycle, but others operate in different time frames. Because of processes put in place through legislation like the National Environmental Policy Act of 1969, the federal government's environmental decisions are on a two-year cycle. Local government comprehensive plans, which set the overall guidelines for how a county or municipality will grow and develop, are often five years in the making. A college or university often has a ten- or even twenty-year strategic plan to govern its institutional priorities.

Citizen activists who do not pay homage to these policy cycles often find themselves on the outside looking in. I am familiar with a group of citizens concerned about the sorry state of civics education in their state who wanted to reform the civics textbooks used in public schools. They received a harsh dose of reality when they learned that the state textbook selection was on a six-year cycle and that the cycle had started just one year before.

Political cycles are critical for three admittedly cynical reasons: First, as elections approach, politicians are interested in advocating policies that make their constituents feel good and thus make them look good. The month of October in an even-numbered year is not the time to go to your state legislator or member of Congress and ask him to visit pain (tax increases or spending cuts) on constituents. Second, if an elected official either cannot or does not run for reelection, she may feel liberated to take risks if she doesn't have to face the voters again. On the other hand, a lame duck politician generally has less power than one who may still be around at the start of the next legislative session. Third, the longer an elected official's term, the more power she has to help you. In the nineteenth century, many state governors served for one year. Today, the usual term is four years with the chance for reelection—a change that has made governors the primary factor in state politics. You will read more about the significance of governors in the chapter 10 case study.

But be wary of any one-size-fits-all approach to political cycles. In some nations, such as the United Kingdom, voters can endorse or reject the status quo by keeping or changing the entire government in a single election, whereas our divided system often produces muddled results. When voters in 2006 returned the Democrats to power in both the House of Representatives and the Senate, many were expecting a sharp turn in policy, especially policy on the war in Iraq. They were disappointed. Because the elections did not produce a new president, or give Democrats a governing 60-seat majority in the Senate, policy changes have been slow at best.

Economic cycles inevitably affect policy matters. If you're not convinced of this relationship, try asking your university administrators for additional spending in a year when the institution is fighting a budget deficit caused by higher inflation, lower enrollment, or a reduction in private or public support. Politics regulates the economy and at the same time is captive to its consequences. This is why the British define the study of government as political economics.

Here is one example of how an understanding of economic cycles powers political success. In the 1980s a group of parents and educators across the nation enthusiastically noted a trend toward commencing children's education before the kindergarten year. They were supported by convincing scientific studies of the brain's development that offered a possible antidote to low student achievement pervasive in secondary schools. But the movement's leadership had the wisdom of patience and waited until the booming prosperity of the 1990s to press their case before school boards, governors, and legislatures. The result in many states was state-funded education for three- and four-year-olds from voluntarily participating families.

Finally, never forget the importance of individual politicians and the cycles in which they played a role. The passion, energy, and inspirational qualities of the individual at the helm can sway the day, whether it is a national leader, such as Winston Churchill, Britain's prime minister in the 1940s, or a visionary mayor in an American city today. But look beyond the question of who's in charge now to who might be in charge down the road. A newly elected legislator without seniority, but also without the time commitments that come with longevity, might be the leader to whom you can entrust your cause. Conservative Republicans found a new representative from Georgia to have those qualities. Rising from a far distant back bench in the early 1980s to become the mastermind of the Contract with America in 1994, Rep. Newt Gingrich for a time transformed American politics and seized the national policy agenda from a president who had taken office just two years before.

CHECKLIST FOR ACTION

- ☐ Manage the clock.
  - Know deadlines and start long in advance.
  - Study the budget.
  - Select the best time to achieve your goal.
- ☐ Take advantage of cycles, trends, and deadlines.

Exercises

TRENDS

Which trends have the greatest chance of influencing your college, local community, state, or nation in the next twenty-five years? What public policies will be most advantaged or endangered by these changes?

CYCLES

Has the problem you defined in chapter 1 been influenced by any political or economic cycles? As you work to address the challenge, is there some way to use that cycle for your benefit? Does the cycle threaten your prospects for success in any way?

Note: I am grateful to the President and Fellows of Harvard College and the John F. Kennedy School of Government's Case Program for allowing me to condense one of their copyrighted case studies for use in this chapter. Harvey Simon originally wrote the unabridged version of this case study, which was entitled "The Orange Hats of Fairlawn: A Washington, DC Neighborhood Battles Drugs" (C16-91-1034.0).

All for One, and One for All

Coalitions for Citizen Success

"We're putting the band back together."

—Jake and Elwood Blues

Case in Point: The Orange Hats of Fairlawn

In 1988 a group of Washington, D.C., residents began standing on the street corners of their working-class neighborhood, attempting, through their visible presence, to drive away the hundreds of drug dealers who had recently invaded the area. Wearing orange hats to identify themselves in the busy, open-air drug bazaar that had established itself on the once-quiet streets of Fairlawn, as their small neighborhood of the Anacostia section of Southeast Washington was known, they gathered nightly in groups small and large. Middle-aged and elderly, male and female, members of the Fairlawn Coalition stood on the sidewalks, and sat there on lawn chairs, among the crowds of drug dealers. Using video cameras, they filmed the drug dealers in action and recorded the license numbers of cars carrying drug-hungry customers from Virginia, Maryland, and other parts of Washington. When the drug business moved, the coalition members moved with it. On patrol, they walked the neighborhood's major thoroughfares and narrow side streets, past its schools and small stores, sometimes catching a glimpse of the floodlit U.S. Capitol, across the Anacostia River.

The coalition's leader, Edward Johnson, knew the group needed another ally: the local police. Although his neighbors had experienced what they perceived to be police indifference to their situation, Johnson believed that the police could be convinced to take a different attitude. If he was wrong, the risks the coalition members assumed in standing face to face with armed drug dealers would be very great.

Before the drug dealers appeared in the mid-1980s, neither residents nor police thought of Fairlawn as a high-crime area.[1] Although a few residents looked out for each other, almost everyone else in the neighborhood was a stranger. "Somebody could break into your house and carry out everything, and somebody would see them and never even say a word, and never call the police," says Johnson. Until the drug dealers arrived, the residents' isolation from one another did not present a major problem. Fairlawn was an island, a quiet little neighborhood surrounded by a sea of crime.

In the mid-1980s Fairlawn lost its island status. Fueled by a rise in the use of illegal drugs, the crime that was rampant in other parts of Anacostia crossed the line into Fairlawn. Ironically, the very qualities that had made the neighborhood a desirable place to live may have contributed to its decline. Drug customers preferred to complete their transactions on Fairlawn's quiet streets, rather than in the surrounding urban jungle. "Instead of driving right into a public housing complex," says a police official familiar with the area, "you'd much rather go into an area like Fairlawn, where you feel more comfortable, but the product is available to you there."

---

[1] This conclusion is based on the impressions of residents and the police. Crime statistics were not kept specifically for the Fairlawn neighborhood during this period.

Rather than hold the DCPD responsible for not being responsive to Fairlawn's needs, Johnson blamed himself and his neighbors. "It was our problem that we didn't get better [police] response, because we didn't complain, like . . . people on Capitol Hill, or the people out in Georgetown," Johnson explains. "We kind of let things ride."

THE FAIRLAWN COALITION: GETTING STARTED

A community rally with a march through the area would be a good way, Johnson believed, to grab the attention of Fairlawn residents and let the police know that the citizens were beginning to take an interest in their neighborhood. His neighbors liked Johnson's idea for a march, but none knew how to go about organizing a demonstration. For advice, they turned to another potential addition to the coalition, the Reverend Richard Dalton, who led the congregation at the Garden Memorial Presbyterian Church.

Reverend Dalton, who shared Johnson's conviction that the neighborhood had to take more responsibility for what was happening on its streets, was struck by how deeply rooted the drug problem was in the area. "I felt, simply because I lived there, and some of the members of my church lived there, that it was necessary for the church to be directly involved," he says.

From Marching to Patrolling

In the early evening hours of a Thursday in mid-August of 1988, an assembly of perhaps eighty local residents marched a preplanned, fifteen-block route through Fairlawn, finishing at the Anacostia High School, where anyone who cared to do so could make a brief speech to the crowd. Along the route prayers were offered, songs were sung, and chants were chanted. Residents, attracted by the crude flyers that had been stuffed in mailboxes and slipped under automobile windshield wipers, were joined by a roughly equal number of supporters from outside the neighborhood. These individuals, who had been invited to join the march by Johnson, Reverend Dalton, and the other organizers, included about twenty ministers from churches around the Washington area; twenty-five members of the Nation of Islam, who provided physical protection; a city councilor; and members from other city organizations, such as Moms on the Move, an organization of mothers whose sons and daughters had been involved with drugs.

The march through Fairlawn was intended as the kickoff to something much bigger. The march was a kind of local publicity venture, an attention-grabbing, participatory advertisement for an idea the organizers wanted to sell to the community. "The march was connected with a plan of action," says Reverend Dalton.

The plan was to get the community interested in and motivated to actively fight its drug problem. By bringing people together—in meetings, at barbecues, and at block parties—Johnson and Reverend Dalton thought they could get their neighbors to have a direct impact on Fairlawn's drug problem.

A community patrol would deter drug dealing through a kind of moral persuasion, Johnson thought. Residents patrolling their neighborhood would send an implicit message to the drug purveyors that the people who lived in the area were taking an interest in their community. As a result, the drug dealers, not wanting to do business in an area of the city where they clearly were not wanted, would stop doing business there. "What I figured is that if the [drug dealers] . . . see community people out there concerned about where they live, and [the residents] don't want that kind of messing around, that this would encourage them to move on."

The work began within a week of the march, when about ten people, all from the immediate area around Johnson's block of Minnesota Avenue S.E., met in the Garden Memorial Church basement and started hashing out Johnson's basic idea for a neighborhood patrol. There, and in meetings combined with cookouts held in Johnson's side yard, coalition members talked about the drug problem in their neighborhood and about possible solutions, beginning and ending each meeting with a prayer circle. They told each other stories of their own experiences and brought in representatives from community organizations around Washington. They talked about requesting help from the Nation of Islam, which had been involved in patrolling some Washington neighborhoods, and from the Guardian Angels, a nationally known group that patrols selected streets in various cities. Coalition members ended up rejecting both groups: They considered the groups' tactics as too confrontational, the groups would not provide a permanent presence, and they were not from the neighborhood.

Apart from getting to know one another for the first time, these Fairlawn neighbors accomplished three things during their months of meetings: They agreed on a name—the Fairlawn Coalition. They put Johnson in charge, after Reverend Dalton decided he did not want the neighborhood organization to become a church group. And the coalition talked with outsiders about the drug problem in Fairlawn. But as James Foreman, who lived a half-block from the heaviest concentration of street narcotics sales lamented, even the so-called experts "had no solutions on how to solve the problem." The group was exactly where Johnson wanted it; the only people they could turn to were themselves.

Bringing the Police into the Process

During these meetings Johnson led the group into a discussion about their attitudes toward the Police Department. "What we had to do was approach this thing from a positive approach and . . . not go back blaming [anyone] for what hasn't been done," says Johnson. He wanted to present the police with a united, well-organized, disciplined community group.

The group envisioned a hand-in-hand cooperation, not only to clean out the drug dealers but generally to deter crime in the neighborhood. The coalition did not just want more respect or faster response times when police answered calls; the group wanted the police to become a presence in Fairlawn. "By them being visible in the community and us out there on the street walking," Johnson says, "this would prevent things from happening before they had to happen."

Capt. Claude Beheler, who had joined the Police Department as a cadet just out of high school in 1971, and had spent half his nearly twenty-year tenure in Anacostia, agreed to come to the Fairlawn Coalition's next meeting. He was soon working closely with the group. He became convinced that they were sincere about their mission and dedicated to cleaning up the neighborhood. On a more personal level, he felt comfortable with the people he met, and this motivated him to work with the coalition. "I got a real positive feeling from them," he recalls.

Feeling that something positive could come from working with the coalition, Captain Beheler attended every meeting he could, and the group, sensing that the captain could be crucial to their success, went so far as to rearrange its meeting time to fit his schedule.

ON PATROL

At the group's last meeting before Christmas 1988, many residents who had assembled in the church basement that evening decided they would stand out on the street where the drug dealers stood. The presence of the coalition members on the street that December night produced a minor disruption in the drug trade there. Some drug dealers left, and some people, apparently on their way to buy drugs, went elsewhere. It showed the neighbors that they could do something.

Two weeks later, approximately forty-one Fairlawn residents walked down the neighborhood's principal street to the end of the block. There they found what they had seen before: a group of young people selling drugs "just like it was an open-air market," according to Johnson. If these dealers were typical, they ranged in age from roughly thirteen to twenty-one, some years younger than their business partners who supplied them with their product. "We stood around right amongst [them]," Johnson says. "A few boys asked me, "What you old church people doing out here?" Johnson's riposte poked gently at their funny bones: "Well, you know, you all seem to be enjoying it so much . . . we figured we'd come out here and enjoy it some along with you." The drug merchants laughed, and, one by one they slowly drifted away.

The next evening when the coalition returned to the same corner, they found that the drug dealing was continuing unabated. But this time the coalition brought along a tool: a video camera. Although the camera was originally intended only to take pictures as a memento of the group's early actions, the coalition quickly discovered that the camcorder spooked the drug dealers. After one week of coalition members standing on the corner with their camcorder, the dealers went elsewhere. Again, they did not go far, setting up just two blocks away. Again, the coalition moved along with them. So the dealers split up, reestablishing their business on several different corners, and the coalition followed suit.

The coalition could tell who the drug dealers were, and soon the dealers and the police had no trouble picking out the coalition. Its members could be seen from blocks away by the bright, engineer-orange baseball caps they started wearing on their patrols, beginning early in 1989. Captain Beheler had suggested this shade of orange during the coalition meeting. The color of the group's signature caps thereafter became known as "Beheler Orange."

Although Beheler had concerns about liability and had not given this kind of activity his full-fledged support, his actions spoke louder than his words. Back at the station, he assigned two officers, Norman Sanders and Richard Perkins, to work hand-in-hand with the Fairlawn group to help the residents eradicate drug dealing from their neighborhood.

The two officers worked with the patrol group—not always walking alongside them but never far away either—and on their own initiative did whatever they could think of to clean up the neighborhood. Although Beheler thought the coalition's patrols had the potential to be effective, he was also thinking about their limitations. "There is no way the patrols themselves could have had a significant impact," he commented.

Sanders agreed to work with the new organization in his old neighborhood, although from his experience with other community associations, he did not believe the Fairlawn group would be active for long. But Sanders soon changed his mind, impressed with what he says was the dedication the coalition members showed to the task they had set themselves of ridding their neighborhood of drugs. After a few weeks back in Fairlawn, "I saw these people were serious," Sanders says. "These were working people who came home from work, they ate their dinner, they met at a certain location, and they patrolled their neighborhood up until well into midnight. It didn't make any difference about the weather, whether it was rain, sun, nice weather, cold weather, they stayed out the duration. That showed me something: that these people were serious about their neighborhood."

Sanders and Perkins took on the neighborhood's problems almost as a personal project: sitting together, thinking about all the things they could do, both to put suspects in jail and to deter criminal activity. They collected all the outstanding felony and serious-misdemeanor warrants for people thought to be living in the area, tracked them down, and took them to jail. They set up roadblocks on neighborhood streets busy with drug traffic, stopping every car that came through and warning the drivers and their passengers that they were on the lookout for drug sales.

The key to their relationship with the criminal community was the personal relationship the two officers formed with the members of the coalition. Every other Tuesday they attended the group's meetings, which continued to be held in the basement of the Garden Memorial Church. They came to the coalition's barbecues, and they attended its parties. They stopped by unannounced at the homes of coalition members, stopped to talk with people on the street, and walked along with coalition members on patrol—all in all making as many as five contacts with residents a night. In this way, Sanders and Perkins began to win the trust of the community. They were "always in the neighborhood!" Johnson exclaims. Once residents were convinced that the officers were interested, that they cared, and that they could be trusted to protect their confidentiality, they started providing information that enabled Sanders and Perkins to close criminal cases that had gone unsolved for months and to make quick arrests in new cases.

Police Patrols and Citizen Patrols

At first, Perkins and Sanders stuck close by the side of the coalition members when they were patrolling the streets at night. The officers, and their superiors, wanted to ensure that the coalitioners were safe on the streets. But this umbilical link was soon loosened: The police team and the Fairlawn patrol would head out in different directions, come together and walk with each other for a while later in the evening, then divide up again. Although Perkins and Sanders—riding motorcycles, on foot, or in a cruiser—might be checking out corners of the neighborhood blocks from the coalition's patrols, they could be readily contacted and could appear at any trouble spot in minutes.

Perkins and the coalition leaders were convinced that the Fairlawn patrols would be less effective if the police were always there with them. If the police were merely the guardians of the patrolling neighbors, the coalition would never gain the respect of the drug dealers, and it would have no effect on them.

Staying Together

Backing from the police was not the only thing the coalition had to keep it going. It also had a network of social relationships that were forming among members. The orange hats were the symbol of a social group as well as an anticrime coalition. But the main social bonding took place on the street. "They . . . were hooking together their social relationships, their religious relationships, their neighborhood relationships, their law enforcement relationships," says Beheler.

The coalition also became a kind of mini-social-service agency. Most of the coalition's activities focused on the young people in the neighborhood.[2] In addition to arranging parties, which were intended for the youth of the neighborhood, the coalition also did informal counseling. "We try to turn them around and show them there is a better way . . . primarily by talking to them," says Johnson. "We are not necessarily just there to see that they go to jail for their illegal activities. . . . [We are] out there to help them, because we care."

On the evening of January 9, 1991, the date the organization considered its anniversary, one member after another drifted over to the street intersection that had been the coalition's initial target. Apart from passersby, the only people standing there that night had orange hats on their heads. Not a drug dealer was in sight.

By Johnson's estimate, the neighborhood was "completely" cleaned up after one year of patrolling. Beheler's more systematic account revealed that the neighborhood saw a 20 percent decrease in serious crimes during comparable eight-month periods in 1988 and 1989.[3] And with the coalition funneling information to Perkins and Sanders about drug houses in the area, the police closed fifteen of them in two years. Less tangible than the police statistics were the "thank yous" that coalition members received from neighborhood children, happy to be able to play on the street again, and

---

[2] In calendar year 1990 the Fairlawn Coalition raised, and spent, approximately $10,000. The group accepts no government funding. All of its money is raised through small donations from members and the community.

[3] Serious crimes included homicide, rape, robbery, assault, burglary, theft, theft from auto, breaking and entering into vending machine, and stolen autos. The number of reported crimes for the area, between January and August 1988, was seventy-one; the number for the same period in 1989 was fifty-seven.

from the many cars that honked their support as they passed the evening's patrol.

Within two years of the Fairlawn Coalition's first night out, 126 neighborhoods in the Washington metropolitan area had adopted its model with a total of 9,500 members. James Foreman summed up the lesson of the Orange Hats: "They know that together they are a force and they can reckon with anything in their community. . . . When they come up, the crooks run. And for anyone, that's power, man."

BUILDING YOUR OWN COALITION: A STEP-BY-STEP GUIDE TO FORGING AN EFFECTIVE ALLIANCE

Whether you want to fight new graduation requirements, demand that your college offer a new course, or urge the local city council to put in a traffic light at a busy intersection, you are much more likely to succeed if you have the active support of a broad base of citizens and interests. The following guidelines will help you create and sustain the coalition that you will need to turn your goal into reality.

1. Define the Problem Specifically and Attract the Widest Possible Coalition

As noted in previous chapters, effective citizenship—including coalition building—hinges on the formulation of a concise, fact-based, and compelling statement of the problem you aim to fix. A well-stated problem helps to recruit and motivate potential coalition members, particularly if the timing and circumstances create a sense of urgency.

Recall the case of the Georgetown University students and their local Advisory Neighborhood Commission. When the commission supported restrictions on student parking and housing, students could summarize their problem in a simple and dramatic way: If the commission had its way, they would have no place to park or live. Similarly, if you are concerned about crime on campus, define that concern in a way that speaks to students, faculty members, university employees, parents, and others who may share your concern. Few if any of those potential coalition partners will be motivated to act if you simply declare that "crime is a problem on campus." But if the facts support your statement that "fifty people have been mugged on campus walkways or in campus parking lots in the past six months," you are more likely to inspire others to help you fix a problem that you all share.

Remember that coalitions form only if multiple parties believe that they will benefit their particular interests by joining forces. Define the problem in a way that appeals to those varied interests. If your college or university were to require all students to take a semester course in nuclear physics in order to graduate, and you wanted to fight that requirement, think about potential coalition partners and why they might want to join you. Students majoring in the humanities and social sciences may not want to take a course so far outside their fields of study. Nuclear physics professors may want to work with small groups of students interested in the field and prefer not to teach those taking the course only because it is required. University budget planners may fear the fiscal implications. You are much more likely to capture the support of those disparate groups if you formulate the problem in a way that broadly yet succinctly targets all these various concerns.

Schedule a brainstorming session to determine potential coalition partners. The meeting should produce a list of individuals and groups you need to contact. Many potential coalitions lose steam at this stage because nobody takes responsibility for turning a great idea into an even greater alliance. Don't make that mistake. Pick up your cell phone or turn on your laptop and start calling or e-mailing your potential partners. Ask them to get together for lunch or coffee at a location convenient to them so that you can discuss your idea in person. Nothing communicates respect like going to a potential partner's neighborhood and asking for input and support for your cause.

2. What Comes First—the Coalition or the Solution?

What comes first, the chicken or the egg? The answer is it depends on your point of view and circumstances. Some coalitions form around a problem and use their membership to generate solutions. Others will emerge in support of a solution and work on transforming that solution into policy.

Just as a clear definition of a problem can attract coalition members who share your frustration about conditions that need to be changed, your identification of well-received possible solutions to that challenge can both motivate new recruits and give them the hope of an outcome to rally around. Recent American history shows how solutions can drive the formation of coalitions. In Virginia in the late 1990s anger over the state's personal property tax—the "car tax"—brought automakers, car dealerships, low-tax crusaders, automobile owners, and others together to rally behind a plan to abolish the tax. Acting from their different positions in the Virginia business and political communities, these coalition partners turned the car tax into the single most important issue of the 1997 gubernatorial election. The candidate who opposed full abolition of the tax—ironically an automobile dealership owner himself—lost in a landslide to the candidate who championed the end of the tax.

The use of proposed solutions to find allies takes place every day right in our own backyards. If a local street or highway is gridlocked from traffic, or unsafe from poor construction or years of wear and tear, a proposal to build a new road or improve public transportation will likely draw the support of motorists, businesses, homeowners, and consumer safety advocates. Similarly, local coalitions are forming and rising up to fight proposed Wal-Mart superstores in their communities. Because those coalitions are broad-based—often composed of small businesses, organized labor, manageable-growth advocates, and potential Wal-Mart neighbors—many of them have succeeded in convincing their city councils and county commissions to deny these proposals.

Perhaps the best example comes from America's largest city: New York. In December 2004 Wal-Mart announced plans to open a 135,000-square-foot store in the borough of Queens. One Wal-Mart executive suggested that the Queens store was just a beachhead in what the company hoped would become a full-scale retail occupation of the Big Apple. "Wal-Mart is eager to make New York City its next frontier," said the executive.[4] But it seems that New Yorkers did not share Wal-Mart's pioneering spirit. A coalition of labor unions, small business owners, community and religious leaders, environmental advocates, city council members, and retail groups sprung up almost overnight to oppose the Queens project. They quickly and effectively raised public concerns about Wal-Mart's alleged penchant for driving local businesses out of business and lowering labor and environmental standards. It wasn't long before the coalition won the first battle: The developers working with Wal-Mart on the Queens store pulled out of the deal.

Of course, the solution need not always precede the coalition. Coalitions can form around a problem and then develop practical solutions that generate public support and lead to the desired change in policy.

The problem you identify and the circumstances under which it exists will help you determine whether the coalition or the solution comes first. If the coalition comes together around the problem, organize a meeting of all the coalition partners— other student organizations, college or university officials, and local community leaders—to brainstorm possible solutions, as the citizens of Steamboat Springs did in bridging the gap between a majority of its residents and the school board. If the solution energizes a coalition, have a similar meeting for those who you have reason to believe support the proposed solution. Then use that meeting to assign specific roles for turning the proposed

---

[4] Steven Greenhouse, "Foes Dig In as Wal-Mart Aims for City," *New York Times*, February 10, 2005.

solution into policy. Previous chapters have already discussed some of the roles—such as conducting research and identifying the decision maker—and future chapters will cover more.

3. Know Your Friends and Your Enemies

As Michael Corleone said in *The Godfather II,* it is wise in coalition building to "keep your friends close and your enemies closer." Although the first step in finding allies is to research and identify potential coalition partners, it is just as important to locate and analyze your probable opponents so that you can counter their arguments.

Many times, it will not be necessary to build a coalition because one already exists. The alliance you need to lower the condominium fees imposed by a board of elected condo officers probably exists within the condo association. Your local Parent-Teacher-Student Alliance (PTSA) or teachers' organization may serve as effective coalition partners on a public school matter. Efforts to improve your city's economy or business climate could find a friendly audience at the area Chamber of Commerce. If you can unite with a group that already shares or could be inspired to share your passion for finding a solution to a problem, don't reinvent the wheel. Join forces and start working toward your goal.

However, if there is no coalition available to join, you can build your own. Some allies will be obvious. If you are concerned about traffic congestion in your neighborhood, your neighbors may feel the same way. Poor trash collection in your dormitory may be a problem that your hallmates and other residents share. You might also find willing allies in proponents of recycling. As you form your coalition, look for individuals and organizations who share your values or who have economic, political, or personal interests in addressing the problem you have identified or the solution you have proposed.

Similarly, as in professional sports drafts, where some teams choose players less for their overall talent and athleticism than for perceived team needs, you may need to select some coalition partners for their expertise. If you have created a coalition around the idea that your state's legislature has not adequately funded your college or university, find an economics professor or graduate student with special knowledge of higher education finance to give your coalition better information about how insufficient funding affects colleges and students. The coalition described in chapter 2—Fair Insurance Rates in Monroe—was very skilled at recruiting experts such as actuaries, engineers, and meteorologists to help make its case.

Effective coalition building must go deeper than finding the most superficially obvious partners. It takes curiosity and creativity to divine less predictable but potentially even more valuable allies. For example, since more than forty states offer prepaid college tuition programs for prospective students, the millions of American families who have bought prepaid contracts have a giant but unrecognized interest in ensuring the quality of their state's public institutions of higher learning. For most of the parents or grandparents who have purchased the contracts, the greatest risk is that the quality of in-state colleges or universities will decline to the point that their child or grandchild, at the time of college selection, will say, "Thank you, but I've chosen an out-of-state institution with a program and reputation superior to any in our state." University presidents looking for sources of increased financial support from state legislatures or private sources need look no further for allies than these families. On another issue, environmental leaders are forging coalitions with business leaders who understand the economic benefits of a healthy environment and religious organizations that find biblical support for protecting natural treasures.

If you're having a hard time stimulating the creative side of your brain, start by examining what individuals or groups with similar interests have done elsewhere. If your concern is funding for universities, and you want to enlist prepaid tuition contract holders, see if you have counterparts in other states who have had the same idea. Your efforts will have more credibility if you can cite precedents. If prepaid tuition contract holders in Michigan have joined in advocating greater university funding, why can't those in your state do the same?

Identifying potential enemies is almost as important as knowing your friends. Once you discover who they are and why they oppose your initiative, you can determine how to turn them around and secure their support—or at least reduce the intensity of their opposition. In some cases, your insights into the opposition may even lead to a compromise that broadens your base of support. When sizing up potential opponents, keep these questions in mind:

- Does the opposition have its facts right? If not, how do you correct those inaccuracies without alienating them and undermining a potential compromise?
- Which individual or group in your alliance is closest to the opposition? Make that coalition member the principal point of contact in an effort to find common ground.
- As you investigate and engage the opposition, remember to think long term. Although an issue may be controversial and intense at the moment, there is no reason to treat opponents with anything but respect. Respect will build goodwill that can be leveraged for your benefit. More important, it will reduce the likelihood that you will trigger a chain of old enemies to retaliate against you in the future.

4. Have a Simple, Direct Message—and Repeat, Repeat, Repeat

Because a coalition is a confederation of independent organizations and individuals, it always runs the risk of dissolving into a Babel-like collection of disassociated talking heads. You can ward off that danger by formulating a clear, coherent message that every member of the alliance abides by and repeats. The Fairlawn case study is a strong example of just how effective a clear message can be in achieving success.

In determining its public message, a coalition should:

- Decide the salient points to be made and determine how best to express them.
- Select a limited number of spokespersons.
- Provide the spokespersons with the factual information needed to make the message credible.
- Exercise discipline in transmitting a coherent message.

Commercial advertisers say that a listener must hear the same message ten times or more before it penetrates. A political message is no different. Whether members of your coalition are talking to campus newspaper reporters, submitting op-eds or letters to the editor to the newspaper, conducting interviews on the campus radio or television station, blogging or sharing information on a social networking site, giving speeches in dining halls or in fraternities or sororities, posting fliers or posters in classrooms and residence halls, or just talking about your issue with other students, they should be saying the same thing every time. Variety may be the spice of life, but in the realm of public messaging, it is the kiss of death.

5. Pick a Strong Champion to Celebrate Your Cause

Every cause needs a public leader whose personal qualities and identification with the problem provide the credibility necessary to win public support. An effective champion can seize the popular imagination and bring needed attention to a cause. The most effective champions are often charismatic citizens whom the public can relate to and will remember.

In 1955 that citizen was Rosa Parks, a seamstress in Montgomery, Alabama, who set in motion a public transportation boycott and launched the modern civil rights movement when she refused to move to the back of a segregated bus. In 2005 that citizen was Cindy Sheehan, the mother of a soldier killed in Iraq, who protested the U.S. occupation of Iraq in front of President George W. Bush's Texas ranch and became a leading figure in turning public opinion against the war. With champions like these, you may worry how anyone in your coalition could measure up.

Stop worrying. While Rosa Parks and Cindy Sheehan are now household names, few people other than their friends and families knew them when they first emerged into the public eye. And though their causes blossomed into larger-than-life crusades, each woman's initial goals were far more basic. Parks was tired of being asked to sacrifice her self-respect and dignity—and tired of being treated like a second-class citizen. Sheehan wanted a meeting with President Bush to express concern about a war in which her son had been killed. People you met in previous chapters—such as Candy Lightner and Barbara Capitman—were similarly anonymous when they started their efforts.

Sometimes, a cause finds a celebrity spokesperson to embrace its issues. If the celebrity is popular, personally motivated, and willing to devote the time, he or she can make a huge difference in building public support. Consider the example of the Save the Manatee Club. In the 1970s and 1980s the threat to Florida's unique manatee population from boat propellers and polluted waters had reached critical levels. Enter Jimmy Buffett. A Florida resident who had previously written a song with a memorable line about manatees—"Sometimes I see me as an old manatee, heading south as the waters grow colder"—Buffett had a genuine personal interest in the issue and was willing to be actively involved in promoting the cause. He had the star quality necessary to be an effective champion for the endangered manatees and was able to secure political support, as demonstrated by the

Florida Legislature's passage of a Save the Manatee license plate that raised millions of dollars for the cause. Finally, he motivated private contributors to lend their support through appeals at his Parrothead concerts and special Save the Manatee benefits.

Think carefully about who should serve as your coalition's public voice. You want someone whose personal story or rhetorical skills are likely to rouse public support. If you are protesting your university's investment of part of its endowment in companies owned by the People's Republic of China, for example, find a student leader whose family suffered human rights abuses at the hands of the Chinese government. If your goal is to reform your college's honor code, find someone who was wrongly accused or convicted in the current system. If you want to fight what you believe to be unfair tuition increases, find a spokesperson who can't afford to stay enrolled in school if the increases take effect. If you want to put an endangered species on the public's radar screen, a celebrity with Jimmy Buffett–like qualities might be the best way to attract support.

6. Be Vigilant in Keeping the Coalition Together

We all know one of the oldest stories in rock and roll: A highly acclaimed new band produces one or two hit albums and then drifts apart out of boredom. Or the albums go nowhere, and the band dissolves from the lack of initial success. Coalitions often have the same problem.

It is almost always more difficult to hold a coalition together than to assemble it in the first place. This is particularly true if the effort experiences an early defeat and then loses the will or urgency to continue. In chapter 10, you will see that an initial loss is not reason for despair—politics has few permanent defeats.

But maintaining the coalition is also important in the face of success. Politics yields few permanent victories, and few victories are ever achieved completely on the first attempt. Your cause requires constant vigilance to achieve the intended results. There are several keys to maintaining tenacity over the long run.

First, a partial achievement of the goal is not a defeat but a victory on which to build. The glass is half full. Don't celebrate a first accomplishment and then disband. Use an achievement as your springboard to even greater success.

Second, the transparent exchange of ideas and data is the lifeblood of any coalition. Don't compartmentalize or play favorites. Provide each member of the alliance with the same information—as did the organizers of the Steamboat Springs initiative in building support for educational enhancements. Solicit coalition members' thoughts and consider their ideas.

Third, lack of growth is death. A coalition that is not continuously expanding is one that is foundering. As circumstances change, through victory or defeat, some coalition members will move on to different issues. Make sure that other individuals and groups are aware of your campaign and treat them as candidates for recruitment.

Fourth, keep stakeholders engaged through an effective division of labor. If alliance members believe their efforts are critical to achieving victory, they are much more likely to maintain interest in and commitment to the cause. Tasks that can be assigned to various stakeholders include outreach to decision makers (for example, organizing letter-writing, e-mail, or telephone campaigns to persuade legislators or other officials) or even to a single decision maker, especially if a coalition member has a pre-existing relationship with that official. Other tasks could involve fundraising to ensure that the coalition has sufficient resources to spread its message, maintaining contact with the local media to generate favorable press attention, building public support, and coordinating efforts to recruit new coalition members

Fifth, organize the coalition to ensure that individual decision makers do not receive varied messages. This step is especially important when your interest in influencing a decision maker will be ongoing rather than limited to a single issue. As I noted in chapter 5, Florida's chiropractors were very skilled in matching each member of the Florida Legislature with a chiropractor from his or her district. Over time, the legislator and the chiropractor built a strong personal relationship, and when an issue affecting chiropractors arose, the legislator heard one message from one person he knew well.

CHECKLIST FOR ACTION

☐ Define the problem specifically and attract the widest possible coalition.

☐ Decide whether the coalition or the solution comes first.

☐ Know your friends and your enemies.

☐ Have a simple, direct message—and repeat, repeat, repeat.

☐ Pick a strong champion to celebrate your cause.

☐ Keep the coalition together.

Exercises

BUILDING A SUCCESSFUL COALITION

Think back to the problem you identified and researched in earlier chapters. No matter how well you have delineated and studied an issue, your chances for success will be limited unless you can build a solid coalition of allies. Take the following steps to win support for your position:

• Using a specific and broadly inclusive definition of the problem you want to solve, make a list of the groups or individuals who are most likely to be your allies. On a scale of 1 to 10, rank each in terms of its likelihood to be an effective partner.

• Identify the human resources you will need for ultimate success. Determine what kind of expertise is necessary and how you can best attract those experts to the team. For example, if you are fighting a threat to the environment, you may need scientists and economists to help you explain the danger and policy experts to help you convince regulators or legislators.

- Starting with the most likely effective partner and working to the least, contact those potential allies to determine how and by what criteria they will decide whether to support your issue. Carefully observe the context and time frame for such a decision. Many groups require regional, state, or even national approval before local units are authorized to get involved. Any such requirements will affect how and when you approach the organization you are hoping to attract.

- Write a strategy memo outlining potential allies' endorsement practices and history of political activism. In that memo, use the insights gained from chapter 5 to make recommendations about how to pursue endorsements.

- Research possible opponents to the solution you are advocating. Why do they oppose you? Is compromise a possibility? You may need to interview potential opponents to answer these questions. Prepare a report for other members of your alliance. Include recommendations for which existing coalition members—and potentially new ones—could influence those likely opponents.

8 All Your News Is Fit to Print

Engaging the Media

"If a tree falls in a forest and no one is around to hear it, does it make a sound?"

—Philosophical riddle

Case in Point: Max Rameau's Mission*

To meet Max Rameau in his faded T-shirt, cargo pants, and sandals gives lie to the typical image of a successful power broker. He has no expense account to woo media clients. In fact, he gets no salary for what he does; his "office" is an aging Honda. Yet Rameau's cell phone number is locked into the speed dial of some of South Florida's most prominent journalists. When he calls, they respond. More often than not news is the result—news presented in the way that Rameau believes helps his cause.

Which is no small thing.

Ask Rameau his mission, and he'll reply that it's Pan-Africanism—the betterment of those with African ancestry worldwide. Grandiose,

---

*My thanks to Tom Fiedler for writing this Case in Point and providing expert advice for this chapter. Tom worked for the *Miami Herald* for more than thirty years as an investigative reporter, a political columnist, editorial page editor, and executive editor from 2001 to 2007. He currently serves as dean of the Boston University College of Communication.

of course, and Rameau, who was born in Haiti and raised in Washington, D.C., and Miami, will concede that the enormity of the challenge is beyond any individual's efforts. But if he cannot embrace that universal cause, he has learned that he can have a bearing on a local piece of it. How? By inducing local government and civic leaders to take action on his behalf.

In recent years Rameau's projects have profoundly moved public policy. Ex-offenders enjoy more productive lives through a group he founded called Brothers of the Same Mind. The poor and seemingly powerless will have greater clout at the polls because he helped focus attention on problems with voter registration and on flawed voting machines that often discarded ballots. Homeless men and women, some of them displaced from old neighborhoods by pricey condos, may soon have access to housing built on what is now vacant public land.

Rameau's success comes in part from his passion for reform, especially as it will benefit the black community. But even passion would be insufficient were it not for his ability to mobilize the news media, which transforms his personal passion into public action. In short, Rameau knows how to make his cause the media's cause. And he knows that the media's cause often becomes the policy agenda for elected politicians.

"Real change occurs by putting pressure on public officials," Rameau said in an interview for this project. That pressure, he adds, comes from the media.

"People presume that when the media picks up what I am doing and covers it, that it is valid," he said. "They presume that the media has done 'due diligence' on the issue to be sure that it's legitimate."

Getting the media to pick up on the issue is the result of a carefully crafted process that takes planning, patience, timing, and, most of all, an understanding of how the news media works, Rameau said.

It typically begins with an individual problem—what he calls "the surface issue"—that is emblematic of a larger and more fundamental one affecting countless others. An example from the civil rights battles of a generation ago, Rameau said, would be the inability in many states of a black man or woman to enter into an interracial marriage.

"The story of a black man who couldn't marry a white woman didn't attract much sympathy, much less the media's interest," he said. "But when that was framed as one example of unequal rights and racial discrimination, then the public became interested."

Rameau said he began working in the late 1990s on behalf of former felons who had served their sentences and were attempting to regain their places in the community—often against deep resistance. Among the barriers they faced was a full restoration of civil rights enabling them to vote. At the same time, Rameau said, other people were being dropped from voting rolls in broad purges for no other reason than having the same name as a felon.

His efforts were largely unavailing until the 2000 presidential election in Florida, when tens of thousands of voided ballots—many of them cast in African American precincts—likely tilted the outcome to George W. Bush. "After that debacle we were able to show people that election reform was linked to democracy being threatened. Everyone could understand that, everyone could connect to the idea that if their vote is taken away, they are powerless in a democracy."

In a strategic sense, Rameau moved the issue from being a problem faced by a few individuals—former felons or people with the same names—to that of democracy at large. "The media comes in only when the broader vision has been established and when they can explain it in terms of fundamental fairness."

The mechanics of reaching the media are also important. Before approaching reporters for coverage, Rameau said he first insists on being able to answer some critical questions: What's the news here? Why should the media care? So what?

The next step is to create an event that both illustrates the central issue and provides a "hook" for the news media. One way is to stage a well-advanced press conference featuring individuals whose stories are deemed newsworthy. Even better, he said, is to provide the media with a dramatic demonstration of the issue in a way that has visual (for television and photo-journalists) and written (for newspaper journalists) appeal. He dubs such demonstrations as "street theater," which, if true to the issue, rarely fails to attract attention.

In 2007 Rameau drew local and national media when a group he organized erected a shantytown overnight on a vacant lot in the Liberty City section of Miami, a predominantly poor and African American neighborhood. The lot had previously been the site of a public housing project that had been bulldozed years before, ostensibly to be replaced by newer buildings. The replacements never came, despite a deepening crisis in low-income housing in the city.

Tipped off by Rameau, reporters flocked to the shantytown to cover its creation and to tell the stories of the homeless people who occupied it—what Rameau would consider focusing attention on the "surface issue." More important, the news media's stories put pressure on city and county leaders to address the overarching issue of low-income housing—or the lack of it—throughout the community. The reaction was almost immediate as city and county politicians scrambled to promise speedy development of that site and others like it.

"The challenge is to be able to reduce a complex argument"—making publicly owned land available to meet public needs—"to a fundamental point about fairness," the young activist said. "Then the media will come."

Max Rameau's blog is http://takebacktheland.blogspot.com.

GETTING TO KNOW THE MEDIA

To most people the news media is remote from their daily lives and as complex and inscrutable as Big Government. But while the media is often perceived as monolithic, it appears in many shapes and sizes—and each of those forms plays some role in helping to bridge the distance between colossal institutions, such as the government, the business community, the entertainment world, organized religion, and everyday citizens. At least in theory, the media exists as a kind of filter—taking in new information from a variety of governmental and private sources; straining out irrelevant data, conjecture, speculation, and rumor; and providing the public with the remaining facts as news. Your efforts to solve the challenge you have identified will be advanced if you can persuade the media to present your story to its readers, viewers, and listeners.

Although some forms of media—such as the television network C-SPAN, which provides live coverage of Congress in action—show their subject without explanation or filtering, members of the media generally gather information by investigating and scrutinizing the subjects they cover and relaying those insights to the reading or viewing public. In this sense, the news media provides a layer of accountability through which citizens can evaluate the actions of various institutions and leading individuals in those institutions. For example, scandals abound in government, business, and entertainment—some with grave consequences, others of only passing importance.

Government. Over the past forty years the American public has been rocked by several major controversies and scandals—the occupation of Iraq, the Iran-contra affair, the Vietnam War, and Watergate—where presidential administrations were found to have abused their power. The news media exposed each of these events. Had *Washington Post* reporters Bob Woodward and Carl Bernstein simply accepted the Nixon administration's explanations about Watergate, or had war correspondents not been present in Vietnam and Iraq to record the actual conditions on the ground, citizens would have had no better information about what happened in these situations than what the presidents in power told them. Watergate would not have spawned major campaign finance reforms. U.S. military forces might have remained in Vietnam for decades, with tens of thousands more soldiers killed or wounded. But because we have an active and independent news media, Americans had the information they needed to demand that elected representatives take action.

Business. When the bottom fell out of several major U.S. business entities in the early 2000s—Enron Corporation, WorldCom, Tyco, and others—shareholders lost billions of dollars in investments and thousands of workers lost their jobs and their retirement savings. The business media uncovered the corporate malfeasance that led to these financial calamities, and both investors and the public at large demanded action. Congress responded by enacting the Sarbanes-Oxley Act of 2002 to enhance corporate accountability.

Entertainment. The media is full of stories about the latest escapades of Lindsay Lohan, Britney Spears, and Paris Hilton. In August 2007 an *Entertainment Weekly* cover story proclaimed that season as the "Summer of Scandal" in Hollywood.[1] Although there is no question that the paparazzi—mostly tabloid photographers trying to take the most lurid photographs possible—are a stain on the media landscape, the mainline entertainment press performs a valuable service: It gives consumers information that helps them decide which movie star or musician is going to receive their hard-earned dollars. When former *Seinfeld* costar Michael Richards, aka Kramer, launched a racist tirade during a stand-up comedy routine in late 2006, the public responded with outrage—but only after entertainment news sources chronicled his actions. In 2005 fans of megastar Tom Cruise had more insights into his beliefs when he launched a direct-to-camera

---

[1] *Entertainment Weekly,* August 31, 2007.

assault on psychiatry, antidepressant medication, and actress Brooke Shields for her use of the latter to treat postpartum depression after the birth of her daughter.

Given the media's historic role in reporting news that can cast a less-than-favorable light on its subject matter, why would any person in his or her right mind risk any contact with reporters? The answer is simple: People who engage the media on a regular basis—public officials, candidates, business leaders, entertainers, active citizens—accept the risk of occasional negative coverage in exchange for access to a low-cost way to communicate their message to thousands or even millions of people. The media offers the same benefit to you. Whether the problem you identified after reading chapter 1 is a statewide issue (such as public education funding); a local issue (such as crime control); or a campus challenge (perhaps housing assignments), you are unlikely to persuade decision makers to address your problem unless you can rouse sufficient public attention. Nothing focuses a policymaker's attention on a problem quite like the prospect of scrutiny into his actions or inactions. Additionally, media coverage of your issue will alert potential allies and help you build the kind of coalition needed to bring about a solution to your problem.

I'll get to the question of how you can most effectively engage the media later in this chapter. First, let's look at the types of media with which you will need to interact if you want to increase public awareness about your issue. Each of these types—newspapers, television, radio, multicultural media, and the Internet—has unique advantages and disadvantages that you should keep in mind as you put together a media plan to focus awareness on the problem you have identified.

Newspapers

Newspapers have a long history of providing details of current and local events, and almost every community in the United States has a newspaper of some kind. Larger cities and towns tend to have daily newspapers (examples are the *Sacramento Bee, Denver Post, Buffalo News,* and *Charlotte Observer*). Smaller communities often have weekly newspapers. Your college or university may have both. It is important to understand the differences between the two varieties in your efforts to attract newspaper coverage. Daily newspapers typically cover large geographical areas and thus a wide range of reader interests. Your "pitch" should mirror this broad coverage. In contrast, weekly newspapers usually have a narrow audience and view the news through a more parochial and personal lens. Adjust your approach accordingly.

Whatever their differences in scope and approach, most newspapers are organized along similar lines. A publisher has overall command, with ultimate oversight over the three main elements of the newspaper. The business side is primarily responsible for generating revenues through newspaper circulation and advertisement sales, as well as for managing costs to maintain a profitable and thus sustainable news organization. The news side consists of editors and reporters who produce news articles. The editorial side conveys the newspaper's opinion on relevant issues of the day. For your purposes, you need be concerned only with the news and editorial functions.

The news staff generally has two types of personnel: reporters, who investigate and write the news stories that appear in the newspaper, and editors, who decide which subjects the newspaper will cover and carefully review and revise the articles that reporters submit for publication. Reporters are organized into "beats." For example, at your daily newspaper, one reporter may be assigned to the police beat, to cover crime; another reporter has the schools beat and is responsible for education coverage; yet another follows municipal government on the City Hall beat; and so on. Pay close attention to which reporters are assigned to the various beats at your college or local newspaper: The reporter who covers your issue can be a valuable ally in introducing your cause to a wider audience.

When you begin your efforts to attract newspaper coverage of your issue, you will first approach a reporter who can produce a news story. But newspapers also have editorial boards that publish pieces giving the newspaper's stance on a particular subject (so-called editorials) and also pieces from professional columnists who analyze and comment on local, national, or international news. Individuals are also given a chance to publish their own opinions (in op-ed pieces or letters to the editor). A newspaper's reporting staff and editorial board are separate and independent entities, a structure that you can use to generate both news and editorial coverage of your initiative.

As you strategize about your media plan, be mindful of the changing influence of newspaper coverage and its relative advantages and disadvantages as a news source. For most of American history, newspapers have been the dominant form of political and governmental media in the United States. In decades past, citizens who wanted to reach policymakers through the press had no choice but to work through newspaper reporters. But times have changed. The advent of broadcast news in the mid-twentieth century and its rapid expansion since then, as well as the more recent explosion of the Internet as a source of news and information, have changed the role of daily and weekly newspapers.

According to the 2008 biennial Pew Research Center for the People and the Press News Consumption Survey, only 34 percent of those polled had read a daily newspaper the day before the survey—down from 40 percent just two years before and way down from 58 percent in February 1994.[2] Although newspapers have recovered a small portion of their lost audience by establishing Internet sites offering online news, broadcast sources still have an advantage. In the Pew survey, 57 percent of those surveyed reported having watched television news the day before.

---

[2] Pew Research Center for the People and the Press, "2008 News Consumption and Believability Study," August 17, 2008, http://people-press.org/reports/pdf/444.pdf.

The shift from print to broadcast and online sources has caused economic havoc in the newspaper industry. As former readers move to new sources of information, advertisers have followed them and significantly reduced their newspaper-based marketing. The global economic crisis of 2008 and 2009 accelerated this trend. As a result, newspapers have suffered huge reductions in revenue. In December 2008 the Tribune Company—which at the time owned eight metropolitan newspapers including the *Chicago Tribune, Baltimore Sun, Los Angeles Times, Orlando Sentinel, South Florida Sun–Sentinel,* and *Hartford Courant*—filed for federal bankruptcy protection. One month later the *Minneapolis Star–Tribune* did the same, and the *Seattle Post-Intelligencer* was put up for sale. In March 2009 the *Detroit Free Press* and *Detroit News* ceased personal home delivery of newspapers except on Thursdays, Fridays, and Sundays. Even the *New York Times,* which has long been the gold standard for daily newspapers, announced in early 2009 that it was accepting a $250 million loan from Mexican billionaire Carlos Slim Helù and mortgaging its Manhattan headquarters for up to $225 million as it grappled with debt exceeding $1 billion. In an effort to cut costs, many daily newspaper chains have either bought out or laid off large numbers of reporters and other news employees. Daily newspaper stories are increasingly generated not by local reporters but by national and statewide news sources, such as Associated Press (www.ap.org), Reuters (www.reuters.com), and Bloomberg News (www.Bloomberg.com).

Despite these financial troubles, the newspaper industry continues to look for new business models that will help daily print journalism survive. We should all hope they flourish, because newspapers offer great advantages to you in communicating your citizen message. The first is credibility. Newspapers are often seen as the medium most likely to "get it right" in terms of accuracy of reporting and fairness to their subjects. A comprehensive newspaper account will help to validate your initiative in the eyes of decision makers, possible coalition partners, and other reporters.

Another advantage is breadth of coverage. Unlike television and radio reporters, who may have two to three minutes to report a story, newspaper reporters have comparatively more room to provide a comprehensive account of the news item or issue in question. Although the facts you gather in support of your initiative will be helpful to any reporter, you are much more likely to see them published in a newspaper than aired by the broadcast media. Additionally, newspapers often shape other types of news coverage. Broadcast news directors often base their decisions on where to send their reporters on national and local newspaper headlines. A front-page story can produce a ripple effect across other media outlets in your community.

At your college or university the daily or weekly newspaper may be your primary or even exclusive source of campus news. You need to establish strong relationships with both reporters and editorial board members. But chances are good that since your fellow students are probably using television, radio, or the Internet to download state, national, and international news, they are also using those sources to learn about university issues.

Television

Television is the dominant source of news around the globe—the 800-pound gorilla of the media world. Its dominance cuts across socioeconomic lines. In the 2008 Pew survey, where 57 percent of those surveyed had used television as a source of news on the previous day, the number was even higher among certain demographic groups—59 percent of nonwhite Americans, including 68 percent of African Americans, and nearly 75 percent of people over the age of sixty-five. Families earning less than $30,000 annually were almost as likely to watch television news as were those making more than $100,000. College graduates and high school dropouts watched in relatively equal measure.

But television, like the media in general, is not monolithic. It consists of several levels of which you need to be aware as you consider how to put your issue in the spotlight. The first level, and the one with which you are most likely to engage, is local television news (which includes campus television programming). Local television stations are referred to as network affiliates when they are affiliated with one of the national television networks (PBS, NBC, ABC, CBS, Fox, and CW). Some local stations are independent with no network affiliation.

Local TV news is best known for half-hour newscasts—usually aired sometime between 5:00 p.m. and 6:30 p.m. and then again between 10:00 p.m. and 11:30 p.m—which provide summaries of the day's local news, weather, and sports. Although local television stations in big cities have larger staffs, almost every local station has a news director, who oversees the news operation; several news anchors, who present the news on set to the viewing public; news reporters, who cover general assignments; and an assignment editor, who directs news reporters to follow up on news tips or cover planned press events.

You are watching national network news if anchors such as Charles Gibson, Brian Williams, or Katie Couric are presenting the day's stories. Unless the problem you have identified has broad, national significance, and has attracted intense interest in Congress or at the White House, you will probably not work with them in airing your initiative.

Cable news is an increasingly popular form of television news coverage. Its mention immediately brings to mind Cable News Network (CNN), Fox News Channel (FNC), and Microsoft/NBC (MSNBC), but those national cable stations present the same problem as national network news. Unless your initiative has controversial national implications, they probably will not broadcast your story. You face another problem in the fact that your name is not that of a celebrity or controversial figure.

However, more and more local cable systems are sponsoring "Headline News" style channels that provide local and regional news, weather, traffic, and sports twenty-four hours a day, seven days a week. For example, Bright House Networks in the Tampa Bay area offers Bay News 9 (www.baynews9.com/Home.html) to its cable subscribers in a six-county region. In the Orlando area, Central Florida News 13—"All Local, All the Time"—performs the same service (www.cfnews13.com). Given the amount of airtime local cable stations have to fill, your issue might be of interest to a similar station if one exists in your community.

As with newspapers, television news offers its own set of advantages and challenges. The scope of television viewership is a major plus. Since Americans overwhelmingly prefer television as a news source, there is no better way to reach a large audience. Television news penetrates almost every household in the nation, including those in your community where citizens live who can bring pressure to bear on decision makers. The more your issue is aired and discussed, the more likely you are to bring about positive action.

Although television remains the best way to communicate with a mass audience, that reach comes with trade-offs in the form of reduced depth and credibility. With limited time available (after commercials, twenty-two to twenty-three minutes of a thirty-minute broadcast), local television reports rarely last more than two or three minutes. That is hardly enough time to introduce, never mind fully present, the challenge you have identified and the solutions you are proposing. The 24/7 local cable stations offer another opportunity for broadcast coverage, but they also present news according to a strict format that does not usually allow in-depth reporting. Local TV stations are notorious for prioritizing stories about murder and mayhem over other subject matter—hence the saying, "If it bleeds, it leads." Cable news has come under increased scrutiny for its breathless coverage of celebrity scandal, and what news it does show is sometimes tainted by allegations of bias (for example, the charges that Fox News Channel is too conservative and CNN is too liberal).

If your campus or local community has one or more television stations that provide news coverage, make an effort to build relationships with each station's news director and key reporters. Like Max Rameau, and using the suggestions in this chapter, convince them that your citizen initiative deserves television coverage. Remember that they don't have the airtime to provide all of the details; it's your job to help them craft stories that can be told in 180 seconds or less.

Radio

Radio may seem an anachronism—a medium that once filled the role that television now plays in our media culture. Recent statistics don't help that impression. According to the 2008 Pew survey, only 35 percent of those interviewed had listened to the radio for news the day before they were polled. That number is substantially down from a 49 percent response in a similar 1998 survey. However, radio remains a potent source of news and commentary. With Americans spending significant time in their cars, millions listen to radio each day. Radio news generally falls into three categories. NPR (National Public Radio); national and state radio news networks; and national, state, and local radio news and talk shows.

The first category, NPR (www.npr.org), provides a variety of programming, including the drive-time national news shows "Morning Edition" and "All Things Considered." In 2008 nearly 25 percent of Americans reported listening regularly or semiregularly to NPR and its network of affiliate stations across the nation. More important for your purposes, individual NPR affiliates in metropolitan areas are often associated with a college or university and are sometimes located on campus. These local NPR stations often provide a steady diet of regional news updates throughout the day. They may give you an opportunity to have your issue aired if you communicate with the station's news director or news reporters.

The second radio news category consists of national and state radio networks that provide regular news updates throughout the programming day for stations that pay for their services. If you listen to your favorite FM station and hear a brief news report at the top or middle of the hour from ABC Radio News or Florida News Network, you are hearing one of these quick national or state news broadcasts. As is the case with network television news, you are unlikely to interact with these types of radio news unless your issue is controversial or of statewide interest.

But the radio news landscape has increasingly come to be defined by the third category: news/talk networks and programs. In the past two decades, national talk show hosts, such as Rush Limbaugh, Neal Boortz, Glenn Beck, and Michael Savage, who present consistently right-wing views, have become household names. Talk show hosts on the other side politically include Ed Schultz, Bill Press, and Stephanie Miller. Local radio news/talk shows have sprung up in the image of these national programs in media markets across the country. Although talk radio no longer has the audience it did in the mid-1990s, when 45–50 percent of Americans regularly or sometimes listened, the 2008 Pew survey showed the regular or sometimes listenership at 40 percent. Any news source heard at least some of the time by four of every ten Americans is worth your time.

Although the programs in this medium do not present the news so much as they comment on it, they attract millions of listeners who in effect use the shows as a source of news. Whether your local radio news/talk station is based on campus or covers the entire local community, you can use it to shape discussion of your issue once it has been introduced into the public arena.

Regardless of the form of radio that is appropriate for your campaign, keep in mind that it has its own pluses and minuses as an information source. Its wide scope is a major advantage. However, it is not always ideal, especially in terms of reach, depth, and credibility. As evidenced by the 2008 Pew survey, radio faces a declining share of the overall news market. Like television, it has limited time available to give airtime to the problem you have identified and the solutions you are proposing. Unless you can convince your local NPR affiliate to produce a comprehensive feature story on your subject, your chances of extensive radio coverage are slim. Finally, although NPR and its affiliates and other national and state public radio networks win high marks for credibility, news/talk programs do not because many come with an inherent political bias.

As you organize the media effort for your initiative, plan to visit your campus radio station, local NPR affiliate, and any talk radio stations in your area and make contact with key reporters, anchors, and hosts. See if your community or state has a radio news station or network not affiliated with NPR that may provide coverage of your initiative. Finally, build a team of supporters who can call into local talk radio shows and create buzz about your concern. If you can find a talk radio host who has particular influence with the policymakers you want to influence—such as a popular conservative to whom Republican lawmakers listen—you may want to see if you can convince that host to champion your cause on air.

Multicultural Media

Increasingly, our nation's unique diversity is reflected in the news media. Throughout the United States, Hispanic, African American, and other multicultural newspapers, radio stations, television stations, and Web sites are integral members of the media. In New York, Los Angeles, Houston, Miami, Chicago, and other major media markets, Spanish-language television and radio stations—either independent or affiliated with a major network such as Telemundo or Univision—consistently have some of the largest audiences and highest ratings. African American networks like Black Entertainment Television and local African American newspapers and broadcast stations also hold significant sway. In some areas, other groups (for example, Haitian Americans in South Florida) have media outlets of their own in which they can discuss community issues.

If your community enjoys this kind of media diversity, include these news sources on your target list. Analyze your issue to determine if it will particularly affect the community you are targeting, and build relationships with those newspapers and stations. Your outreach will make a difference with key segments of the overall audience you hope to reach.

The Internet and Blogs

At the time of the Pew survey in 2008, the Internet still paled as a news source compared with newspapers, television, and radio. According to the poll, 29 percent of those surveyed received news online on the day prior to the poll. While that is a smaller percentage than for daily print or broadcast sources, the real story in these numbers is the increased use of online news. From 1998 to 2008 the number of people in the general public who went online for news at least three times a week increased from 13 percent to 37 percent. Since the 2006 version of the biennial Pew survey, the number of Americans going online for news daily increased approximately one-third. As more and more people, especially younger people, use Internet search engines to find news stories, spend time on blogs to comment on the news, and read online newspaper sites, the Internet continues to grow as a news source.

The stunning decline of the newspaper industry has heightened the influence of online news. Most newspapers are looking for profitable ways to transition from the traditional printed edition—which comes with huge operating costs in the form of printing presses and employees required to operate the machinery—to a sleeker, more cost-effective online model. Although the shift from printed to online articles will not significantly change your basic approach to newspaper reporters, it may mean that fewer reporters are still employed at your local daily and available to cover your initiative. You'll have to work harder and be more creative to attract their interest. On the other hand, the change in model means that news sources like AP, Reuters, and Bloomberg News will have even more influence than they do now. Even if your issue is a campus or local community matter, you may need to engage statewide news sources more than you would have during the heyday of newspapers.

The most profound revolution in the use of Internet sources for news, however, is the blog. Until the mid-2000s blogs were few and far between. Now blogs are everywhere. Most follow the same format: A blogger posts a story or opinion on a subject and invites fellow bloggers to respond with comment. This invitation usually leads to a stream of back-and-forth on the issue posted and may even produce online discussion of other subjects.

Blogs are important to your initiative for three reasons. First, the sheer number of blogs means that bloggers are hungry to report stories like yours. Second, as newspapers reduce their reporting staffs, blogs are assuming more of the responsibility for original reporting, some of which the traditional press later picks up as newsworthy. Third, blogs were designed in a way to attract the attention of Web search engines. If someone searches Google, Yahoo, or another search engine for a particular issue, he or she will quickly encounter blogs that reference that issue.

Blogs that primarily discuss government or politics fall into three main categories. Some are derived from existing news media outlets. Examples are the *Washington Post*'s political news blog "The Fix" (http://blog.washingtonpost.com/thefix), the *St. Petersburg Times*'s "Buzz Blog" (http://blogs.tampabay.com/buzz), the *Chicago Tribune*'s "The Swamp"(www.swamppolitics.com/news/politics/blog), the *New York Times*'s "The Caucus" (http://the caucus.blogs.nytimes.com), and the *Wall Street Journal*'s "Capital Journal" (http://blogs.wsj.com/capitaljournal). For these types of blogs, reporters post news stories, videos, and opinion columns and encourage reaction from their audiences. Other newspapers across the nation, possibly including the one you read, host similar news blogs.

Others are ideologically based. For example, the left-leaning Daily Kos (www.DailyKos.com) advertises itself as a "daily weblog with political analysis of US current events from a political perspective." RedState (www.redstate.com) calls itself a center-of-right blog. Your local community undoubtedly has several blogs from a variety of ideological perspectives that discuss the news of the day.

Engaging these blogs is more about becoming a part of their community. Most of the ideological sites allow users to create "diaries," or individualized blogs. Create one and engage directly. Post comments and participate in the existing discussion. Then, when you have a news story that you want Daily Kos or RedState or another blog to cover, the goodwill you have established may help your pitch succeed. Finally, keep in mind that most ideological bloggers are half-journalist, half-activist. Conduct research and identify those bloggers who are already talking about your issue or a related issue. If they're already active in your space, you should be able to persuade them to discuss your initiative.

Other blogs are issue oriented, focusing their attention on a single policy matter or related set of issues. For example, the Health Care Blog (www.thehealthcareblog.com) defines itself as "Everything you ever wanted to know about health care but were afraid to ask." The Center for Rural Affairs, which describes itself as "a private, non-profit organization that is working to strengthen small businesses, family farms and ranches, and rural communities," hosts an agriculture-related blog at http://cfra.blogspot.com.

Even more so than talk radio, blogs are an extremely accessible information source: Anyone with a computer and Internet access can contribute to a blog discussion. This lack of filters (such as reporters, editorial writers, radio call screeners, and the like) helps to explain why blogs are an increasingly popular way of sharing information. But the same accessibility also generates concerns about their reliability. Because traditional reporters have to verify information before they print or air it, the printed or televised news is often seen as much more likely to be accurate. On a blog, even if the original post is reliable, the resulting commentary is not always perceived to be dependable. However, many of the most widely read and established blogs take their credibility very seriously. They have their own editorial processes, writers, and retraction policies. On some of the major blogs, for example, writers are required to strike through mistakes and make corrections on the original story.

Policymakers are increasingly paying attention to blogs as a way to keep their finger on the pulse of public opinion. Although bloggers are not yet a representative sample of the entire community, they tend to be more active in public affairs than is the average citizen. A blogger is more likely to provide small donations to political campaigns, send e-mails to local elected officials, stoke the fires of a controversial issue, and send out mass communications over the Internet.

Don't ignore the blog culture as you seek to raise awareness about your initiative. Take advantage of its growing influence by establishing your own blog about the problem you are trying to solve. Visit other blogs to create sympathetic diaries, encourage discussion about your issue, and direct bloggers to your blog. In so doing, you may help to build a core of committed online allies who can help spread the word about your challenge and proposed solutions.

PERSUADING THE PRESS: DESIGNING AND IMPLEMENTING YOUR MEDIA PLAN

In 2007 a Pew Research Center survey on public perceptions of the press found that, by 69 percent to 23 percent, Americans believed that the news media is "often influenced by powerful people and organizations," rather than being "pretty independent." [3] In other words, the news media appears to most Americans to be a tool available primarily to the elite and the powerful, not the champion of ordinary people with their everyday concerns.

---

[3] Ibid., "Views of Press Values and Performance, 1985–2007," August 9, 2007, http://people-press.org/reports/pdf/348.pdf.

Unfortunate as it may be, there is some basis for this view, despite the fact that most journalists want to give a voice to the powerless and stand ready to take up worthy causes. To repeat that well-worn phrase, what we have here is a failure to communicate.

As the Pew survey shows, the major news media all too often fails to show a welcoming face to outsiders. But contrary to that perception, the media is neither impenetrable nor a tool exclusively of the elite. With some basic planning and a better understanding of how to attract press interest, you can use the media to advance your citizen agenda and promote solutions to the challenges you have identified. Try the following steps to engage the attention of the media.

1. Know Your Goals, Message, and Media Audience

The worst possible way to engage the media is a backward "Fire . . . Ready . . . Aim" approach. Before you even begin to think about which reporters you might contact, you need to decide how you want the media coverage to benefit your cause. Are you simply trying to bring an issue to light because a decision maker is keeping it in the dark? Are you trying to sway administrators or legislators in advance of an important decision or vote? Do you want to identify others who share your concerns and build a strong coalition? Is your goal to alert the general public about a problem that they should be aware of but are not? Do you hope to build support for a particular piece of legislation that would solve your problem? Are you belatedly attempting to rebut the public arguments your opponent has already made? Think carefully about what you want your media campaign to accomplish, and stay focused on that goal in all of your upcoming interactions with the media.

But simply articulating a media goal is not sufficient. You must also develop a basic message, one that can be summarized in a single sentence. For example, assume that a wave of violent night-time muggings has spread through your college community and students are afraid to walk through campus after dark.

Angered by what you feel is a lackadaisical response from the administration and local authorities, you want to use the media to stir public outrage and force action. Your every interaction with the media—whether through newspapers, television, radio, or the Internet—must drive home the same message: The crime spree has put students, faculty, staff, and community members who walk across campus at risk, and the university administration and local law enforcement officials must eliminate the danger.

After you develop your basic message, consider which members of the media are best suited to help you convey it. Marshall McLuhan, who many have called the father of the electronic age, explained this conceptualization in a now-famous phrase: "The medium is the message." Some stories are visual in nature—a house crushed by a fallen tree, a hurricane battering a beach, a SWAT team storming a suspected crack den, a rat-infested government apartment complex. These stories make compelling television.

However, other important stories lack a live, visual dimension. For example, it may be hard for television to present a comprehensive account of a major government decision or conduct an investigative report into government misspending. These stories could be page-one features in your newspaper, but they will do little to excite a television viewer's interest. How is your story best told? Is it visual? If so, a television journalist is likely to be receptive to doing that story. On the other hand, if telling your story requires a reporter to dig through government records or privately interview many people who don't want public attention, it may be best suited for the newspaper or the Internet.

2. Do Your Homework

Once you have settled on a message and analyzed which medium—it could be more that one—will help you effectively communicate that message, identify specific reporters who can best help you talk to the public at large.

For example, if you have decided to target print sources, try to match reporters with their beats so that you can identify those who are likely to be most receptive to your concerns. Many newspapers, from national dailies to your campus newspaper, now list reporters and their beats on the paper's Internet site. If you can't find them there, look for recent articles on your issue and identify the reporter assigned to that beat by looking for the byline. If all else fails, telephone the newspaper's newsroom and simply ask which reporter is assigned to your beat. You can repeat the same process to discover which member of the newspaper's editorial staff is responsible for writing about your issue.

The set-up for broadcast reporters is similar, although only a few are as highly specialized as their print counterparts. Moreover, most television and radio stations do not have nearly enough news personnel to staff a full beat system. In most cases, you'll want to start with the news director or assignment editor and have that person guide you to the correct reporter. If your local television stations are among the few that still broadcast editorials—a station's position on an issue usually presented by its general manager or editorial director—contact the stations and arrange a meeting with the appropriate personnel. As for the Internet, you may find Web-based publications as well as local, state, and perhaps even national blogs that write about your issue.

3. Walk a Mile in the Media's Shoes

After you have identified the reporter (or reporters) you want to approach, take time to wire yourself into their brains before you make contact. Put yourself in the place of a journalist who is learning about your issue for the first time. Ask these questions: What makes this a story of community interest? How would I tell it? Why is this newsworthy? Why should other people care? If you can't answer these issues on your own, you're going to have a hard time convincing a reporter that your story is news.

Don't limit yourself to questions a generic journalist might ask. Review this particular reporter's previous stories on the subject and see if you can detect a common thread. For example, if your goal is to expose a property insurance company that is illegally denying claims, it would help to know if the reporter you want to target has previously investigated insurance claims practices of any kind. What has he or she written about property insurance carriers?

If you have thought through the general and specific interests in your story, you're ready to approach the reporters who can help you convey your message to the public. But don't go empty-handed. Instead, rely on a phrase that is a fundamental precept of journalism: "Show me; don't tell me." To focus the news media's attention on your issue, gather supporting information, line up contacts, or provide helpful leads. The more tangible information you can provide, the more likely the reporter will write your story. For example, in the case of the campus safety issue mentioned earlier, if you were able to put the reporter in touch with robbery victims who could describe their harrowing experiences, and also provided minutes from administration meetings that demonstrated a heel-dragging response, you would enhance the reporter's interest in the issue.

Don't wait until you're about to engage the media to collect supporting information. As you employ the research methods described in chapter 2, consider how the data you have already gathered might be useful to a reporter. But don't just focus on the past—envision and pursue new lines of research that could result in positive press coverage.

Especially when you are working with television reporters, it helps to take this proactive approach one step further and create the powerful visual images they need to tell your story. You should not manufacture news. But it makes sense to present your concerns in a setting that is visually compelling. For example, if you want to focus attention on your state's chronic underfunding of its public universities, bring television reporters to campus so that they can film and talk with students forced to stand in overcrowded lecture halls. Walk them to the registrar's office and introduce them to seniors frantic with worry because the courses they need to graduate aren't being offered.

Finally, as you stick carefully to your basic message, think about which applications of that message might catch a reporter's interest. The media values the good of the many over the good of the few—or of the one—and reporters are most likely to take up the causes of people to whom most others in their audience can relate. They are not inclined to act as an advocate for an individual whose concerns aren't widely shared by others. For example, a job seeker who loses out to a rival isn't likely to persuade a TV reporter to make that story the subject of the evening news. But if that job seeker was rejected because of his race and not his qualifications—and there is evidence to that effect—that's newsworthy. Suddenly this isn't about one person's grievance; it's a matter of group discrimination, which most people won't tolerate.

4. Make Contact

Become a person to journalists, not just the faceless author of a text message or a voice mail. Once you've identified the reporters most likely to be interested in your issue, find a way to communicate directly with them. An e-mail may crack the door, but barely. A phone conversation is better, perhaps followed by an e-mail. Best of all is a face-to-face meeting followed by an e-mail summarizing your key points.

Don't stop with reporters. Find out who oversees the reporters who cover the subject area in which you're interested. In many newspapers the names and contact information for supervising editors are printed on the front page of the relevant sections. Again, send an e-mail, make a phone call or, if possible, schedule an in-person appointment. Remember to be specific about the subject and emphasize why you believe your story is newsworthy. Building independent relationships with editors is important for another reason: Individual reporters come and go, frequently moving from beat to beat. Editors are more likely to stay in one place and can be the key to an ongoing relationship.

As you discovered in chapter 6, timing is everything—and that precept is no less true when you are dealing with reporters. The pace of a news reporter's day generally accelerates as the day goes on. So if you want to make initial contact with a reporter, do it during a "slow" part of the day. For most reporters, the later in the day it is, the more hectic things become as deadlines close in for the evening television news, the drive-home radio, or the morning newspaper. Think also in terms of when your story would receive the most (or least) attention. Weekday news will normally have a larger audience than weekend coverage. Because readership, viewership, and listenership have traditionally been down at the end of the week, government officials and companies often release bad news late on Friday. Timing is also a question of context. If your concern is that the university has not allocated enough football tickets to students, you may want to raise that issue with the news media in the week before the season starts.

If a reporter is not able to cover your initiative right away, don't worry. Be patient. Some matters require lengthy investigation. For other matters, at least in the opinion of the news media, the timing isn't right for your story to be told. This example may sound familiar: Some citizens warned for years that punch-card ballot machines disenfranchised many voters in every election. They had the data and the evidence to back up their allegations and to support their demands for new machines. But only when the result in the 2000 presidential election was too close to call in Florida were those machines discredited and ultimately replaced.

5. Take Multiple Bites at the Apple

Even when a reporter has written or broadcast your story, don't consider your work done. That initial media coverage is usually just a launching pad for additional press interest. When the daily newspaper publishes a story about your initiative, immediately contact local radio and television stations and interested Internet sources and blogs to provide copies of the article. If you can also provide them with facts, people to interview, and compelling audio and visual depictions of your message, your story may start off in the morning papers and end up on the evening news and all over the Internet. The reverse is also true. In this era of new media, your first hit may occur on a blog before more traditional sources pick up the story.

Additionally, don't forget that media outlets often offer more than one avenue to print coverage. Once your story becomes news, ask for a meeting with the editorial writer responsible for the issue. Persuade him or her that the newspaper should adopt your position as its own. If you are successful, the paper may produce a favorable editorial that validates your cause as you seek allies, funding, and even more media attention. Similarly, contact your local TV stations if they still broadcast editorials.

Finally, take advantage of opportunities to argue your case using your own words. In addition to publishing the opinions of syndicated columnists (writers like George Will, David Broder, and Ellen Goodman) whose work appears in newspapers across the nation and world, and local columnists who write primarily for a particular newspaper, newspaper editorial pages often reserve space for op-ed pieces where policymakers, community leaders, and everyday citizens can express their views on a particular issue— usually in about 600 words. Once your initiative has become a news story, a published op-ed in which you argue your position can not only extend the life of the story but also generate public discussion. Conversely, if reporters have not yet paid significant attention to your cause or issue, an op-ed can help you present it to the public directly. If the newspaper won't publish your op-ed, drop down to the smaller size (150–300 words) letter to the editor to express your views.

6. Stay Credible at All Costs

Never exaggerate, lie, or deceive, even by omission. Chances are that a good journalist will discover the deception and your credibility will be forever damaged. When that happens, your chances of engaging the media on this or any other issue will be gone.

Additionally, remember that you are pursuing this initiative to be a good citizen, not to supplement your income. News isn't for sale. Ask for nothing in return, even if your story has potential as a blockbuster. Reputable journalists will not pay for news. Those that do pay, such as supermarket tabloids, generally have little credibility with the public, just as a paid police snitch has little credibility with a jury. The converse of this is to never offer to pay or to provide gifts to a journalist in exchange for reporting on your issue. A reputable journalist will consider such offers— even if made in good faith—as tantamount to bribes.

7. Distribute Your Own Message

Traditional media outlets serve as a filter of sorts between news-makers and the general public. As discussed earlier in this chapter, the Internet has given citizens more direct access to making, reporting, and reacting to news than at any other time in history. Take advantage of these unique opportunities. Box 8-1 explains how you can communicate directly with supporters and the general public through your own Web site and Internet program.

Tips from the Pros: Putting Your Grassroots Campaign on the Internet

JOSH KOSTER

1. *Forget the hype.* Most news reports about the use of the Internet in politics focus on the exceptions to the rule—Howard Dean, Ron Paul, Barack Obama, and other high-profile candidates whose fame allowed them to use the Internet in revolutionary ways. Don't try to replicate those efforts as you establish your own Internet program. You can't. Instead, your goal should be to use the Internet to make your campaign or initiative more efficient—giving you faster research, better fundraising, and enhanced communications capabilities. Period. If you are hell-bent on trying all sorts of "new approaches" or discovering the next big innovation, you will lose sight of your real needs and probably fail in your campaign.

2. *Make your Web site a hub for supporters.* Citizens who visit campaign Web sites tend to be politically engaged in general or personally engaged with your initiative. Either way you need to communicate with them throughout your campaign and encourage them to share those messages with others. Design every part of your Web site with the goal of enticing would-be supporters to provide contact information so that you can keep them engaged. In other words, make sure that your e-mail sign-up form and action items (volunteer, donate, or host) are big, noticeable, above the fold, and on every single page.

3. *Remember that good content matters.* Give Web site visitors something worthwhile to read. This means using eye-catching graphics and putting effort into your issue positions from the first time you draft them. Invest in a Web site that can be easily updated so that your campaign team can change the site and keep visitors coming back to see new content.

4. *Promote your Web site.* This isn't *Field of Dreams*. Even if you build it, there is no guarantee they will come. The Internet is a big place, and your job is to make sure people find the site. Ask every

blogger who writes a good story about your initiative to add a link to the site. Post links in the comments fields of articles related to your campaign. Purchase cost-effective Internet advertisements to drive traffic to the site. Instruct your candidate or spokespeople to hype the Web site at every public appearance.

5. *Build good lists.* The Internet provides users with unprecedented opportunities to communicate with others. But the key word is *others.* Your campaign can have the best message ever crafted, but it won't matter if you fail to build a constantly expanding list of e-mail addresses to receive that message. Make this an all-hands-on-deck operation. Instruct your fundraisers to collect e-mail addresses from donors and potential donors. Put your field organizers in charge of doing the same with volunteers. Ask your coalition partners to gather e-mails from their networks. As more and more people learn about your initiative, visit your Web site, and take an interest in your cause, they will encourage others to do so—and your e-mail list will grow even more.

6. *Respect your e-mail subscribers.* Communicate with subscribers only when you have something worthwhile to report or have a significant request to make. Nobody likes frivolous or pointless e-mails; so yours had better be important. Never, ever, under any circumstances, send an e-mail because it has been a long time since you last sent one.

7. *Invest in a good bulk e-mail program.* These programs are dirt cheap and help your communications avoid spam filters. The better bulk-mail programs also provide valuable information—the number of intended recipients who opened your e-mails, clicked on links in your e-mail, and forwarded your e-mail. These metrics help you determine which issues motivated your supporters the most and which actions you should ask them to take.

Josh Koster is the managing partner at Chong Designs LLC (www.chongde signs.com), a new-media firm based in Washington, D.C., that specializes in digital marketing and brand management. He has consulted for a presidential campaign, House and Senate races, numerous local and municipal campaigns, and a ballot initiative as well as for companies and nonprofits.

CHECKLIST FOR ACTION

- ☐ Know your goals, message, and media audience.
- ☐ Do your homework.
- ☐ Walk a mile in the media's shoes.
- ☐ Make contact.
- ☐ Take multiple bites at the apple.
- ☐ Stay credible at all costs.
- ☐ Distribute your own message.

Exercises

MEDIA SAVVY

Identify a citizen in your community (college campus, town, county, or state) who has advanced her policy goals through effective interaction with the media. Interview her and determine how she persuaded newspaper, broadcast, or Internet reporters to take an interest in her issue, and how that engagement has affected her initiative. Present your findings in class.

THE NEWS IN PRINT

Call a local newspaper editorial writer to visit your class and explain what influences the newspaper's editorial opinions. Ask him how the newspaper determines which op-eds and letters to the editor to publish.

Following his presentation, write an op-ed (no more than 600 words) arguing the case for your citizen initiative and submit it to the newspaper for consideration. Your professor might provide extra credit if the op-ed appears in print.

THE MESSAGE AND THE BEAT

Consider the problem you identified early in our work together. How could media attention help to solve that problem? Develop a basic message about the challenge that you want the general public to understand. Which of the media—print, television, radio, or Internet—are best suited to help you convey that message and why? Be prepared to discuss.

For whatever issue you have chosen, identify the beat reporter for your campus newspaper (if applicable) and for the local daily or weekly newspaper. Call the campus radio station, the local NPR affiliate, and each of the local television and radio stations and determine the name and contact information for their respective news directors, assignment editors, and key reporters. Determine if local, state, or national bloggers or other Internet outlets are discussing the issue online.

9

The Price of Progress

Finding the Resources to Support Your Initiative

"Money is a terrible master but an excellent servant."

—P. T. Barnum

Case in Point: Nothing But Nets

The campaign to save children in Africa started in Italy with a writer from Denver. Rick Reilly, best known for his wry back-page *Sports Illustrated* columns, had found an activity even more exhausting than the sports he usually covered: shopping alongside Venetian canals with his teenage daughter. At the end of that tourist marathon, Reilly returned to his hotel room and collapsed on his bed, with only enough strength to turn on television and tune into a British Broadcasting Company documentary on malaria in Africa. Expecting to be asleep within seconds, Reilly was instead captivated by a single sentence: "Up to 3,000 children die needlessly each day of malaria—and all they need is a net."

Reilly's mind immediately flashed to all of the sports that use nets: tennis, basketball, soccer, hockey, and lacrosse. He envisioned Wimbledon finalists shaking hands across the net. He saw blaring red sirens when hockey pucks slipped past the goalie into the net. He saw Michael Jordan launching a perfect shot ending with a swish. And then it hit him: What the children of Africa needed was nothing but nets.

Before rushing to his keyboard, Reilly did some research. He found that malaria killed between one and three million people each year, primarily in Africa. A child somewhere in the world died of malaria every thirty seconds. Scientists had developed a new device that reduced the incidence of malaria by 50 percent or more: It was an inexpensive insecticide-treated net, easily installed over a bed, and it killed or repelled mosquitoes for three to five years.

In April 2006 Reilly located an organization already deeply involved in reducing the malaria toll: the United Nations Foundation, which had been established in 1998 with money donated by CNN founder Ted Turner. Since 2001 the UN Foundation had collaborated with five private organizations and the U.S. government to raise and distribute $29 million to fight malaria. But it had not found similar success with the public at large. In partnership with Reilly, the UN Foundation created a new fundraising entity called Nothing But Nets. Through the Foundation's fast Web site—it could be navigated in forty-one seconds—people could make donations for insecticidal bed nets quickly and easily. Even better, the UN Foundation agreed to purchase and coordinate delivery of all the nets funded by Internet contributions. In other words, 100 percent of all donations would go straight to saving lives. All each donor had to do was visit the site, complete a short contribution form, enter a credit card number or send a check to the UN Foundation, and more nets were on their way to Africa.

Nothing But Nets was unveiled to the world in Reilly's column on May 6, 2006. He urged readers to skip two trips to Starbucks or postpone buying the latest Britney Spears album and instead contribute $10 or $20 to fighting malaria. The public responded. Within a few weeks, Nothing But Nets had raised nearly $1.6 million from thousands of donors. The average contribution was $60.

Nothing But Nets soon attracted a large and diverse organizational following. The National Basketball Association and United Methodist Church were the initial partners. Major League Soccer, the Union for Reformed Judaism, and the Lutheran Church in America joined the team as well. As a tangible demonstration of their commitment to helping children, the Methodist and Lutheran Churches—two of the largest Protestant denominations in the United States—each pledged to raise $100 million. The Gates Foundation agreed to match the first $3 million, which was quickly fulfilled.

But as grateful as the leaders of Nothing But Nets were to receive these large contributions, they were touched and awed by the innovative methods that many supporters used to generate funds. These included the following:

- At the April 2008 United Methodist general membership meeting, church leaders auctioned off a basketball signed by all the church's bishops for $430,000.
- Advocates organized Nothing But Nets teams to fundraise through athletic competitions and other activities. These "Netraisers" generated more than $150,000.
- At Howard University, in Washington, D.C., the African Student Association raised $2,300 through a fashion show.
- Yoni D. P. Rechtman, a seventh grader in Brooklyn, New York, organized a "mitzvah project" basketball tournament, which raised $1,900.
- Georgetown University students, in Washington, D.C., created a Netraiser Team appropriately named "Operation Bug Off." In advance of World Malaria Day on April 25, 2008, the Hoyas held seven events, including a 5K race, a trivia night, a bar night, a three-on-three basketball

tournament, a restaurant night, and two pizza nights that together raised over $2,000.

- Seven-year-old Katherine Commale of Hopewell, Pennsylvania, may be the most valuable player. After seeing the same documentary that had stirred Rick Reilly in Venice, she told her mother: "we have to do something." After building a diorama of an African family in a hut, with the children protected from swarming mosquitoes by a net over their beds, Katherine cultivated interest among her elementary school peers. Her presentation to neighborhood churches raised almost $2,000. Katherine and friends made presentations to churches and crafted hand-decorated gift cards that read, "A mosquito net has been purchased in your name." In total, her team—named "One Bed Net at a Time"—raised $73,000 for the purchase of mosquito nets.

Six months after his column appeared, Reilly visited villages in Nigeria and saw the results of the initiative—in his words, "nets like crazy." The numbers also tell the story. Since its creation in 2006, Nothing But Nets has attracted 100,000 individual supporters. Those supporters, along with Net Raiser teams and corporate and foundation donors, have generated more than $23,000,000 for the purchase of 2,300,000 nets. Because the World Health Organization believes that each net saves two lives, the math is simple: 4.6 million lives have been saved. That's something from Nothing But Nets.

THE MOST POPULAR LABOR-SAVING DEVICE

An oft-repeated political maxim holds that "money is the lifeblood of politics." Although success in the political system depends on much more than the size of your wallet, virtually every campaign—from the presidential race to a statewide ballot initiative to an effort to alter university policy—requires at least some financial resources to succeed.

The good news is that the amount starts small and increases only as you seek to accomplish more complex aims or move up the political and governmental ladder. For example, if your goal is to reform your college or university's housing assignment process, the necessary budget may be as small as the funds needed to pay for the printing costs of petitions, refreshments at meetings, and any advertisements necessary to build and demonstrate support for your position. In that situation, where you are trying to persuade administrators and other academic policymakers to adopt policy changes, you will spend mostly time and energy rather than money. A bigger and more complicated campus initiative, like the Georgetown University students working to win seats on their local Advisory Neighborhood Commission, may cost more.

As initiatives affect more and more community members (residents of a municipality or citizens of an entire state, for example), the cost of victory escalates. This is especially true when an election is involved and voters will decide the fate of your issue or candidate. As evidenced by the huge sums that presidential and congressional candidates raised and spent in 2008, elections are expensive. If you have to put your initiative on the ballot, or run a political candidate who has promised to champion your concern, you'll have to find enough financing to succeed.

In short, don't assume that you are destined for success just because your idea has merit or you are operating from the best of intentions. The political graveyard is littered with worthy candidates and ideas that didn't have sufficient financial backing to win. This chapter will help you prevent your initiative from suffocating from a lack of resources.

PAYING FOR YOUR INITIATIVE: A USER'S GUIDE TO SUCCESSFUL FINANCING

For many of you, this first effort to make democracy respond to your concerns will also be your first attempt at raising money for a cause. If you feel nervous, you're not alone: The idea of asking for financial contributions makes even the most experienced politicians suffer anxiety pangs. Calm your nerves by thinking of fundraising in a larger context. Financial contributions are one way that citizens participate in our democracy, and asking someone for money is a way of asking them to fulfill a civic duty. Although some may choose to participate in other ways, those who view monetary contributions as civic engagement will appreciate the opportunity. Asking for financial help is also a good way to measure your chances of success. It is one thing for friends and potential supporters to applaud your efforts and express verbal support but quite another for them to put their money where their mouth is. Finally, the fundraising process gives you additional chances to argue your case with individuals or entities that may later be in a position to influence the decision maker you have targeted. Even if they give little or no money, they will remember the initiative.

Past fundraising experience is helpful but not decisive. If you methodically follow the steps in the next section, you should be successful in generating the necessary resources. As you follow these steps, keep an open mind. Many of the best innovations in political fundraising occurred because fundraisers were struggling with traditional methods and were forced to think creatively. You may pioneer a new fundraising method in your own citizen initiative. (See "Creative Fundraising: The Sean Tevis Story.")

1. Determine How Much Money You Will Need to Meet Your Goals

More citizen campaigns have unraveled because they did not adequately gauge their financial needs at the start of the effort.

Creative Fundraising: The Sean Tevis Story

Arlen Siegfreid is a senior and respected Republican member of the Kansas House of Representatives—a Goliath in the politics of the Sunflower State. In 2008 his reelection to a fourth term seemed assured. And then his David appeared in the form of Sean Tevis, a Web programmer.

Tevis, thirty-nine, had never run for office before. He didn't have a great deal of name recognition or financial support in the suburban Kansas community in which he was running (Olathe—birthplace of the cowboy boot). He was running as a Democrat in a district in which Republicans outnumbered Democrats almost two to one.

At first, Tevis ran a traditional campaign. He spent the first weeks of his campaign asking friends and family for financial contributions and knocking on doors for support. But the people being asked, like many Americans, were drowning under high gas prices and mortgage payments and lived in fear of losing their jobs. Tevis's efforts raised $1,525—a drop in the bucket compared to the resources his opponent would have.

Tevis was a realist. He recognized that he had to do something to enhance his name recognition and to finance the campaign. So Tevis turned back to what he knew best and designed a campaign Web site that he hoped would turn heads.

On July 16, 2008, Sean launched his Web site: http://seantevis.com. Some of the features were standard political fare. The front page showed a serious man making direct eye contact with site visitors. The easily navigated page had two hallmark messages: "Let's Make Government Work for US" and "No Sales Tax on Food." From there, the viewer was led to crisply written positions on three issues: no tax on food, best schools in the U.S.A., and transparency in government. The other drop-downs implored visitors to join the campaign, make direct contact with Sean, read Sean's succinct biography (concluding with "He loves Olathe"), and take advantage of the opportunity to donate to his campaign.

But what set Tevis's Web site apart was his commitment to innovation. Visit http://seantevis.com/kansas/3000, and you'll see a comic strip that tells the story of the campaign. In the comic strip, stick-figure candidate Sean receives advice from a bearded stick-figure strategist. At one point, as Sean frets about the need to raise money, his bearded strategist consoles him. "Relax," he says. "You just need 52 people who can contribute $500." A dispirited Tevis replies, "I know two."

He then hatches a new plan to raise the needed campaign funds. Rather than ask for $500 from each supporter, he would ask for $8.34. Why that small amount? Tevis had been told that the cost to run as a challenger for a Kansas House seat was $25,000. Most candidates would try to follow the bearded stick figure's advice and seek $500 to $1,000 from 25 to 50 supporters. Tevis calculated if he could get 3,000 contributors the cost would be only $8.34 per donor.

Moreover, targeting large numbers of small donations from everyday people would also highlight his decision to forgo donations from lobbyists—and serve as a contrast to his opponent, who was accepting lobbyist contributions.

Tevis's page also featured his own blog—a day-by-day diary of what it is like to run for public office the first time. Located at http://seantevis.com/weblog, the blog gave visitors a real-time sense of the campaign. It made his efforts both accessible and authentic.

But the best Web site that nobody sees is like the tree falling in the forest. So Tevis sent his Web site to a network of 200–300 fellow Web programmers and asked it they would link to it from their sites. The results were stunning. In a week, almost ten people per second were visiting his site. In thirty-five days, over 750,000 individuals had visited. More than 6,200 visitors contributed in excess of $100,000—eighteen by check and the rest through credit cards. In that same period, Tevis received almost 3,000 e-mails of support and encouragement. His creative efforts won the attention of state and national news outlets including the *Los Angeles Times, Wall Street Journal,* and National Public Radio. You can watch a national television description of the effort at http://seantevis.com/weblog/story/television-interview-hdnet-world-report.

On Election Day on November 4, Democrat Barack Obama lost Kansas by 57 percent to 41 percent. Sean Tevis didn't win either—but he almost did. Of 10,000 votes cast, a mere 425 votes separated him from his opponent. But while this modern-day political David may have lost in 2008, don't count him out for the future. The day after the election, he told the *Kansas City Star* that he may run again. Goliath, beware.[1]

---

[1] Mike Hendricks, "Web-Savvy Loser Has Much to Teach Other Candidates," KansasCity. com, November 6, 2008.

Don't make that mistake. Schedule a brainstorming session with your core supporters to answer the following questions:

- What are your goals? Are they realistic or have you exceeded your reach?
- Having established realistic goals, have you conducted a hard-nosed and itemized assessment of the funds required to achieve those goals?
- How much money will be required to win the election?

If the answer to the second question is no, and the answer to the third question is that you don't know, begin your assessment by thinking about each of the major citizen skills identified in this book. Assess whether conducting research, surveying public opinion, building coalitions, engaging the media, or other tasks will cost money. Here are other questions to consider:

- Does meeting your goals require you to participate in an election? In other words, will you have to put your initiative on the ballot for voter approval, or back a candidate (or a slate of candidates) to advocate your position once elected?
- If you are running a formal campaign in which a candidate or an issue will appear on the ballot, does the election authority levy any costs? Is there a qualifying fee or any other fee?
- What goods or services will you have to purchase? Are all of those items absolutely necessary? How much will the truly essential items cost?
- Can you identify anyone to donate ("in kind") any of these goods or services to the campaign or initiative so that you don't have to pay for them?
- How many paid staff members do you really need to hire? Which campaign roles can instead be filled by unpaid volunteers?

When it comes to fundraising, history can signal what will and will not work:

- What have similar initiatives or campaigns had to raise and spend in the past, and how did they spend their funds?
- Have you spoken with the organizers who led those efforts to determine whether they would make different spending choices if they could revisit their elections?
- In retrospect, what expenditures would they prioritize if they had another opportunity? Has the cost of goods or services increased since then?

The most critical questions of the entire process are these:

- What is the time frame for your campaign or initiative?
- When do funds need to be available for priority spending items?

In many campaigns the bulk of expenditures—and usually the most important ones, like broadcast advertising—are made in the closing weeks or even days of the race. If money has not been reserved for these items, the campaign will run out of gas within sight of the finish line. Just ask Sen. John McCain. In the summer of 2007 his presidential campaign nearly collapsed because it had already spent millions of dollars on its large staff, campaign consultants, and other questionable expenditures. Although his resurrection following that near bankruptcy is now the stuff of political legend, 99 percent of campaigns in that position would have died. Don't let yours become a statistic.

Keep in mind that campaigns—particularly electoral campaigns—are changing. During the 2008 general election some states saw as many as 50 percent of registered voters cast ballots *before* Election Day through early voting or absentee voting. Candidates or initiatives that require voter approval must now raise and spend money on voter communications earlier than ever to avoid missing a large chunk of the electorate. The law of supply and demand also applies. If a campaign waits too long to raise money, it may miss out on opportunities to secure the highest-rated television time, the most competent petition gatherers, or other critical resources.

Early fundraising is also critical because it signals viability. Since the 1980s EMILY's List (www.emilyslist.org) has been raising money for prochoice, Democratic women candidates in congressional and gubernatorial races. (The organization's name derives from an apt slogan: Early Money Is Like Yeast—it makes the dough rise.) When a candidate or issue campaign raises early money, it is easier to convince other potential donors that their contributions will go to a campaign primed for victory.

As you discuss and research these questions, keep in mind the critical distinction between initiatives that do not require an election campaign per se and those that must be achieved through electoral means. If you want to amend your state constitution, alter your county or city charter or comprehensive plan, reform a university policy that requires student approval, or change policy through the election of officeholders who share your goals, you will need significant financial resources. It is time-consuming and expensive to affect public opinion, and successful initiatives or candidates must have enough funds to communicate with voters. As we shall see in the next sections, securing those resources requires legal compliance, organization, and persistence.

2. Know the Law—or Enlist the Help of Someone Who Does

Campaign financing is heavily regulated at the federal, state, and local levels, and it is very important that you comply with the letter of those laws, rules, and regulations. Otherwise, you will be subject to legal punishments, which could include fines and, in some extreme cases, disqualification. Furthermore, the media often report campaign finance violations, and this negative press coverage will cast your initiative in an unflattering light. A few essential steps will help your campaign avoid the consequences of poor compliance.

First, determine which level of government has jurisdiction over your campaign and review the applicable finance laws and regulations. The Federal Election Commission (FEC), the independent agency that regulates federal elections, provides immediate access to election laws and regulations at www.fec.gov/law/law.shtml. State law generally governs elections for state and local office, and state and local ballot initiatives, although county or municipal ordinances may provide additional requirements for local candidates and initiatives. For more information on your state's election officials, laws, and regulations, find the Web site for your state elections board, division, or commission. In some states, the secretary of state oversees the elections process. Your county elections board or supervisor of elections can provide details on any additional local requirements.

Second, as you are reviewing the rules and regulations that govern your election, take special note of certain key provisions:

Has the law changed since the last election? Campaign finance rules are jurisdictionally specific and change frequently. Don't expose your initiative to costly and embarrassing penalties and fines because you weren't aware of recent election law developments.

Does the law restrict who can give to your campaign? For example, some jurisdictions (like the federal government) prohibit direct corporate and labor union contributions. Others impose age requirements. Federal law bans foreign nationals from making campaign donations in local, state, or federal elections (www.fec.gov/pages/brochures/foreign.shtml). Study the law to ensure that you do not take money from someone not authorized to give it.

Is there a cap on how much a donor can give? At the federal level for the 2010 elections, contributors may give candidates $2,400 in a primary election and an additional $2,400 in a general election. States and municipalities impose their own contribution restrictions. More campaigns run afoul of the law in this area than in any other; so be sure you know the applicable donation ceiling in your campaign. Check before each campaign because some federal, state, and local limits are now adjusted for inflation and may increase over time.

Additionally, decide whether it is in your campaign's political interest to impose your own restrictions. Florida political legend Lawton Chiles imposed a $10 limit on contributions to his successful 1970 campaign for the U.S. Senate. His subsequent campaigns for reelection (1976 and 1982) and for governor (1990 and 1994) operated under a $100 cap. The limitations reinforced Chiles's populist message that he answered to everyday Floridians rather than to big-money donors. Similarly, President Barack Obama's campaign for the White House, in which he pledged to change the political culture of the nation's capital, refused contributions from Washington lobbyists and political action committees (PACs).

When does the law require that you report your contributions and contributors? To keep voters informed about who is giving money to your campaign, many jurisdictions require regular public disclosure reports that detail the name, address, occupation, employer, and amount contributed of each donor. (See "Practice Tip: Reporting More than Contributions.")

Does the law draw a distinction between candidates and issue campaigns? Don't assume that one size fits all. The campaign rules for a state legislative race may differ sharply from those that govern county charter amendments.

Can you set up an "issue committee" to influence an election? Known in some cases by reference to the section of the Internal Revenue Code that governs their existence ("527"), and in some states as electioneering communication organizations (ECOs), these sometimes controversial entities usually can accept unlimited donations with some restrictions on how they spend their contributions. In

Practice Tip: Reporting More than Contributions

Don't view campaign disclosure deadlines and reports simply as operational requirements imposed by law. In truth, fundraising reports are opportunities for you to share news about campaign progress. If you raise substantial amounts of money during a fundraising period, the press will view that achievement as tangible evidence of your campaign's strength. Conversely, if you don't have success in a fundraising period, you'll need to present that data to the media in a way that minimizes any harmful public perception.

In campaign financing, few things demoralize the campaign staff more than having what you thought was a successful fundraising period, only to read in the newspaper that you raised "less than expected." When it comes to political contributions, you should set expectations carefully. No sane professional football coach would guarantee a Super Bowl victory in his first year, and you shouldn't promise the moon and the stars in political fundraising. Keep your expectations at a level where you can surpass them.

Money raised and spent is the immediate focus of any campaign report, but reports provide you with other opportunities to share good news about your initiative. Especially in local campaigns, the sheer number of people who have made contributions, regardless of the amount, can be a critical sign of community support. Your goal should be to collect donations from as many different individuals, organizations (if legally permissible), and interests as possible. Pay particular attention to contributors whose support will create positive buzz for the campaign. These include well-respected community members, significant numbers of donors from a highly regarded profession or occupation ("Small business owners support our campaign"), members of a particular demographic ("More women gave to our campaign than to the other side"), or geographic group ("At least one person from every precinct has contributed").

federal elections, so-called 527 advertisements may mention candidates and discuss issues, but they may not directly advocate the election or defeat of a candidate or coordinate with any political candidate they want to help. Some states, like Florida, ban ECOs from direct advocacy but allow them to coordinate with candidates. Unfortunately, some special interests have at times used these "issue advocacy" entities to launch factually questionable attacks on candidates they oppose. In states that permit direct coordination, some observers have accused candidates of using issue committees to escape campaign contribution limitations and personal responsibility for dubious attacks on their opponents. But if your initiative involves the promotion of policy issues rather than political candidates, a 527 committee or ECO may be well suited for your needs.

Third, if at all possible, consult an attorney with election law expertise to help your campaign navigate the often tangled web of finance laws and regulations. Sound legal advice will help you avoid common pitfalls that bedevil many campaigns. If you don't have sufficient funds to pay for an attorney, see if you can find one who will volunteer or donate his or her time. At your college of university, this might be the campus legal clinic, if one exists, or a law school professor who is willing to advise you on the campaign's financial and legal issues.

3. Establish a Campaign Finance Infrastructure

Poorly led and unorganized campaign finance operations are doomed to failure. As you create yours, make sure that trustworthy and competent people hold the key positions and that each of them has clear lines of authority. In most campaigns, the finance hierarchy looks something like this:

- **Treasurer:** Most jurisdictions require campaigns to appoint a treasurer, who is accountable for money management. The treasurer also works closely with the candidate, the finance chair, and the staff to record all donations and report them in the legally required manner. Please keep in mind that the appointment of a treasurer can have political implications. For example, in Florida, a

Practice Tip: Don't Mess Around with the Bookkeeping

Campaign accounting is inherently complicated, and mistakes can put a candidate or initiative in serious legal and political jeopardy.

• Don't be penny wise and pound foolish. If you need to hire a qualified treasurer to make sure the books are properly managed, do it.

• For small grassroots campaigns that cannot afford to pay staff, ask someone you would trust with your life—or someone whose strong integrity can be verified by others—to serve as treasurer.

• As Ronald Reagan said, "Trust, but verify." Buy personal-warranty insurance against the risk of inappropriate behavior. Ask former U.S. senator Dennis DeConcini of Arizona why this matters—his treasurer stole hundreds of thousands of dollars from the campaign coffers.

candidate must publically appoint a treasurer as soon as he or she qualifies to run for office. When I first ran for governor in 1978, my aunt Ina Thompson served as my treasurer. In addition to being someone I trusted—a prerequisite in the selection process—Aunt Ina was well-known as the first woman appointed to head a Florida state agency. She also lived in North Florida, which complemented my status as a South Florida resident. If your campaign is required to appoint a treasurer, look for someone who is both financially responsible and politically beneficial. (See "Practice Tip: Don't Mess Around with the Bookkeeping.")

• Finance Chair: The person with ultimate responsibility for the overall fundraising effort is the finance chair. This individual works with the Finance Committee and the finance director to establish and execute the fundraising strategy in compliance with finance laws.

- Finance Committee: Members of the Finance Committee, who serve at the request of the finance chair, advise the overall fundraising effort and take personal responsibility for soliciting campaign funds. On most campaign finance committees, each member pledges to raise a designated amount in contributions for the candidate or initiative.

- Finance Director and Staff: Large campaigns usually hire several staff members who focus exclusively on raising money for the campaign. These staffers generate contributions by planning fundraising events and managing the campaign's telephone and Internet communications with potential donors. Make sure that at least one finance staffer has the skills needed to direct your Internet fundraising operation.

4. Ask, Ask, and Ask Again

Thomas P. "Tip" O'Neill of Massachusetts, who served as Speaker of the U.S. House of Representatives from 1977 to 1987 and enjoyed a thirty-four-year congressional career, was a noted storyteller. In his autobiography, O'Neill recounts his very first election, a race for the Cambridge City Council. Although O'Neill ran hard, like Sean Tevis six decades later, he lost by a narrow margin. The day before the election, O'Neill ran into his neighbor and former high school teacher, Mrs. O'Brien.

Mrs. O'Brien told O'Neill that she was planning to vote for him the next day even though he had not asked for her support. O'Neill was shocked. He pointed out to Mrs. O'Brien that they had been neighbors for nearly two decades and that he had cut her lawn in the summer and shoveled snow from her walk in the winter. He didn't think that he needed to ask. But Mrs. O'Brien corrected him. "People like to be asked," she said.[2]

---

[2] Thomas P. "Tip" O'Neill with William Novak, *Man of the House: The Life and Political Memoirs of Speaker Tip O'Neill* (New York: Random House, 1987).

Successful campaign fundraising operates on the same principle. The campaigns that raise the most money are those that ask for money frequently and in a variety of different ways. Every fundraising effort should, at a minimum, include the following steps.

First, develop a list of the initial supporters of your cause. Start with your own individual and organizational contacts and solicit them for financial support. This includes your personal circle—family, friends, and close contacts will give to the initiative because they trust and want to help you. If you cannot raise enough from this core group to support the campaign during its initial phases—at least sixty days—you may need to reconsider whether the campaign is feasible. But if you are successful, you can build outward from those initial contacts. Designate your strongest initial supporters as members of the Finance Committee and brainstorm with them to create an even bigger list of donors who may be interested in the initiative. Ask them to raise money for your effort from their own contacts, relationships, and networks. If they are successful, the new contributors they recruited can reach out to their contacts, relationships, and networks for even more potential donors. The goal is to have this process of soliciting new contributors who then find even more new donors take on a life of its own and become self-perpetuating. Meet frequently as the Finance Committee to continue brainstorming and discussing opportunities.

Second, look for individuals or groups who may have an economic interest in your success. For example, if your goal is to put your state on a program to reduce greenhouse gas emissions, companies that produce alternative fuels (like ethanol) or specialize in "clean" technology may want to contribute to your cause. If potential customers in your area are more likely to patronize a "green friendly" business, you may also receive contributions from companies wanting to establish that reputation. Similarly, if your initiative seeks to give commercial property owners the same tax benefits given to residential owners, businesses that own commercial property, as well as real estate agents who broker its purchase and sale, will have every incentive to make sure that you are well funded.

Third, consider potential ideological allies. If your plan aims to create low-cost health insurance for uninsured working families, unions may want to lend a hand. If your aim is to reduce alcohol-related driving deaths by restricting local liquor sales to certain days or locations, socially conservative groups may assist you. A school-related initiative might win the support of the local Parent-Teacher-Student Association and relevant teachers' organizations.

Fourth, take advantage of low-cost fundraising tools. You and your fellow initiative leaders likely belong to clubs, neighborhood associations, fraternal and service organizations, and other groups that may provide names of potential donors. Additionally, look for previous campaigns with political, economic, or ideological interests similar to your own. If the law allows it in your election, and if the previous candidate or initiative is willing, see if you can use or purchase their fundraising lists.

Fifth, if your key supporters are unenthusiastic about calling friends and contacts to ask for checks, suggest that they host fundraising events at their homes or offices where potential donors meet candidates or cause leaders, learn the about the initiative and its progress, and leave contributions. If you have an event, and the law allows, see if the main host or the co-hosts will agree to donate the cost of refreshments so that the campaign does not have to spend money on food and drink.

Sixth, find a supporter with event-planning experience to oversee fundraising parties like those mentioned above. Without proper planning, a political fundraising event can easily end in failure. Additionally, a skilled and creative organizer may be able to schedule events that raise both money and awareness. For example, if your campaign is advocating the construction of a new professional baseball stadium in your community, it might work to schedule a high-profile fundraising game pitting current players against retired players. Fans would buy tickets and generate proceeds for the campaign, and media coverage would communicate a message of player support to voters.

Seventh, use the mail. Although direct-mail fundraising is expensive (there are costs of printing, postage, and handling), it can be productive. If you take this approach, try to find accurate mailing lists for individuals and organizations with an interest in seeing your campaign succeed. Some lists can be obtained for free. Others are available for purchase from organizations that have compatible interests. Don't waste time on groups with little stake in your issue or candidate. If your goal is to preserve endangered species in Alaska, the mailing lists of the local chapters of the Audubon Society and National Wildlife Federation would be valuable. The state dental society would not.

Eighth, use celebrity endorsements as a way to generate support. If your celebrity is willing to host or appear at campaign fundraisers, hold benefit events, sell autographs or signed photographs, lend his or her name to direct-mail or Internet solicitations, or otherwise raise money, these efforts can have a powerful effect on the bottom line.

Ninth, invest in campaign finance software that allows you to stay in close contact with donors and potential donors. The key to successful fundraising is not the initial "ask" but rather the follow-up. A contributor's promise to provide funds is of little benefit to the campaign until it becomes money in the bank. Keep in touch with potential donors through e-mails, telephone calls, and written correspondence until their checks or credit card authorizations arrive. After the money is in the bank, send thank you notes and continue to keep donors engaged in the campaign. It is the polite thing to do, and it just might result in additional contributions. Constantly update financial commitments, contributions received, and donor and potential donor contact information in the campaign database you have purchased.

Tenth, solicit volunteers in addition to dollars. Quality volunteer assistance reduces your staff budget and increases the resources available to your campaign. You can "raise" volunteers in the same way that you raise financial contributions: Start with your core supporters and work outward to bring others into the cause.

5. The Special Case of the Internet

The Internet is the new wave of campaign fundraising—and for good reason. The Internet allows campaigns to reach thousands of donors with campaign news and solicitations almost instantaneously. In recent years, presidential candidates such as Barack Obama, Howard Dean, and Ron Paul have raised hundreds of millions of dollars in campaign contributions online. Candidates for governor, the U.S. Senate, the House of Representatives, and other offices are also successfully using the Internet to raise funds.

In the past, robust Internet fundraising has usually been more practical for high-profile campaigns that attract significant media attention. The traditional model involves sizeable start-up expenditures of money, time, and energy: hiring or finding dedicated volunteers to design and host a campaign Web page; purchasing and maintaining necessary computer systems and software for contribution collection; buying or renting e-mail lists of individuals and organizations that might have an interest in the campaign; updating the Web page continually; composing and distributing campaign news; and sending fundraising solicitations.

Yet Internet fundraising is also emerging in small, grassroots initiatives like that of Sean Tevis and those you are likely to pursue. More and more pioneering Web engines have emerged to power low-cost Internet fundraising efforts for political and nonprofit groups and campaigns. Keep your expectations in check—you almost certainly won't be able to raise money on the scale of Obama, Dean, and Paul and some other national or statewide campaigns— but online fundraising can be a useful complement to your other efforts. The easiest way for you to raise money online may be to focus on bringing potential small-dollar donors into the campaign through more traditional methods while fastidiously collecting their e-mail addresses. For example, if you hold a fundraising event that fifty people attend, and each of them pays $25 to support your candidate or cause, you will have raised $1,250 and ensured that those individuals are now invested in your initiative. Having laid that foundation, you can resolicit them by e-mail in the future and expect that at least some of those supporters will donate again.

The Internet can also be a robust tool for recruiting volunteers who expand your resources and lower your costs. Web sites such as VolunteerMatch.org, SERVE.net, and networkforgood.org match eager volunteers with like-minded causes. Additionally, the rise of telecommuting allows volunteers to help from home with conducting research, drafting press releases and other campaign materials, developing potential volunteer and donor lists, and performing other campaign tasks.

CHECKLIST FOR ACTION

- ☐ Determine how much money you need.
- ☐ Know the law—or enlist the help of someone who does.
- ☐ Establish a campaign finance infrastructure.
- ☐ Ask, ask, and ask again.
  - Recruit core supporters—and ask them to use their contacts and networks.
  - Look for shared economic interests.
  - Consider ideological allies.
  - Take advantage of low-cost fundraising tools.
  - Organize fundraising events.
  - Find a trained event planner to help.
  - Use the mail.
  - Make use of celebrity endorsements.
  - Invest in a reliable campaign finance database.
  - Solicit volunteers as well as dollars.
- ☐ Don't forget the Internet.

Exercises

ASSESSING WHERE YOU ARE

Congratulations. By this point, you have completed nearly all of the steps necessary to put your initiative in a position to succeed. You first defined the problem you wanted to solve. Next, you carefully researched the issue to determine how others have championed it and to discover possible solutions. Then, after identifying the level of government, the agency or department, and the person who was responsible for your issue, you tested public opinion and set an action plan to win the support of the decision makers—at all times taking into account critical trends and deadlines so that your work would not begin either too early or too late to be effective. Realizing that you couldn't do it all alone, you built a coalition of like-minded allies. In order to build broad public support, you engaged the media to disseminate information about your initiative. Now you have learned how to raise the financial resources needed to support your initiative.

PAYING FOR YOUR INITIATIVE

Let's make sure that all of your hard work thus far was not in vain. Take the following steps to ensure that you will have sufficient resources to make your effort successful:

1. Find individuals who have successfully raised money for a political or citizen campaign and interview them. What were their goals and how did they pursue them? Which techniques worked and which ones failed? How would they refashion their efforts if they were to embark on another campaign?

2. Brainstorm to determine the goods or services you will need to facilitate your initiative, as well as their approximate costs. Draft an initial budget.

3. If your goal involves an election, look up the rules governing that election.

4. If the initiative does not require an election—for example, you hope to persuade the university administration to install more lights and emergency phones on campus—you will need to appoint only one member of your coalition to handle the relatively small amount of money required. However, if you will have to raise money for a campaign, you should select several members to serve as your Finance Committee and appoint one of those members to direct the fundraising effort as chair.

5. Unless you are willing to finance the entire initiative from your own pocket, make a list of all potential supporters. Starting with your colleagues, coalition partners, and closest allies, and making sure at all times to comply with any applicable rules, laws, or regulations, ask each of them to make a financial contribution to the effort. Be prepared to report on your progress.

10 You've Won! You've Lost

Preserving Victory and Learning from Defeat

"In victory be not proud. In defeat be not depressed."

—Chinese proverb

Case in Point: A Victory Born in East L.A.

It appeared that July 13, 1987, would be a date to live in infamy for the residents of East Los Angeles. That afternoon the California Senate had voted 29–6—an overwhelming majority—to join the Assembly in authorizing construction of a 1,450-bed prison in the heart of one of Southern California's most economically troubled communities. Prison opponents already knew that their last hope was a lost hope. Gov. George Deukmejian, who had campaigned in support of the prison, would not veto the bill. Five grueling years after East Los Angelinos had banded together to fight the addition of more than a thousand felons to their neighborhood, it seemed their efforts had ended in defeat.

But if the history of the proposed East Los Angeles prison debate proves anything, it is that the status of the battle was never as it seemed. Unbeknownst to prison opponents, the state Senate's vote on July 13, was not the end but just another of the twists and turns in a roller-coaster ride more treacherous than Space Mountain in nearby Disneyland. East Los Angeles had lost but could still win, just as it had previously won but had still lost.

The roots of the debate began growing in the late 1970s, when California, like many other states, adopted tough new criminal-sentencing guidelines to keep lawbreakers behind bars for longer periods than in previous times. California's policy worked—almost too well. Correctional officials estimated that the statewide prison population, which was counted at 21,000 in 1976, would grow to 95,000 by 1991. Since overcrowded prisons could subject California to constitutional challenges for violating federal confinement standards and were breeding grounds for dangerous inmate riots, legislators ordered the construction of six new state prisons to house the inmate overflow.

Despite the huge expense of prison construction, mandating and financing the new facilities was the easy part. Identifying communities to host the new prisons was much harder. Although Californians were generally concerned about crime and supported both the tougher sentencing guidelines and the new prisons, the NIMBY syndrome—not in my back yard—was a powerful force. It was especially strong in Northern California, which produced only 40 percent of the state prison population but was home to 60 percent of the prison facilities. Los Angeles County, which generated 35 percent of the entire state's prisoners, did not have a single state prison. To placate Northern California legislators, the 1982 law mandated that one of the new prisons be located in Los Angeles County.

After fierce debate within Los Angeles County, the California Department of Corrections (CDC) eventually decided to place the new prison on what was known as the Crown Coach site—a parcel of land that once hosted various industrial buildings—located across the Los Angeles River from the East L.A. neighborhood of Boyle Heights. The CDC initially signaled that the Crown Coach site was too small for a full-scale prison and announced that it would instead host a prisoner-intake facility. But in March 1985 the CDC shocked East L.A. residents with the news that it had purchased land adjacent to the Crown Coach site—enough land to build a full-scale, 1,700-bed, medium-security prison.

Overwhelmingly Latino East L.A. reacted with outrage. State assemblywoman Gloria Molina and residents of the area argued that the local and state governments had repeatedly dumped unattractive public projects—such as highways, junkyards, and landfills—in their neighborhood. Even worse, the new prison wouldn't be the first in East L.A. Five other federal or county prisons were located within four miles of the Crown Coach site and held 75 percent of the total Los Angeles County prison population. East L.A. felt it was being forced to carry more than its fair share of what other county residents didn't want in their backyards. Worst of all, the construction of a new state prison would prevent the Crown Coach site from being included in an economic empowerment zone that could create thousands of new jobs and offer economic hope to a community that had long suffered from serious unemployment woes.

East L.A. had been unable to repel those previous projects and prisons, and many residents thought the odds of reversing the CDC decision were insurmountable. But Molina and local business and neighborhood leaders took action. They formed the Coalition Against the Prison—a group that eventually swelled to include forty-seven community organizations—and set out to show state officials that East Los Angeles was unified in its opposition to the Crown Coach prison.

The consensus in Sacramento, the state capital, was that the coalition's efforts were dead on arrival. Despite the odds against them, Molina and her allies refused to go away. They aggressively lobbied state legislators with personal visits and impressive briefing books to make the case against the Crown Coach site. This investment of time and energy paid off in 1985. Although the California Senate approved the prison, and Deukmejian threw his gubernatorial weight behind it in an effort to secure quick passage, maverick Assembly Speaker Willie Brown refused to play along. He held the bill until 1986 so that Assembly committees could review it fully, giving the coalition more time to build opposition in Sacramento. For the moment, East L.A. was winning.

However, victory in politics can be fleeting. Allies shift constantly. Although Speaker Brown had saved the coalition in 1985, he refused to meet with members when they resumed lobbying efforts the following year. In July 1986 the Assembly overwhelmingly approved the Crown Coach prison. The fight now moved to the Senate, which had previously been hostile territory for the coalition.

Molina and company had learned a thing or two since their first unsuccessful interaction with the California Senate in 1985. Although their previous member-to-member lobbying had been a good start, success depended on convincing enough senators that they had something to lose in supporting the prison: political support from across the state, especially among Latino, Roman Catholic, and women voters. Fortunately, the coalition had a weapon that reached each of those key demographics.

The weapon was the Mothers of East Los Angeles, also known as MELA. Father John Moretta, a respected Catholic priest, had organized MELA as a way to rally women to oppose the Crown Coach prison. At first, MELA focused its efforts within East L.A. Thousands of women participated in MELA neighborhood marches to raise local awareness about the issue. Many of the marchers were thirty-something housewives who could help spread the word through their family, school, and church networks, and who had the flexibility to organize on a moment's notice.

In the summer of 1986, 300 MELA members descended on Sacramento. Dressed in T-shirts, wearing message buttons, and holding up masks depicting a child behind bars, they beseeched individual legislators for support, attended committee hearings on the issue, and held rallies to garner press attention. By the time of the Senate vote, it was clear that MELA had influenced the debate. The only question was whether it had changed enough minds to block the two-thirds majority needed for approval. When the vote occurred on August 14, the final tally showed twenty-three senators in support and twelve opposed—exactly one vote short of the necessary supermajority. Once again, East L.A. had won an important battle.

But 1986 was an election year in California, and the war over the prison raged on. Governor Deukmejian ran for reelection and highlighted his support for the Crown Coach prison as part of his anticrime credentials. Deukmejian and his team also argued that the proposed prison would provide an economic boost to East L.A., because prison jobs paid relatively high wages. The coalition against the prison gathered high-profile support from César Chávez, the United Farm Workers president and civil rights legend, and Roger Mahoney, the Catholic archbishop of Los Angeles. It even convinced the influential *Los Angeles Times,* California's largest newspaper, to withdraw its previously unconditional support for the prison and instead to demand an environmental review of the Crown Coach site before the CDC purchased the additional land needed to build the prison.

The roller coaster continued unabated for the rest of 1986. On November 4 California voters dealt the coalition a major blow when they reelected Deukmejian as governor in a landslide over L.A. mayor Tom Bradley. The coalition's nemesis would be in Sacramento for another four years. But December brought better news. California's state auditor criticized the CDC for its procedures in selecting the Crown Coach site and questioned the state's appraisal of the property. For the first time the coalition had official documentation to bolster its case. Then, all of a sudden, the issue appeared to become moot. The Crown Coach property owners, opting to side with the neighborhood over the CDC, announced that they would sell the site to a private industrial developer. The property was off the market, and East L.A. reacted jubilantly. The CDC could not build on what it did not own.

The coalition members then learned that elections really do matter. Riding the wave of popularity from his reelection triumph, Deukmejian ignored the damning state auditor's report and reiterated his determination to build the Crown Coach prison. In his eyes, the property sale was inconsequential. He announced that California would buy the land from the new owners, take the property through eminent domain, or simply build a high-rise prison on the smaller East L.A. parcel the state already owned. His perseverance led a *Los Angeles Times* editorial writer to wonder "why Deukmejian is so determined to continue his political mano-a-mano with the Eastside."[1] Whatever the reason, the governor would not give up the fight.

Any governor, but particularly the governor of a large state, has enormous power to shape the public agenda. Legislators who ignore this executive's power do so at their own peril, because a governor's influence and veto pen can kill legislators' priorities and make them appear ineffective. California's lawmakers understood this political reality and worked to find a compromise. On July 13, 1987, just months after East L.A. thought it had dodged the bullet, the California Senate voted 29–6 to approve the so-called pain for pain legislation. The plan called for the CDC to build two prisons: a 1,450-bed prison in East L.A. and a 2,200-bed prison in Lancaster, a Republican area in the northern part of Los Angeles County. After both houses of the California Legislature approved the bill, Deukmejian signed it into law. The coalition had lost what seemed to be the final battle over the Crown Coach prison.

For East L.A. community activists, defeat had been snatched from the jaws of victory. The compromise bill was devastating and demoralizing. But the coalition and MELA did not surrender. Against all odds, and in the face of certain construction, they continued their public efforts to block the prison.

---

[1] Franklin del Olmo, "Is the Governor Crossing Macho Line on Prison?" *Los Angeles Times*, January 15, 1987.

California's elected governor and legislators had repeatedly disappointed East Los Angeles, but appointed public officials had provided evidence that was helpful to the cause. Although the governor ignored the 1986 auditor's report, its findings had given the coalition's arguments new credibility around the state. After the July 1987 vote, state regulators again came to the coalition's rescue. When California conducted an environmental study of the Crown Coach site, the survey found significant soil contamination left over from the property's former industrial use. The environmental report gave the Coalition and MELA additional ammunition, since the cleanup would require the state to spend more money on the site than had originally been anticipated.

The environmental study and its aftermath also consumed significant time. Deukmejian decided to retire after two terms, and Pete Wilson succeeded him as governor in January 1991. In September 1992, following more intense pressure from East L.A. residents and facing an expensive cleanup of the Crown Coach site, Governor Wilson signed a bill terminating prison construction. At long last, the coalition had triumphed.

No prison would be built in East L.A., but the Crown Coach property did not remain empty for long. In 1998 California gave the Los Angeles Community Redevelopment Agency permission to restore the contaminated site back to productive use. After another environmental study and a $3.3 million soil cleanup, Los Angeles turned the property over to Alameda Produce Market, Inc., for the development of more than one million square feet of industrial and retail space. Instead of 1,450 prisoners, the site would attract 2,500 jobs and more than $80 million in private investment. Thirteen years after its formation, the coalition had achieved its economic empowerment goals.

The highs and lows of the Crown Coach debate are common to the task of influencing decision makers: East Los Angeles activists experienced victory, defeat, victory, again defeat, and then victory. When citizens engage democracy, there are few permanent triumphs or setbacks. There is no rest in participatory democracy. Winning brings new responsibilities, and losing presents new opportunities. This chapter will help you understand what lies ahead after winning or losing.

IF YOU HAVE WON: CAPITALIZING ON VICTORIES

Nothing is more satisfying than victory in a cause that you have passionately and energetically championed. But don't let winning seduce you. Your triumph among the electorate, through the favorable action of your state legislature or city council, or your success in winning over your school or college bureaucracy is not the end of your efforts. If you want this euphoric moment to be the start rather than the end of a winning streak, take steps now to preserve and extend your victory.

1. Look over Your Shoulder

It feels like you have won, but are you sure? While you shouldn't cross the line into paranoia, you should be vigilant in ensuring that your "victory" isn't suddenly reversed. Electoral campaigns often seem like the surest of triumphs—after all, one candidate or position won more votes than the other—but recent history tells us that the Election Day results are often far from the final word. For example, the 2000 presidential campaign was supposed to end with the election of a new chief executive on November 7, 2000. Indeed, at one point during that night, Vice President Al Gore called Texas governor George W. Bush to concede victory. But the results in Florida and New Mexico were so close that the nation needed thirty-six more days of recounts and litigation before it had a president-elect. More recently, in the race for the U.S. Senate seat in Minnesota in November 2008, Republican incumbent Norm Coleman and Democratic challenger Al Franken experienced an even longer delay before the election was resolved. If you have just concluded what you think is a successful political campaign, don't let the fact of winning the most votes lull you into a false sense of security. You haven't won until your county or state election officials certify the results as official. Make sure that the attorney you engaged after reading chapter 9 is helping your campaign take the steps necessary to facilitate election certification.

The risk of unexpected reversal is even greater when your victory is the result of actions taken by a state legislature, city council, or other governmental body or agency, including administrative offices in colleges or universities. East L.A. residents learned this painful lesson many times, as various "wins"—the unexpected alliance with Speaker Brown, the initial Senate triumph, the state auditor's report, and the property owner's refusal to sell the property to the CDC—suddenly became losses. This danger is ever present at every level of government.

For example, assume that your college's Public Works Department has just ratified a long-time student demand for a new parking garage located close to campus. Can any other department or administrator—perhaps the college president—countermand that decision? Alternatively, assume that you have persuaded your city council to set up a special taxing district to raise funds for children's programs. Does the mayor have the power to veto that district, or does the council have to put the issue before voters for final approval? Finally, imagine a scenario in which you have persuaded your state legislature to enact a sales tax rebate that will help your business retool its manufacturing plants. Can your opponents use any parliamentary tactics to derail the bill after final passage?

Felix Unger from the 1970s television sit-com *The Odd Couple* said it well: "Don't assume, because you'll make an ass out of 'u' and 'me.'" As soon as you feel certain that your cause has won, that's exactly when you are most likely to become the unwitting victim of an unexpected loss. Look in the rear-view and side mirrors immediately.

2. Close the Doors Correctly

Some citizen efforts don't require as much paperwork as others. You may not need a full-blown political campaign, with the accompanying rules and regulations, if your goal is to persuade your college administrators to keep the student center open all night, convince the school board to alter boundaries so that your children can attend a different elementary school, or motivate a town official to clean up your local park. But if you put a candidate or an issue on the ballot, you must strictly follow the legal procedures set forth for the operation and conclusion of the campaign.

In chapter 9, I said that your campaign's greatest vulnerability is in financing—in other words, legally and ethically raising, allocating, and accounting for the money you need to be successful. The second greatest vulnerability is completion—properly shutting down the official campaign apparatus. Most states have very specific procedures for winding down the affairs of the campaign, and you can experience problems if you are not faithful to the execution of those procedures. These can range from the inconvenient to the serious. For example, I once received an official notice for state taxes due for a campaign that was three years in the past—long after the records were warehoused and the people familiar with them had left for destinations unknown. But that challenge pales in comparison to former candidates and campaign staff members who are forced to defend themselves against civil or even criminal charges related to paying insufficient attention to campaign shut-down regulations. Your state's election commission is certain to take a dim view of violations, forcing you to spend thousands of dollars in legal fees to rectify the problem.

Fortunately, you can take several steps to avert disaster. First, appoint a competent and experienced person to manage the campaign shut-down, and ensure that she has plenty of assistance from trusted volunteers. Second, do not allow your campaign attorney to go home until he has provided you with the expert legal advice necessary for a proper conclusion to the campaign's affairs. Third, if your campaign is in the position of having spent more than it raised, develop an aggressive plan for speedy satisfaction of any outstanding debts.[2]

Don't take this third job lightly. When I served in the U.S. Senate, one of my colleagues struggled every year just to pay interest on the debt from his unsuccessful presidential campaign. He did not erase his obligations until he left the Senate and could devote himself full-time to the task. The debts were paid nearly fifteen years after the campaign in which they were incurred. Since you won your campaign, your path to solvency is easier. You can avoid the stress my colleague experienced if you meet with your primary creditors right away to discuss debt relief. Don't be surprised if they are willing to help. For a variety of reasons—support for your campaign goals, excitement at having backed a winner, or wariness of the long hassle likely needed to secure full repayment—campaign creditors are often reasonable about repayment.

Once you have established how much you owe from the campaign, consult your campaign attorney to determine the legal fundraising procedures for retiring the debt. Depending on the applicable campaign laws and regulations, the same money-raising techniques identified in chapter 9 may be available after the campaign to close your deficit. Take advantage of them before you or your candidate has to devote full time to governing, or you have to focus exclusively on proper implementation of the successful results of your initiative.

3. Say Thank You

Unbelievably, the easiest post-campaign task is the one most often ignored: expressing thanks to the many people who aided your success. More triumphant candidates and issues lose supporters

---

[2] Before you run, determine if the federal, state, or local election laws that govern the election even allow your campaign to incur debts. Some campaign laws strictly prohibit spending more than what has been collected in campaign contributions.

over this omission than any other. No matter whether you organized a big or small effort, you can follow several simple steps to ensure that nobody becomes an enemy for lack of gratitude on your part.

First, send a mass mailing—either by U.S. mail or the Internet—to every single person who played a role, no matter how big or small, in your campaign or citizen initiative. Second, devote adequate time to appreciative telephone calls. Just as you spent hours each day dialing for dollars, volunteers, or votes, invest the time to call those individuals who helped you the most—fundraisers who hosted events or collected significant numbers of donations, donors who gave substantial financial support, precinct or county leaders who organized and rallied supporters, elected officials who were particularly outspoken in their support, and others. These calls are important not only because you owe these friends your thanks but also because they will help to solidify your network of supporters for future campaigns or citizen initiatives.

Third, give your most diligent supporters a campaign memento to capture the spirit of the campaign and encourage long-term enthusiasm. Many Americans who helped Jimmy Carter's successful 1976 bid for the presidency still treasure the peanut pin he distributed after victory. When I was elected Florida's governor in 1978, I sent my supporters "Graham Crackers" and copies of the book—*Workdays*—about the 100 jobs I took during the campaign.

Fourth, if your campaign was large enough to hire staff members, and you have enough remaining financial resources to pay bonuses, make sure to give monetary thanks for a job well done. Campaign staff members typically work long hours for little pay, and the financial gratitude will be warmly received.

Just remember: You can't say thank you enough or to too many people. The person you forget to thank for helping you reform university financial aid policies, rezone real property for charitable purposes, block the state legislature from placing a prison in your community, or elect you to office is the person least likely to help when you seek assistance in the future.

4. Chronicle the Campaign

As philosopher and poet George Santayana said, "Those who cannot learn from history are doomed to repeat it." Your successful campaign or citizen initiative should have a slightly different take on those timeless words of wisdom: Those who do not chronicle their success won't remember how to replicate it. With the help of others who are intimately familiar with the topic, prepare a written end-of-campaign history while the effort is still fresh in your mind. That document should answer several questions: How and why did the campaign begin? Who were its leaders, and how can you contact them in the future? What key events define the campaign chronology? What were the high and low points? What lessons were learned? Which decisions paid positive dividends and which were mistakes? What actions would you replicate in the future, and which would you avoid? Because this successful initiative is not likely to be the last in which you will be involved, you can dust off the written history in two, four, or more years as you prepare for the next campaign.

But as valuable as that written narrative is to long-term success, it isn't enough. You are sitting on a gold mine of information, and now is the time to safeguard that hard-won treasure. Over the course of the campaign, you have accumulated hundreds or thousands of names, addresses, e-mails, and telephone numbers of volunteers, contributors, consultants, policy experts, and others—data that will be extremely valuable in the future. You also have a wealth of documents, research, fliers, letters, campaign forms, and other papers. Using the appropriate computer program, organize and archive all of this information so that you have ready access to it in the future.

Campaigns are supposed to be fun; so take care to protect those items that symbolize the enjoyable part of the experience.

Paraphernalia, buttons, bumper strips, slate cards, posters, and DVDs containing television advertisements have both historical and sentimental value. If you keep them, they will help you recapture the positive feelings that both inspired and accompanied your victory.

5. Turn Opponents into Friends

In the aftermath of your victory the advice to keep your friends close and your enemies closer is worth following. Even if the contest was tough and the debate was heated, purge any lingering anger or bitterness you feel toward your opponents. Politics should not be a blood sport, and enemies' lists are a waste of time and energy. The partisan gridlock in Washington, D.C., and in various state capitals in recent years can be attributed in part to individuals in power who care more about demonizing and ruining the opposition than working together to bolster our democratic institutions.

You are better than that. Be magnanimous in victory, and reach out to those who opposed you. Start with a phone call to the leader of the other side on the day after your victory, and work over time to find opportunities for common ground. If you can turn your opponent into an ally, or at least minimize long-term animosity, you are less likely to face opposition in the future. Even more important, since politics is an ever-shifting chess board, you may need that former opponent on your side in a future battle.

Former Senate majority leader Bob Dole delivered a particularly gracious concession speech when he lost the 1996 presidential election to President Bill Clinton. He spoke to his supporters and a national television audience: "I've said repeatedly in this campaign that the President was my opponent and not my enemy. And I wish him well, and I pledge my support in whatever advances the cause of a better America." [3] Celebrate your victory with an outstretched hand—not a swinging fist.

---

[3] "Remarks by Dole in Conceding Defeat by Clinton," *New York Times*, November 6, 1996.

6. Think about Next Month and Next Year

Your campaign triumph is well worth celebrating, but it does not mark the conclusion of your efforts. Winning has given you the responsibilities of a parent with long-term obligations for leading your candidate or issue into political adulthood. These parental responsibilities include the following:

Keep your coalition together and look to add new members. You can use the same techniques discussed in chapter 7 to expand the coalition in this post-victory period and make sure it does not wither.

Engage the individuals who will execute your idea. Here are three examples: If you have persuaded your college to provide soap-dispensing machines in dormitory bathrooms, you should reach out to enlist the support of the employees responsible for maintaining the building. Your county school board's decision to give free books to elementary students for after-school reading should prompt you to contact the administrator in charge of reading instruction. If the voters have passed a constitutional amendment that prohibits smoking in restaurants, you will need to contact state legislators and regulators who will be charged with implementing the ban.

These contacts are important because your victory gives you credibility, and your advice and encouragement will help to keep the execution of policy decisions in line with your original goals. But expect to encounter bureaucratic resistance and antagonism. Your initiative may have altered a program or pattern with which officials were comfortable, and they may drag their heels in making any changes. Treat them with respect, but develop a plan in advance so that you can dodge any obstacles placed in your path.

Devise methods for measuring the implementation of your idea. Governments routinely fail to have metrics that are clearly expressed and understood, a failing that often impedes progress. Don't make that mistake. Let's assume that the county government has just approved your plan to clean up a local lake. You will be able to track the plan's success if you develop a short list of quantifiable standards. For example, what are the levels of contaminants in the water? In the past month, how many days was the lake closed to fishing or swimming? How healthy are the wildlife populations that depend on the lake? Take these metrics to the legislators who enacted your idea and the appointed officials charged with implementing it, and persuade them to use those metrics to track progress. Seek agreement on who will gather, analyze, and report the relevant data. When the report is ready to be released, engage the media so that the public knows whether goals are being met or missed.

Recognize those who are helping you. Again, success really boils down to regular expressions of thanks. Say thank you early and often. Schedule an annual event to boost your cause. Present the most supportive elected and appointed officials and the most diligent volunteers with awards, plaques, trophies, or other tangible signs of appreciation. Never fail to write or call with thanks when a legislator or other government official shows interest in your citizen initiative, and make sure that constituents or voters who support your cause do the same. Reward your friends and remind your opponents that you are alive and kicking.

Reach beyond your original territory. Mothers Against Drunk Driving started in a single California town. Before long, it was a statewide, then national, and now international force. With each expansion, MADD became more powerful in its original town. Don't worry if you can't or don't want to go global, national, or even statewide. If you were able to win in your community, you will almost certainly find support for your cause in a nearby one.

IF YOU HAVE LOST: RECOVERING FROM DEFEAT

Defeat on the playing field is never easy, whether it is in sports, business, law, or politics, and it stings the most when you care deeply about your cause. But a loss is not the time to surrender. As the residents of East Los Angeles discovered more than once, initial defeat can serve as the foundation for future victory if you learn from the experience and refuse to go quietly into the night. Your steps for rehabilitation will include the following:

1. Apply the Same Techniques as the Winners—but Sometimes in Reverse

Regrettably, losing does not free you of the obligation to close your campaign in accordance with the appropriate local, state, or local procedures. Closing down will be painful, but it is nonetheless necessary. However, some of the same post-victory actions suggested in the previous section can also work to your long-term advantage—especially if the winning side arrogantly or negligently fails to implement them.

First, don't miss this opportunity to thank and recognize your supporters just as fervently as you would have done in a winning campaign. Your words of appreciation will help to comfort very disappointed people who have given freely of their time, energy, skills, and financial resources, and those words will also help to motivate them to engage in future campaigns. The process of writing, calling, or e-mailing allies will also be therapeutic for you. A reminder of why you originally engaged in the battle can be the best medicine for overcoming a loss, and supporters can provide a healthy dose of inspiration.

Second, take advantage of the situation if the winning side is not looking over its shoulder. Does a higher authority at your university, locality, or state have the power to derail what appears to be a victory? What parliamentary maneuvers, if any, can you employ to block final legislative passage of the opposition's agenda? Although you don't want to display a sour grapes attitude, contribute to gridlock, or obstruct simply for the sake of obstruction, the victorious campaign has the burden of securing final triumph. There is nothing inappropriate in championing your position until the last possible moment.

Third, even if you cannot stop the opposition from achieving victory in theory, you may still be able to slow down the implementation process. If victors do not skillfully engage the officials charged with carrying out policy decisions, then you may find natural allies in the bureaucratic forces that often prefer the status quo to change, or in agencies that want their interests represented in the process. For example, the hopes of the East L.A. Coalition Against the Prison were dead in the water until California environmental regulators reported that pollutants had contaminated the proposed prison site. Had Governor Deukmejian preemptively addressed concerns about the property's environmental health, he may have succeeded in forcing prison construction. But Deukmejian ignored that constituency and paid for his mistake with the failure of his plan to build a prison.

2. Diagnose the Problem and Fix It

A defeat is the proper time for some serious introspection. Was your cause inherently flawed and thus unlikely ever to achieve victory? Or did the campaign make mistakes that struck down an otherwise winnable idea? The typical errors that sink a campaign involve all of the skills that we have previously outlined: failure to define the problem sufficiently, inadequate research, absence of a broad base of support, efforts that start too late or too early, incomplete public understanding of your issues or equally dangerous overexposure to them, or a lack of financing. Your most trusted campaign colleagues and impartial outside observers can help you perform this necessary analysis. Take heart: Most of these problems can be remedied before you undertake future efforts.

3. If at First You Don't Succeed, Try, Try Again

Some of the best ideas in American politics didn't succeed on the first, second, or even twentieth attempt. We wouldn't have direct election of U.S. senators, Social Security, the minimum wage, NASA, women's suffrage, or universal civil rights if the champions of those causes hadn't persisted. Defeat does not mean that you don't have what it takes to succeed, but it does mean that you need to recalibrate for the next shot at the target. Remember that politics does not bring permanent victories or losses. Certain defeat comes only when you have thrown in the towel.

CHECKLIST FOR ACTION

- ☐ If you have won:
  - Look over your shoulder to avoid a reversal.
  - Close the campaign correctly.
  - Say thank you.
  - Chronicle the campaign.
  - Turn opponents into friends.
  - Think in the medium and long term.
- ☐ If you have lost:
  - Close the campaign correctly.
  - Say thank you.
  - Seek opportunities for reversal or legitimate delay.
  - Diagnose and fix what went wrong.
  - Keep trying.

Exercises

THE JOURNEY CONTINUES

If you have read and assimilated the text to this point, it means that you have now learned and practiced the ten skills most vital to successful citizen leadership. You have defined the problem; conducted research on your issue; identified which officials have the power to address your concerns; gauged public opinion; persuaded the proper decision maker; used deadlines, trends, and cycles to your advantage; built a coalition; engaged the news media; looked for ways to raise campaign resources; and learned to protect victory and rebound from defeat.

Before this journey began, many of you—like many Americans today—were spectators in the great arena of democracy. But now you have the knowledge and skills to be a robust democratic participant—one of the men or women in the arena. With that new awareness comes two final assignments.

1. Think back over the past ten chapters. What aspects of active citizen engagement most surprised you? Why? If you were helping to lead a future citizen initiative, which of these skills would most likely be your specialty? Be prepared to discuss your answers.

2. The challenge you defined in chapter 1 may still be a problem. Don't let it escape your focus and attention simply because you have finished reading this book. Using the insights you have gained, prepare an action plan to solve that problem and start executing it as soon as possible.

Congratulations and good luck. Democracy awaits!

Index